Smart, Sustainable and Inclusive Growth

NEW HORIZONS IN REGIONAL SCIENCE

Series Editor: Philip McCann, *Professor of Urban and Regional Economics, University of Sheffield, UK*

Regional science analyses important issues surrounding the growth and development of urban and regional systems and is emerging as a major social science discipline. This series provides an invaluable forum for the publication of high quality scholarly work on urban and regional studies, industrial location economics, transport systems, economic geography and networks.

New Horizons in Regional Science aims to publish the best work by economists, geographers, urban and regional planners and other researchers from throughout the world. It is intended to serve a wide readership including academics, students and policymakers.

Titles in the series include:

Smart, Sustainable and Inclusive Growth

Political Entrepreneurship for a Prosperous Europe

Edited by

Charlie Karlsson

Professor Emeritus of the Economics of Technological Change, Jönköping International Business School, Jönköping University and Professor Emeritus, Blekinge Institute of Technology, Sweden

Daniel Silander

Associate Professor, Department of Political Science, Linnaeus University, Sweden

Brigitte Pircher

Senior Lecturer, Department of Political Science, Linnaeus University, Sweden

NEW HORIZONS IN REGIONAL SCIENCE

Edward Elgar
PUBLISHING

Cheltenham, UK • Northampton, MA, USA

Published by
Edward Elgar Publishing Limited
The Lypiatts
15 Lansdown Road
Cheltenham
Glos GL50 2JA
UK

Edward Elgar Publishing, Inc.
William Pratt House
9 Dewey Court
Northampton
Massachusetts 01060
USA

A catalogue record for this book
is available from the British Library

Library of Congress Control Number: 2019935387

This book is available electronically in the **Elgar**online
Social and Political Science subject collection
DOI 10.4337/9781788974097

ISBN 978 1 78897 408 0 (cased)
ISBN 978 1 78897 409 7 (eBook)

Typeset by Servis Filmsetting Ltd, Stockport, Cheshire

Printed and bound in Great Britain by TJ International Ltd, Padstow, Cornwall

Contents

Contributors

Helena Ekelund is Senior Lecturer of Political Science at Linnaeus University, Sweden. Her research focuses on the EU agencies, migration and border policies and human rights.

Anne Haglund-Morrissey is Associate Professor and works as Senior Policy Officer at the DG Research and Innovation at the European Commission, Belgium. Her research involves EU research and innovation policy and EU international and development cooperation.

Charlie Karlsson is Professor Emeritus of Economics at Jönköping International Business School, Sweden. He has focused on infrastructure, urban, regional and small business economics, spatial industrial dynamics and entrepreneurship.

Martin Nilsson is Senior Lecturer of Political Science at Linnaeus University, Sweden. His research focuses on European environmental and climate change politics, the European Union and prerequisites to sustainable democracy.

Mats Öhlén is Senior Lecturer of Political Science at Dalarna University, Sweden. His research includes EU institutions, transnational European parties and Swedish party politics.

Anna Parkhouse is Senior Lecturer of Political Science at Dalarna University, Sweden. Her research interests include the European Union as regional and global actor, the impact of the EU membership incentive on rule adoption in minority rights legislation and European policies on asylum-seekers and refugees.

Brigitte Pircher is Senior Lecturer in the Department of Political Science at Linnaeus University, Sweden and Lecturer at the University of Vienna, Austria. Her research includes European integration, EU institutions, EU decision-making processes, and EU law and its implementation in the member states.

Charlotte Silander is Senior Lecturer of Political Science at Linnaeus University, Sweden. She works at the Department of Didactics and Teachers

Practice. Her research focuses on higher education and the European Union, including gender issues and research policy.

Daniel Silander is Associate Professor of Political Science at Linnaeus University, Sweden. His main areas of interest are political entrepreneurship on a domestic and international level, international politics, democracy and state and human security.

Sam Tavassoli is post-doctoral researcher at the CIRCLE, Lund University, Sweden and Assistant Professor at Royal Melbourne Institute of Technology in Melbourne, Australia. His research focuses on economics of innovations, technological change, entrepreneurship and the evolution of industries.

PART I

Europe 2020 and framework of study

1. The European Commission and Europe 2020: smart, sustainable and inclusive growth

Daniel Silander

This book focuses on European political entrepreneurship in the Europe 2020 strategy. The aim of the book is to analyse the Europe 2020 strategy and the role of European political entrepreneurship in debating, shaping and implementing the strategy within the EU's political levels of governance. In 2010, the European Commission released an official communication titled 'Europe 2020 – A strategy for smart, sustainable and inclusive growth'. It succeeded the European Single Market programme (1986–92) and the Lisbon Strategy (2000–10) and was decided on by the European Council at a meeting on 26 March 2010, chaired by President Herman Van Rompuy. The Lisbon Strategy aimed to transform Europe into the most competitive economy in the world, but it was more or less a failure due to an overloaded agenda, lack of member state commitment, lack of ownership and political steering, conflicting priorities and the 'one-size-fits-all' strategy in a socioeconomically and politically heterogeneous Europe (Stec and Grzebyk, 2018: 120–22; Fura et al., 2017: 969; see also Kotz, 2005; Erixon, 2010; European Commission, 2010). In the new Europe 2020 strategy, the Commission called upon EU institutions, member states, regional and local authorities and the private sector to address the economic crisis (Wandel, 2016: 10; Zeitlin and Vanhercke, 2014: 8–9) by promoting smart, sustainable and inclusive growth. It referred to *smart growth* as promoting an economy based on knowledge and innovation, *sustainable growth* as economic growth based on resource efficiency and a greener economy and *inclusive growth* as growth that provides for social integration. The Commission further argued that fundamental measures, beyond day-to-day and regular political and economic activities, had to be implemented by engaged European actors seeking new economic and social models and presenting the state of the world, on all political levels of European governance (see Silander, 2018; Barbier, 2011). From 1995 and up to 2010, the Commission and member states had played different powerful roles as driving engines behind socioeconomic reforms (see Barbier, 2011: 13–17). However, in 2009–10, the Commission pushed for Europe 2020 and the idea of EU governance. It was stated how the European Council had 'full ownership' of the Europe agenda, how the Commission would 'monitor progress towards the targets', and how the European Parliament should 'mobilise citizens and act as co-legislator on key initiatives', but also how the strategy had to engage EU committees, national parliaments and local and regional authorities 'in delivering on the vision' (all cited in European Commission, 2010: 4).

In addition, the crisis was argued to be a wake-up call for the EU and an alarming signal that business as usual would lead the EU along with member states into further recession and to the second rank in the new global economic order. However, a European crisis could also serve as an opportunity for European integration as had been the case throughout the many decades of European politics (see Cross, 2017). This time, the EU had to engage new, innovative politics and to be bold and ambitious by showing leadership and entrepreneurship to determine Europe's future. In 2010 the former chair of the Commission, José Manuel Barroso, called for what this study refers to as European *political entrepreneurship* by politicians, bureaucrats, officers and institutions within the publicly funded sector. With innovative approaches, *political entrepreneurship* encourages entrepreneurship towards a goal of growth and employment for the common good (see Karlsson et al., 2016; 2018; Silander and Silander, 2015). As stated by the former Chair of the Commission,

> The condition for success is a real ownership by European leaders and institutions. . . . European leaders have a common analysis on the lessons to be drawn from the crisis. We also share a common sense of urgency on the challenges ahead. Now we jointly need to make it happen. . . . We must have confidence in our ability to set an ambitious agenda for ourselves and then gear our efforts to delivering it. (Barroso, 2010: preface)

POLITICAL ENTREPRENEURSHIP

A large bulk of studies in economics have for more than half a century stressed how entrepreneurship and entrepreneurs are vital aspects of a growing and dynamic economy (see Schumpeter, 1934; Kaiser, 1990; Carroll, 2017). In the academic literature entrepreneurship plays a crucial role for growth by focusing on entrepreneurs as the important risk-takers, innovators and responders to market disequilibria and so on. Although research on entrepreneurs and entrepreneurship has mostly taken place within economics, there has been a growing bulk of studies on entrepreneurial activities in the public sector. Such a growing body of literature has been inspired by core elements of entrepreneurs and entrepreneurship from the business sector such as the importance of knowledge, innovation, opportunity, implementation and risk-taking (see discussion by Carroll, 2017: 115–19; see also Jones, 1978). Europe 2020 also calls for immediate innovative, risk-taking political actions to seek new opportunities to improve the conditions for entrepreneurship and growth in Europe.

Although the concept of a public entrepreneur had already been identified in 1965 (see Ostrom, 1965), it took about three decades until the concept of entrepreneurship in the public sector was further developed in academia (for example, see Osborne and Plastrik, 1993; Baumol, 1990). Studies have identified *public entrepreneurs* as innovative and creative actors within municipalities and public corporations who seek implementation of innovations in the public sector practice (Ostrom, 1965; Roberts and King, 1991). Studies have also pointed out *social entrepreneurs* are innovative and goal-oriented citizens with the objective of promoting normative good that does not have to be economically oriented, but rather they can have social goals in cooperative associations, interest organizations and movements and so on (Gawell et al., 2009; Borzaga et al., 2008; Brickerhoff, 2000). Such normative good could be to improve welfare services for the young and the elderly, promote human rights issues, work for sustainable development or organize sports and leisure. In addition, *policy entrepreneurs* have often been used as a description of actors outside the formal positions of government who seek to introduce and implement new ideas into the public sector (Roberts and King, 1991) or for politicians and/or government employees who see a window of opportunity to improve government policies. Policy entrepreneurs may or may not be formally or directly engaged in legislative policymaking, but based on know-how, reputation, money and time, they are in a position to develop and present alternative policy solutions to existing problems facing policymakers (Kingdon, 1995). Finally, another concept of entrepreneurship has been the *bureaucratic entrepreneur*, referring to actors as public servants or similar who gain power from policymakers to influence the policy process by initiating a political process, setting priorities and interpreting the implementation phase and so on (Silander, 2016: 11–12; Carroll, 2017; Nakamura and Smallwood, 1980; Roberts and King, 1991).

The different types of conceptual approaches to entrepreneurship are summarized in Table 1.1. Many different types of entrepreneurs and entrepreneurship are described in the literature, and the definitions of these types have differed from one study to another. This has led scholars to argue that 'perhaps the largest obstacle in creating a conceptual

Table 1.1   Types of entrepreneurs

Term	Common Definitions
Economic/Business Entrepreneurs	Actors within the business sector acting as risk-takers, innovators and responders to market disequilibria to seek economic gains for their companies/organizations
Social Entrepreneurs	Actors within the civil society who seek societal changes within cooperative associations, interest organizations, aid branches and rights and liberties movements
Policy Entrepreneurs	Actors inside or outside the formal positions of government/politics who seek to introduce and implement new ideas into the public sector for development of the public good rather than for individual profits
Public Entrepreneurs	Actors within public corporations within the public sector who seek implementation through innovations in public sector practice
Bureaucratic Entrepreneurship	Actors who gain power from policymakers to influence the policy process and/or the public sector by initiating a political process, setting priorities and interpreting the implementation phase
Political Entrepreneurs – traditionally used	Actors (politicians) within the political arena, driven by the common good or individual profit from the political system, acting to receive political support, votes, campaign contributions or improved political status
Political Entrepreneurs – applied in this study	Actors and institutions (politicians, bureaucrats, officers and institutions) within the publicly funded sector that with innovative approaches encourage entrepreneurship/business and where the goal is growth and employment for the common good

framework for the entrepreneurship field has been its definition. What the many different studies on types of entrepreneurship have in common is the main focus on how entrepreneurship includes knowledge, innovation, opportunity, implementation and risk taking as core elements' (see Carroll, 2017: 115). But what has differentiated private/business and public sector entrepreneurs and entrepreneurship has been the lack of entrepreneurial profit (see Boyett, 1996: 49) in public sector entrepreneurship.

In more recent studies, the developing multidisciplinary approach to entrepreneurship has also referred to political entrepreneurs and political entrepreneurship (Silander, 2016; 2018; Silander and Silander, 2015;

Scheingate, 2003). Such conceptualization was introduced by Robert Dahl, who focused on resourceful and masterful political leaders and how the political entrepreneur was 'the epitome of the self-made man' (1974: 25, 223–7, 282). According to Dahl, *Homo politicus* are people formally engaged in politics. Political entrepreneurs could be driven by the common good and by providing collective benefits to the many, but they could also be oriented towards individual profit seeking from the political system by, for instance, receiving political support and votes, campaign contributions or improved political status (see Dahl, 1974; McCaffrey and Salerno, 2011; Simmons et al., 2011). In Dahl's discussions, individual leaders have often been referred to as *entrepreneurial politicians* (Scheingate, 2003), but others have used political entrepreneurship to refer to individuals trying to individually profit from the political system (see McCaffrey and Salerno, 2011).

This study focuses on European political entrepreneurship in the Europe 2020 strategy, but conceptualizes political entrepreneurs and political entrepreneurship based on existing criticism of previous research. First, it has been argued that studies on political entrepreneurship have focused on political entrepreneurs from an actor-oriented perspective by only analysing individual motives and perceptions with institutions as a forgotten dimension. Second, such studies have often started from the assumption that political entrepreneurship is about individual profit-seeking activities within the political/public system, rather than the common good. Third, it has also been argued that fuzzy distinctions have been made between what actually defines political entrepreneurship; that is, what political entrepreneurship is all about compared to regular, day-to-day political/ public activities in the public sector. From a political entrepreneurship perspective, studies have focused on how politicians and bureaucrats may change tax distribution, regulations and implementation procedures, but they have forgotten to argue for why such regular activities in politics would be defined as political entrepreneurship or not (Salerno, 2008; Scheingate, 2003; Holcombe, 2002; Schneider and Teske, 1992).

Following recent studies on political entrepreneurs and political entre-preneurship (see Karlsson et al., 2016; 2018; Silander and Silander, 2015), our perspective focuses on politicians, public servants, bureaucrats and institutions that seek to create new, innovative and favourable formal and informal institutional conditions (see North, 1990; see also Kingdon, 1995) for growth and employment. Political entrepreneurship is about approaching and challenging traditional formal institutions in political steering, leadership, strategies, policies, rules, regulations, laws and budgets for entrepreneurial activities and/or in traditional informal institutions' ideas, attitudes, values, perceptions, images and symbols in ways that structure public day-to-day activities and culture around entrepreneurship (see North, 1990; Morgan, 1986; Putnam, 1993; Casson, 1995; Finnemore and Sikkink, 1998; McCaffrey and Salerno, 2011: 553). Political entrepreneurship occurs when traditional institutions, formal and/or informal, are challenged and changed by new institutions, formal and/or informal, better suited to promote entrepreneurial activities and economic growth. As argued in a previous study, 'The political entrepreneur operates beyond traditional and routinized procedures and is innovative and creative in using formal and informal institutions and networks to improve the public sector's activities towards entrepreneurs and entrepreneurship by developing and promoting new norms that have not been embedded in traditional day-to-day public activities' (Silander, 2016: 10).

EU GOVERNANCE AND EUROPE 2020

The Commission has set out how the European Council must play the role of guiding the EU member states towards the objectives set out in Europe 2020. The European Council should steer the work on Europe 2020 as the political body that could promote integration and collaboration and ensure member state interdependence and collaboration between the EU and member states. On the other hand, the Council of Ministers should be responsible for the implementation of Europe 2020 and making sure that all objectives are met. The progress made by member states with regional and local authorities would be monitored and assessed annually by the European Commission to ensure the development of smart, sustainable and inclusive European growth. It would also be the role of the Commission to set out policy recommendations, warnings and proposals based on these assessments of individual member states. The European Parliament would be co-legislator with the Council of Ministers, but also mobilizer of European citizens into the agenda, and it would have national parliaments include debate over how Europe 2020 could be implemented in the best way possible on a national level as well as regional and local levels, including domestic authorities in relation to private actors and the civil society (European Commission, 2010: 26–7).

> All national, regional and local authorities should implement the partnership, closely associating parliaments, as well as social partners and representatives of civil society, contributing to the elaboration of national reform programmes as well as to its implementation. By establishing a permanent dialogue between various levels of government, the priorities of the Union are brought closer to citizens, strengthening the ownership needed to deliver the Europe 2020 strategy. (European Commission, 2010: 28)

Multiple actors have been involved in the Europe 2020 strategy because of the nature of the EU as an organizational hybrid of international and supranational decision making and steering. Over decades, the EU has widened and deepened, and today EU politics is conducted on different levels of authority and networks, formally including political authorities on a European, national, regional and local level, together creating European governance. The EU has embedded top-down and bottom-up political policies to communicate between the national and local. The most obvious political symbol of EU governance has perhaps been the transfer of sovereignty from sovereign individual member states to the EU institutions. Over time, the EU has become a significant political power in individual member states' politics (Hix and Goetz, 2000). This has been the case foremost in policy areas where the EU has received supreme authority, but the EU has also influenced policy areas where shared competence and supporting competence has existed.

Based on the Treaty of Lisbon of 2009, the EU with member states has a division of competences (Lisbon Treaty, 2009). The Treaty explicitly sets out EU competences and therefore policy areas not mentioned in the Treaty are under the sovereignty of each member state. The Treaty identifies three main categories: exclusive competences, shared competences and supporting competences.

First, *exclusive competences* are mentioned in Article 3 of the Treaty of Lisbon on the Functioning of the European Union (TFEU), which sets out areas where the EU is the supreme authority to legislate and adopt binding acts. The individual member states have transferred all sovereignty to the collective will of the EU, and member states are only involved in decisions when they are called upon by the EU to implement policies. The Commission initiates and implements laws and regulations based on the authorities in the Treaty. In addition, the Council, the Parliament and the European Court assess the rights of the Union in relation to what the Treaty says. The EU possesses exclusive competence on the customs union, the establishment of competition rules in the internal market, monetary policy for the euro area, conservation of marine biological resources under the common fisheries policy, common commercial policy and international agreements (EUR-Lex: Distribution of competences, 2018).

Second, *shared competences* are institutionalized in Article 4 of the Treaty of Lisbon and refer to where the EU and member states share authority to legislate and adopt legally binding acts. Individual member states are sovereign to decide and legislate if the EU has not exercised authority or has addressed intention to exercise authority. Additionally, in those cases when individual member states have laws and regulations in place, the EU has no authority to decide on laws and regulations that could harm or challenge existing national regulations. Shared competence is exercised in the

> internal market, social policy (specifically defined in the Treaty), regional policy, agriculture and fisheries (except conservation of marine biological resources), environment, consumer protection, transport, trans-European networks, energy, area of freedom, security and justice, shared safety concerns in public health matters (defined in the TFEU), research, technological development, space and development cooperation and humanitarian aid. (EUR-Lex: Distribution of competences, 2018)

Third, *supporting competences* are mentioned in Article 6 of the Treaty of Lisbon and delegate the main authority to the individual member states with the supporting role of the EU. The EU has no authority to act for harmonization of state policies, laws and regulation, but may only assist member states through coordination. Supporting competences refer to protection and improvement of human health, industry, culture, tourism, education, vocational training, youth and sport, civil protection and administrative cooperation (EUR-Lex: Distribution of competences, 2018).[1]

The Europe 2020 strategy covers a wide range of policy areas and therefore refers to all three categories of competence. Parts of the strategy are under the regulation of exclusive EU competence, whereas most parts are under shared or supporting competences. This leaves the Europe 2020 strategy to be decided on and implemented by several EU actors in the framework of European governance.[2] The specific role of the EU only in policy areas designated as its exclusive competence has traditionally led to

---

[1] The categories of competences portray the formal hybrid structure of the EU and the official way politics is handled. In day-to-day activities, however, these formal competences are often challenged by practical political hindrances. For instance, despite the EU's exclusive competence in specific policy areas, does the EU embed member states in the Council of Ministers and national politicians in the Parliament who have a say and decide on political issues and policies to be implemented by national politicians and public servants at home in the individual member states? In addition, in those policy areas where member states have full authority, is politics often influenced by the EU institutions due to the networks of local, national and European actors of official and unofficial ties?

[2] The EU categories of exclusive, shared and supporting competences are rooted in two fundamental principles of the EU as set out in Article 5 of the Treaty. The first principle is proportionality and refers to how all EU actions must be proportional to the goals to be achieved (that is, EU actions must only be necessary). The second principle relates to subsidiarity and refers to how the EU in areas of non-exclusive competences must refer decision making to appropriate levels of authority. It requires the EU not to act in policy areas of non-EU competence, but only participate if EU member states are unable to reach identified goals and if such goals can be fulfilled on an EU level. This is regulated in Article 352. It is important to acknowledge that in those policy areas that are not explicitly mentioned in the Treaty, all competences are in the hands of the member states. To change competences from

policymaking in the EU that is complemented by the use of 'soft' governance tools, in terms of benchmarking, recommendations on best practices
and guidelines through the Open Method of Co-ordination (OMC)
process. The OMC was initiated at the Lisbon meeting in 2000 together
with the European Employment Strategy as a method for the EU to
influence policy areas where member states had major national differences
and/or where the EU had limited competences in terms of influence. The
decision on OMC in Lisbon was a compromise between leaving member
states with the main responsibility in a policy area and at the same time
opening up for the EU to coordinate policies (EUR-Lex: OMC, 2018).
The OMC has primarily been about the EU initiating benchmarking and
exchanging best practice between member states based on the voluntary
and intergovernmental mode of cooperation.

However, the OMC process leaves the Commission with substantial
influence through the monitoring and agenda-setting role (see Silander,
2018). In addition, the Council of Ministers also plays a central role by
setting the policy goals and guidelines by unanimity. The OMC process
allows member states to submit annual reports on progress made, and all
reports are commented on and evaluated by the Commission. Although
the OMC process differs in content due to different policy areas, there are
common steps: Step 1 is fixing the guidelines for the union combined with
a timetable (what is to be completed in the short, medium and long term).
Step 2 is to establish quantitative and qualitative indicators and benchmarks. Step 3 consists of translating the European guidelines into national
and regional policies by setting specific targets and adopting measures
for reaching such targets. Step 4 is periodic monitoring and evaluations
organized as mutual learning processes (see EUR-Lex: OMC, 2018).

SMART, SUSTAINABLE AND SOCIAL INCLUSIVE GROWTH

In 2010, after a few years of economic recession globally and in Europe,
the European Commission officially stated *Europe 2020 – A strategy
for smart, sustainable and inclusive growth*. Europe 2020 was a strategic
concept from the Commission on how to promote and protect European
growth, jobs and social integration in times of political, economic and
social challenges (see Stec and Grzebyk, 2018: 119–20; Liobikienė and
Butkus, 2017: 299; Hoedl, 2011: 11–12; Walburn, 2010: 699). The Europe

---

individual member states to the EU level demands an approval by all member states and
from the European Parliament and a new ratification of a treaty.

2020 strategy stressed the importance of developing and consolidating a European social market economy model (see Chapter 2). This model had previously been stressed within the EU, but Europe 2020 re-emphasized the importance of such a model by focusing on smart, sustainable and inclusive growth (Budd, 2013: 274–6; Gros and Roth, 2012: 1–2; Hoedl, 2011: 12). The Europe 2020 strategic targets were: (1) employment; (2) research, development and innovation (R&D); (3) education; (4) poverty reduction and social inclusion; and (5) climate change and energy. As stated,

> The Europe 2020 strategy has been developed as the successor to the Lisbon Strategy as a long-term approach to dealing with structural weaknesses in Europe's economy. One aspect that is supposed to differentiate the Europe 2020 strategy from the Lisbon strategy is the concentration on five key specific targets. These five targets are supposed to be representative of the overall goal of smart, sustainable and inclusive growth. (Gros and Roth, 2012: 77)

The Europe 2020 strategy established main objectives to be reached, implementation tools for handling the serious structural economic weaknesses in the European economy, and ways to turn the European economic recession of 2010 into prosperity and growth in 2020 by focusing on major reforms for smart, sustainable and inclusive growth. As stressed by the Commission, 'Smart growth: developing an economy based on knowledge and innovation. – Sustainable growth: promoting a more resource efficient, greener and more competitive economy. – Inclusive growth: fostering a high-employment economy delivering social and territorial cohesion' (European Commission, 2010: 3).

First, *smart growth*, in developing an economy based on knowledge and innovation, refers to new know-how and technology as main drivers for a future prosperous European economy. The main themes identified would be innovation, education and digital society. Smart growth requires improved education, research and innovations to provide a skilled workforce and new products and services, but also innovative entrepreneurship and financial investments to identify new needs, demands, markets and so on. The Commission argued for greater spending on research and development and foremost targeting private investments by facilitating improved conditions for private sector research and development in Europe. The Commission further identified the importance of improving education, training and lifelong learning by promoting better reading competences and increased numbers of people with university degrees, improving the standards and status of European universities, and matching education with labour market demands. In addition, Europe had to improve its competitiveness in the digital society by reaching out to the fast-expanding demands for communication technologies and increasing investment of European societies in the Internet and providing for more Internet-based goods and services (European Commission, 2010: 9–10). Smart growth was planned to be implemented through targets on the thematic areas, one on R&D and two for education. These targets were to increase public and private investments in R&D to 3 per cent of gross domestic product (GDP), reduce school drop-out rates to less than 10 per cent, and increase the share of the population in the 30–34 age group having completed tertiary education to 40 per cent or more (Eurostat, 2018a; see also Hudrlikova, 2013: 1).

Second, *sustainable growth*, through a transition to a greener economy, refers to building a European economy of resource efficiency and sustainability and staying globally competitive based on new greener technologies. The main themes in focus would be climate, energy and mobility and competitiveness. This requires innovative European political entrepreneurship to foster competitive entrepreneurship, new businesses and networks and to promote a consumer culture that values resource efficiency and a greener low-carbon economy. The Commission stated the importance of continued open trade of exports and imports but also that Europe had to become more competitive and with higher productivity of partner states. Europe must also continue its early initiatives to become a global green economic actor by pushing for green technologies to safeguard resource efficiency. The push for green technologies would lead to fulfilled climate change goals, with significant decreased emissions, but would also open up for a transition to a new environmentally friendly economy of new innovations, products and services that all together would create new jobs and a growing economy. A transition to a greener economy would also lead to lowered costs for import of expensive oil and gas and would be beneficial for European security because of lowered dependency on specific foreign governments (European Commission, 2010: 12–13). Sustainable growth would be approached based on three climate change and energy targets. The so-called 20-20-20 targets set out by the EU include reducing greenhouse gas emission by 20 per cent, increasing renewable energy in gross final energy consumption by 20 per cent and increasing energy efficiency by 20 per cent. Such targets not only provide for important measures against ongoing climate change, but also provide new jobs in a transformed, greener economy with green products and services and makes the EU become a green, global competitive actor (Eurostat, 2017: 15).

Third, *inclusive growth*, with a high-employment economy providing economic, social and territorial cohesion and integration, refers to empowering Europeans by offering job opportunities, an improved labour market, lifelong training, education and social protection from poverty and marginalization to all of Europe and all Europeans regardless of age, gender and so on. The main themes to prioritize were employment and skills and fighting poverty. The Commission clearly stated in 2010 the challenge of demographic change in Europe with a future limited workforce beside an unemployment rate that is higher than in the US – about two-thirds of Europe's working-age citizens being employed compared to about 70 per cent in the US. The Commission further stressed challenges in economic and social marginalization of women, older workers and young people, all facing different hindrances to entering the labour market and/or finding opportunities for education and financial support for building and developing businesses and so forth. The Commission estimated that about 80 million Europeans had only low or basic skills, 80 million European faced the serious risk of poverty (among them 19 million children), and the grave consequences of unemployment and poverty in social exclusion and health inequalities. The Europe 2020 strategy should focus on growth and jobs to sustain and develop Europe's social market economy (European Commission, 2010: 16). Inclusive growth would be approached based on targeting employment, poverty and social exclusion. These targets were established to increase the employment rate to 75 per cent in the 20–64 age group and to prevent at least 20 million people from living under the threat of poverty and/or social exclusion (Eurostat, 2017: 15).

The different natures of these objectives were all embedded in the overall framework of promoting and protecting smart, sustainable and socially inclusive growth in Europe. It was argued in the 'Europe 2020' communication that smart, sustainable and social growth were interrelated and had to be focused at once and as a reinforcing strategy. For example, the Commission stated that smart growth in greener technologies, through research and development, also implied new and sustainable growth and social development and that educational improvements in the lower levels to higher education provided for employability and job creation, as well as social integration, reduced poverty and so on. It was argued that 'educational improvements help employability and reduce poverty – R & D/innovation and more efficient energy use makes us more competitive and creates jobs – investing in cleaner technologies combats climate change while creating new business or job opportunities' (European Commission, 2010).

The Europe 2020 strategy set out the overall goals to be met by EU member states on a national and regional level and translated them into national contexts and objectives to be assessed. These overall objectives were to reach 7 per cent employment among people aged 20–64; secure

3 per cent of the overall EU GDP invested in research and development; lower emission levels by 20 per cent compared to the overall European greenhouse gas emissions in the 1990s; provide renewable energy sources that account for 20 per cent of all energy supply; and increase energy efficiency by 20 per cent by focusing on climate change and energy reforms for a greener economy. In addition, the main objectives were also to improve education standards by pushing down early school leavers to below 10 per cent, support enrolment in higher education by aiming for 40 per cent of people aged 30–34 to have finished higher education, and reduce the number of those who face poverty and social exclusion by at least 20 million people (European Commission, 2010: 3; see also Renda, 2014: 4; Hudrliková, 2013: 450–60).

The objectives were to be reached within a 10-year period of time with reforms taking place from 2010 to 2020. The reforms were to be conducted on different European levels of governance with the main focus on EU governance in EU institutional actions, as well as with national-, regional- and local-level actions at the member state level. The Europe 2020 strategy implied numerous actions by numerous European actors framed by the objectives set out in the Europe 2020 plan and assessed by annual national reports to the Commission and through the EU statistics office, Eurostat and so on (European Commission, 2010: 3–4).

THE SEVEN FLAGSHIPS

The Commission initiated seven flagships to be implemented to provide for a smart, sustainable and inclusive European economy. It was declared that such flagships had to be focused on an integrated policy based on a European/EU and individual member state perspective (see Bongardt and Torres, 2010: 137; Armstrong, 2012: 288–9). The Europe 2020 communication identified the following flagships:

- 'Innovation Union' to improve framework conditions and access to finance for research and innovation so as to ensure that innovative ideas can be turned into products and services that create growth and jobs.
- 'Youth on the move' to enhance the performance of education systems and to facilitate the entry of young people to the labour market.
- 'A digital agenda for Europe' to speed up the roll-out of high-speed internet and reap the benefits of a digital single market for households and firms.

- 'Resource efficient Europe' to help decouple economic growth from the use of resources, support the shift towards a low carbon economy, increase the use of renewable energy sources, modernize our transport sector and promote energy efficiency.
- 'An industrial policy for the globalization era' to improve the business environment, notably for SMEs, and to support the development of a strong and sustainable industrial base able to compete globally.
- 'An agenda for new skills and jobs' to modernize the labour market and empower people by developing their skills throughout the lifecycle with a view to increasing labour participation and better matching labour supply and demand, including through labour mobility.
- 'European platform against poverty' to ensure social and territorial cohesion such that the benefits of growth and jobs are widely shared and people experiencing poverty and social exclusion are enabled to live in dignity and take an active part in society. (European Commission, 2010: 3–4; see also Stec and Grzebyk, 2018: 123)

In the area of smart growth, the Commission identified three flagships of reforms in Innovation Union, Youth on the Move and a Digital Agenda for Europe. The flagship Innovation Union initiative focused on research and development and innovations to promote a transformation of Europe's economy away from industrialization based on oil and gas and towards a greener economy of energy and resource efficiency and new jobs, products and services based on high-tech reforms. Smart growth also embedded health and ageing and how to meet the demographic challenges that exist in Europe with a shrinking workforce and an ageing population that create dire straits for European welfare societies. The flagship Youth on the Move initiative focused on the importance of improved educational institutional capacities and European know-how and skills. This flagship sought to improve smart growth by improving higher education among European universities, enhance researchers' strategic programmes, promote increased mobility among students and trainees, facilitate improved chances among young Europeans to enter the labour market and gear learning outcomes in course syllabuses to contemporary labour market requirements. Finally, under the smart growth objective, the flagship Digital Agenda for Europe initiative focused on how to make use of digitalization, based on a digital single market to provide sustainable economic and social benefits through development of the use and supply of the Internet and broadband in an improved online infrastructure for all of Europe and for all Europeans. This required political and financial support for research, innovations and online services for private and public sector activities (European Commission, 2010: 10–12).

In the area of sustainable growth, the Commission pinpointed two flagships to focus on: the resource-efficient Europe initiative and the industrial policy for the globalization era initiative. The first flagship initiative stated the importance of transforming the European economy into a resource-efficient and low-carbon economy. Europe's economic growth had to be decoupled from inefficient resource and energy use and embed a sustainable approach that prioritized reduced CO_2 emissions, while remaining competitive. The transformation to a greener economy should focus on the transport sector, on the road, in the air and at sea, including a change of the car industry in the production of electric and hybrid cars. The overall objective was to turn the European economy into a low-carbon economy with high emissions reduction providing for real measurements against global climate change. The second flagship on sustainable growth, in the industrial policy for the globalization era flagship initiative, addressed the economic recession and its impact on industries and SMEs in Europe, the competitiveness that comes with globalization and the demand to transform industries to meet climate change challenges. Although some sectors face major changes to survive in the market, other sectors may grow intensively by new market demands and technological solutions. The Commission set out to address the need for industrial transformation by supporting entrepreneurship and new ideas and innovations in a new industrial policy to assist the manufacturing and service industries to survive and develop a competitive and diversified base. The Europe 2020 communication also called for a reduction in transaction costs for businesses in Europe as well as in the administrative burden and dysfunctional business legislation, and improved access to finances, the Single Market and new markets internationally.

Finally, in the area of inclusive growth, two flagships were announced in the agenda for new skills and jobs and the European platform against poverty initiatives. The agenda for new skills and jobs flagship initiative focused on modernizing the labour market and consolidating the social model in the European economy by focusing on work hours, health issues, work safety and so on, as well as empowering Europeans with increased skills and know-how to lower the unemployment rate and make citizens prepared for new jobs and career changes as the economy is transforming. The Commission also stated the importance of providing financial support to promote intra-EU mobility, to assist in adjusting labour supply to labour demand in Europe and to promote improved cooperation between labour market institutions and social institutions in different member states and on national, regional and local levels. In addition, the Commission also focused on an overview of gender equality and existing work–life balance as well as tax levels and benefit systems to keep low-skilled people from social and economic marginalization and to encourage self-employment and entrepreneurship. The second initiative, the European platform against poverty, addressed measurements to combat poverty and socioeconomic marginalization and to promote integration. The Commission stressed the importance of cooperation between institutions, member state authorities and private actors to decrease social exclusion and to implement programmes for those at risk of poverty and/ or social exclusion by providing education, training and job opportunities among groups and in neighbourhoods in dire straits. Such an approach should also include reforms against discrimination based on disabilities, gender and/or migration (European Commission, 2010: 16–18).

The Europe 2020 strategy's main objectives and flagship initiatives are summarized in Box 1.1.

EUROPE 2020: IMPLEMENTATION AND IMPACT?

In 2014–15, the Commission conducted a mid-term review of Europe 2020 based on a public consultation of stakeholders' perceptions of the first years of Europe 2020 and lessons learned. Such consultation took place from May to October of 2014 (Eurostat, 2017: 17). It was summarized that the Europe 2020 strategy was viable and relevant and should continue to be the framework for promotion of growth, jobs and so on. Based on the mid-term review, the Commission initiated an assessment process named the European Semester to promote tighter alignment between the EU and individual member states (Gros and Roth, 2012: 79; Armstrong, 2012: 290). The European Semester policy cycle included several steps:

1. adoption of the Annual Growth Survey (AGS) by the Commission, identifying the socioeconomic priorities;
2. publication of the Commission's Alert Mechanism Report (AMR), but also the Joint Employment Report and recommendations to the Euro area;
3. publication of country reports to assist individual member states to launch reforms and initiatives to serve the Europe Agenda and reach national objectives;
4. submission of National Reform Programmes (NRPs) and Stability of Convergence Programmes (SCPs) from each individual member state, including measures and policies to implement country-specific recommendations from the Commission on a national basis; and

5. adoption of recommendations from the Commission and the endorsement of such recommendations by the Council of Ministers and the Parliament. (Tusińska, 2016: 190–91; Zeitlin and Vanhercke, 2014: 3–4; Eurostat, 2017: 18–19)

The established European Semester was to focus on ensuring healthy public finances to limit macroeconomic inequalities and imbalances within the EU, promoting strategic investments, and assisting necessary structural reforms to seek new jobs and overall economic growth (European Commission, The European Semester). The main function of the Commission has been to analyse EU member states' overall progress and to provide individual national recommendations on macroeconomic and structural reforms and investments to be endorsed and adopted by the Council (European Commission, The European Semester, 2018). As stated,

> Unlike the Europe 2020 strategy, the European semester has a stronger and more complete framework to monitor, discuss, evaluate and enforce policy goals set at the European level to achieve growth, competitiveness and stability in the EU. The European semester has thus been established to cover both the Europe 2020 and the overall economic situation in the member states, including the short-term challenges. (Gros and Roth, 2012: 79)

There has been great scholarly interest in discussing Europe 2020 and its core concepts, but foremost is forecasting whether the EU has been/can be successful in implementing some or all of Europe 2020's identified targets at one time or over a broader time range (Fura et al., 2017: 969–70). Such studies have focused on the different targets set out in Europe 2020 (see Moreno and García-Álvarez, 2018; Liobikienė and Butkus, 2017: 298–9; see also Fura et al., 2017; Renda, 2014; Gros and Roth, 2012; Theodoropoulou,

---

BOX 1.1   AGENDA 2020

- Raise the employment rate of the population aged 20–64 from 69% to 75% or more.
- Achieve the target of investing 3% of GDP in R&D.
- Reduce greenhouse gas emissions by at least 20% compared to 1990 levels and increase the share of renewable energy in our final energy consumption to 20%, and achieve a 20% increase in energy efficiency.
- Reduce the share of early school leavers to 10% from the current 15% and increase the share of the population aged 30–34 having completed tertiary education from 31% to at least 40%.
- Reduce the number of Europeans living below national poverty lines by 25%, lifting 20 million people out of poverty.

Smart Growth	Sustainable Growth	Inclusive Growth
Innovation The EU's Innovation Union flagship initiative targeted improving framework conditions and access to finance for research and innovation so as to strengthen the innovation chain and boost levels of investment throughout the Union.	*Climate, Energy And Mobility* The EU's resource efficient Europe flagship initiative targeted decoupling economic growth from the use of resources, by decarbonizing our economy, increasing the use of renewable sources, modernizing our transport sector and promoting energy efficiency.	*Employment And Skills* The EU's agenda for new skills and jobs flagship initiative targeted modernizing labour markets by facilitating labour mobility and the development of skills throughout the lifecycle with a view to increasing labour participation and better matching labour supply and demand.
Education The EU's Youth on the Move flagship initiative targeted enhancing the performance of education systems and reinforcing the international attractiveness of Europe's higher education institutions.	*Competitiveness* The EU's industrial policy for the globalization era flagship initiative was designed to improve the business environment, especially for SMEs, and to support the development of a strong and sustainable industrial base able to compete globally.	*Fighting Poverty* The EU's European platform against poverty flagship initiative was designed to ensure social and territorial cohesion such that the benefits of growth and jobs are widely shared and people experiencing poverty and social exclusion are enabled to live in dignity and take an active part in society.
Digital Society The EU's Digital Agenda for Europe flagship initiative targeted speeding up the roll-out of high-speed Internet and reaping the benefits of a digital single market for households and firms.		

Note: Adapted from European Commission (2010, Annex I).

2010). In 2014/2015, during the mid-term analysis of Europe 2020, the overall progress made on the objectives of the strategy was analysed.

First, focusing on employment and increasing the employment rate in the 20–64 age group had improved, but did not reach the 2020 target of 75 per cent. In 2015, the employment rate had increased to about 70 per cent. In 2008, during the peak of the economic recession and preceding the Europe 2020 strategy, the employment rate for this age group had increased to 70.3 per cent. The ongoing economic crisis resulted in a declining employment rate to about 68.4 per cent in 2013. However, in 2015, the employment rate had increased again, symbolizing a possible turning point (Eurostat, 2017). In the latest Eurostat evaluation of progress made in 2017 (data on 2015 and/or 2016), it was stated that the rate had increased to 71.1 per cent, showing a positive trend of growing employment and getting closer to the Europe 2020 target of 75 per cent. However, Eurostat indicated that there were higher unemployment rates for people aged 20–29 and people aged 55–64, those citizens with limited education, and migrants to the EU who became citizens, as well as an existing gender employment gap. In addition, Eurostat also addressed major imbalances in employment rates between EU member states, with a north–south division on a national and regional level, Sweden, Germany, Austria, the Netherlands and the UK having high levels of employment. For example, in 2016 employment in Greece was about 56.2 per cent compared to 80.1 per cent in Sweden (Eurostat, 2017: 8–9, 27, 30; see also Gros and Roth, 2012: 32–43). As stated, 'Northern and central European countries recorded the highest rates; eight countries even exceeded the 75% EU employment target. With employment rates below 65%, Mediterranean countries dominated the lower end of the scale' (Eurostat, 2017: 30). Finally, there were also variations on employment rates based on age, gender, education and migration. In short, a general employment gap existed between the young and middle aged, men and women, educated and less educated people and natives and migrants, although in some cases, such as gender balance, the employment gap is decreasing (Eurostat, 2017: 29–33, 36–8).

Second, when studying progress made on research and development and the promoted objective to increase gross domestic expenditure on R&D, Eurostat identified a minor increase as a percentage of GDP from 2008 and forward. In 2008, R&D expenditure was 1.85 per cent of GDP and had increased to 2.03 per cent in 2014, indicating an increased level of public expenditure on R&D. With the Europe 2020 stated objective of 3 per cent of GDP, the level reached in 2014 was 0.97 per cent below the identified objective (Eurostat, 2017: 57). In the latest evaluation of 2017, Eurostat expressed concerns for the continued low level of expenditure on research and development throughout the EU, at a level of about 2 per cent over some years. With a slowly rising level from 2008 and forward, statistics showed halted progress, with more or less status quo in level of investments between 2013 and 2015 (Eurostat, 2017: 10, 59). In a global comparison, the EU is behind the US, Japan, China and South Korea, advanced or fast developing economies, regarding R&D. For example, in 2014, China passed the EU on percentage of GDP invested in R&D. There are also regional variations within the EU with regions in Germany, the UK, Austria, France, Belgium and the Nordic countries with the highest levels of spending on R&D. Within the EU, regions varied on R&D intensity from 0.46 per cent to 3.26 per cent, with highest spending in regions in the Nordic countries and lowest in eastern and southern states such as Croatia and Romania (Gros and Roth, 2012: 9–10, 14–16; Eurostat, 2017: 59–61). As stated,

> Estimates show that to meet the 2020 target, EU R&D intensity would need to grow three times as fast as it did between 2007 and 2014. . . . According to these projections, if the 2007 to 2014 trend continues, investment in R&D is forecasted to rise to only 2.28% by 2020. . . . Progressing more rapidly towards the 3% target would require a faster structural shift to more knowledge-based economic activities. (Eurostat, 2017: 79)

Third, on climate change and energy, estimations of 2014 on greenhouse gas emissions showed a decline in the EU by 22.1 per cent compared to emission levels in 1990. In 2008–09, the emission level dropped sharply by 7.2 per cent, indicating a decline in the overall economic growth in Europe due to economic recession, but also a transformation into a greener European economy that has indicated a great opportunity not only to reach, but also to exceed the Europe 2020 target on greenhouse gas emissions (Eurostat, 2017: 85). Europe 2020 established 80 per cent, a drop of 20 per cent emissions in 2020, showing a successful EU strategy on greenhouse gas emissions. This has mostly been due to structural changes from a manufacturing-based economy to a service-oriented one, reduction in the use of coal in favour of gas and overall reductions of emissions in all sectors except transportation and aviation (Eurostat, 2017: 83–5). In a comparison between EU member states, Luxembourg scored best on reduction of emission per capita between 2005 and 2015, with good practice seen also in Denmark, Greece, Belgium, Finland and Cyprus and poor practice seen in eastern EU member states. In 2015, 16 out of 28 member states had reached their national objectives as set out in relation to Europe 2020 (Eurostat, 2017: 89–90; see also Liobikienè and Butkus, 2017: 299–305).

In addition, the share of renewable energy in gross final energy consumption increased between 2008 and 2014 from 11 per cent to 16 per cent due to biofuels and renewable waste, hydropower and wind, and solar energy. The Europe 2020 target of 20 per cent was not reached in 2014, falling 4 per cent behind in the share of renewable energy in gross final energy consumption, but with signs of fast progress. However, all EU member states have increased their levels of renewable energy, and ten member states have met their national objectives as set out in relation to Europe 2020 (Eurostat, 2017: 96). Another target is declining primary energy consumption. This consumption level had fallen between 2008 and 2014 by 11 per cent, leaving the oil consumption level in the EU lower than in 1990 and almost reaching the Europe 2020 objective by only falling 1.6 per cent below it (Eurostat, 2017). In the Eurostat assessment of 2017, a minor increase of emissions over the last few years was noted, but an overall significant decrease over time was observed, leaving the EU with a great chance to meet the Europe 2020 Agenda target of decreasing gas emissions by 20 per cent in 2020 – a target that had already been met in 2014 and now had to be consolidated. Eurostat explained this EU progress in terms of reduction of gas emission in all sectors except fuel combustion in transport and aviation as follows: 'The share of renewable energy in gross final energy production, the Europe 2020 strategy's second climate change and energy target, increased from 16.1 percent in 2014 to 16.7 percent in 2015. Therefore, the EU remains 3.3 percentage points below the Europe 2020 renewable energy target of 20 percent' (Eurostat, 2017: 10).

Fourth, on education and early leavers from education and training in the 18–24 age range, Eurostat indicated in 2008 a level of 14.7 per cent and in 2015 11 per cent, consistently closing on the Europe 2020 objective of 10 per cent. On tertiary education attainment in the 30–34 age group, Eurostat also identified a consistent increase from 2008 to 2015 from 31.1 per cent to 38.7 per cent, almost reaching the Europe 2020 objective of 40 per cent by 2020 (Eurostat, 2017: 109). The Eurostat analysis of 2017 showed a continued decline in number of early leavers, from 11 per cent in 2015 to 10.7 per cent in 2016, stating that 'Europe is steadily approaching its headline target for 2020, which envisages reducing the rate of early leavers from education and training to less than 10 percent' (Eurostat, 2017: 11; see also Gros and Roth, 2012: 44). It was also argued that women as early leavers were already below the target and that men, although lagging behind, are closing the gap. The most challenged groups were recent immigrants. Early leavers tend to be at a higher risk than others of becoming unemployed, with about 58 per cent of early leavers in the 18–24 age group being unemployed or inactive in 2016 (Eurostat, 2017: 11). In 2016, 15 EU member states had already reached their national objectives based on the Europe 2020 strategy and 17 states had reached the EU objective of 10 per cent, but variations existed among the other member states. In Luxembourg, Croatia, Lithuania, Poland and Slovenia, the early leavers were less than 6 per cent, compared to Malta, Romania and Spain with 18.5 per cent or even more, although such numbers were declining from previous years (Eurostat, 2017: 112; see also Istvan et al., 2016). In addition, younger people were generally more educated compared to older people, and migrants born outside the EU showed a lower level of education compared to European-born people in the EU. Member states also showed variations in the amount of money spent on education for their citizens. The highest public expenditures on education are found in Denmark and Sweden (8 per cent of GDP/7.7 per cent), compared to Romania (2.8 per cent) and Czech Republic (3.8 per cent) (Eurostat, 2017: 123). However, EU member states overall showed progress, as stated by Eurostat:

> The EU average early school leaving rate in 2010 was 13.9 percent and would need to be below 10 percent by 2020, ten years later. It follows from a basic calculation that the minimum annual progress required for the EU as a whole during this period is −3.5%, whereas the observed annual progress for the EU between 2010 and 2016 has been −3.8%. This means that overall the EU is on track. . . . (Eurostat, 2017: 127)

Fifth and finally, focusing on people at risk of poverty and/or social exclusion, the economic crisis had a negative impact, leaving an increased number of people living at risk of poverty and/or social exclusion (see discussion by Gros and Roth, 2012: 56–62); from 118 million people in 2010 to 124 million in 2012. After a few years of crisis, a decline was recorded, leaving about 122 million Europeans at risk in 2014. That is almost one in four people in the EU, and 25 million people too many to reach the Europe 2020 objective (Eurostat, 2018b). In the Eurostat analysis of 2017, about 118.8 million people were affected, showing a decline in the number of people at risk (Eurostat, 2017: 133). The Europe 2020 target, however, was to decrease the number identified in 2008 by 20 million people, leaving the EU in 2017 still with a major challenge. As stated by Eurostat,

> Although the share of poor or socially excluded people has recently decreased and is approaching the levels observed before the economic crisis in 2008, almost every fourth person (23.7 percent of the population) in the EU remained at risk of poverty or social exclusion in 2015, which means that the gap to the EU target was 22.9 million people. (Eurostat, 2017: 11)

Risk of social exclusion has embedded several related challenges, foremost in monetary poverty, but also material deprivation and low work intensity. While monetary poverty has slightly increased over time since 2010, with about 17.3 per cent of citizens challenged in 2015, people in households with low work intensity stayed more or less the same, with a decreased level of people with material deprivation. However, people at risk of poverty and social exclusion remained high in 2015: 86.6 million Europeans were at risk of monetary poverty, 40.3 million at risk of severe material deprivation and 39.6 million at risk of very low work intensity (Eurostat, 2017: 12, 132–6). As stated by Eurostat,

> [t]he number of people living in poverty or social exclusion has fallen since the economy started recovering in 2013. Nevertheless, almost every fourth person in the EU still experiences at least one of the three forms of poverty or social exclusion, showing there is some way to go to meet the Europe 2020 Strategy target. (Eurostat, 2017: 132)

It should be stated that there is great variation within Europe on the risk of poverty and social exclusion. The Czech Republic (14 per cent), Sweden (16 per cent), the Netherlands (16.4 per cent) and Finland (16.8 per cent) scored lowest on risk in 2015, while some southern and eastern European EU member states such as Bulgaria (41.3 per cent), Romania (37.4 per cent) and Greece (35.7 per cent) scored highest, with about one-third or more of the population at great risk of poverty and/or social exclusion. Overall, in 2015 16 member states saw increased numbers of citizens facing poverty and/or social exclusion compared to 2008, leaving these states far from their Europe 2020 national targets. The most negative trends were identified in Greece, Cyprus and Spain (Eurostat, 2017: 136–7). People's risk of poverty and social exclusion in EU member states was higher for women, the young, less-educated people and the unemployed. Although the gender gap has decreased on poverty, women's rate of being challenged by poverty or social exclusion was about 1.4 per cent higher than men's; 31.3 per cent of young people in the 18–24 age group were at risk, compared to 17.4 per cent among the elderly of 65 or older. The economic recession led to young people facing major challenges to enter the labour market or only finding poor-quality and low-paid jobs with temporary contracts. Migrants were another group at risk: native citizens of EU countries comprised 21.7 per cent of the at-risk population, with 25.2 per cent from other EU countries and an additional 40.2 per cent born outside the EU territory (Eurostat, 2017: 143; Chung et al., 2012: 301–306, 314).

The overall achievements made on Europe Agenda targets in 2015/2016 are summarized below in Table 1.2. It should, however, be stated that the implementation of Europe 2020 has varied between EU member states, with a great amount of implementation in Sweden, Finland, Denmark and

Table 1.2   Europe 2020 targets, EU-28

Topic	Target Indicator	2008	2013	2014	2015	2016	2017	Target
Employment	Employment rate, age group 20–64	70.3	68.4	69.2	70.1	71.1	72.2	75.0
R&D	GDP on R&D (%/GDP)	1.84	2.02	2.03	2.04	2.03	–	3.0
Climate change & energy	Greenhouse gas emission[a] (Index 1990: 100)	90.6	82.4	77.4	78.0	77.6	–	80.0
Education	Early leavers from education/ training (% of population aged 18–24)	14.7	11.9	11.2	11.0	10.7	10.6	<10.0
Poverty & social exclusion	People at risk of poverty or social exclusion, EU-27 (million people)	116.1	121.6	120.8	117.8	116.9	–	96.2

Note: a   Total emission, including international aviation, but excluding emissions from land use, land use change and forestry.

Source: Adapted from Eurostat (2018a).

Austria and lower levels of implementation in Romania, Bulgaria, Italy, Malta, Spain and Greece (Stec and Grzebyk, 2018: 128–9).

The Eurostat statistics on progress made on Europe 2020 were summarized in the 2017 edition with the following:

> Since 2008, substantial progress has been made in the area of climate change and energy through reduced greenhouse gas emissions and increased use of renewable energy sources. Positive developments are also visible in the area of education, where the EU is within reaching distance of both headline targets. While the EU remains at a significant distance from its targets on R&D investment, employment and poverty alleviation, the most recent developments in the latter two areas are encouraging and the targets are still within reach for 2020. (Eurostat, 2017: 8)

Europe 2020 is soon to be concluded after a decade of embedded initiatives and flagships for European governance to be implemented. There have been discussions on the content and potential consequences of the agenda on European smart, sustainable and socially inclusive growth. Many scholars have addressed concerns over Europe 2020 based on the limited progress made from 2000 to 2010 and the Lisbon Strategy (see Tusińska, 2016; Makarovič et al., 2014; Gros and Roth, 2012; Prijon, 2012; Borghetto and Franchino, 2010). Many other scholars have provided different forecasts pointing out more or less progress to be expected on R&D, employment, education, climate, poverty reduction and so on (see Gros and Roth, 2012: 2–4). Scholars have also shed light on potential hindrances to successfully implementing Europe 2020 (see Renda, 2014: 5–10; Budd, 2013: 285; Bongardt and Torres, 2010; Tilford and Whyte, 2010).

One such first obvious hindrance to the implementation of Europe 2020 has been the economic recession in Europe. The reason or context of the Commission Communication of 2010 was the global and European recession that had begun in 2007–08 (Bongardt and Torres, 2010: 136). The European economic crisis, which began in the US and spread around the world, challenged the EU, individual member states, regions and communities throughout Europe from 2009 forward. The economic recession influenced more or less all EU member states on a national, regional and local level and challenged political, economic and social survival in Cyprus, Greece, Portugal, Ireland and Spain, among other states. The severe negative impact of the economic crisis required immediate political and financial assistance to these member states from other EU member states, the European Central Bank (ECB) and the International Monetary Fund (IMF) among others. As a consequence of the economic recession, most EU member states faced declining growth, rising unemployment and social tension.

The economic crisis is still damaging European integration and prosperity. The Commission stated that the economic recession had not only halted European economic growth but also wiped out previous progress in Europe to such an extent that Europeans in 2010 were under severe political, economic and social stress. In a few years, European GDP had fallen by 4 per cent; industrial production levels were back to the levels of the 1990s; 23 million – about 10 per cent of the European active population – had faced unemployment; and public finances averaged a deficit of 7 per cent of GDP. In addition, the fragility of the financial system and the banking sector imposed serious restraints on companies and households to access money for investments, borrowing and spending, further paralyzing the European economy (European Commission, 2010: 5). The Commission argued how 20 years of European fiscal consolidation had been wiped out in two years of economic crisis:

Europe faces a moment of transformation. The crisis has wiped out years of economic and social progress and exposed structural weaknesses in Europe's economy. In the meantime, the world is moving fast and long-term challenges – globalisation, pressure on resources, ageing – intensify. The EU must now take charge of its future. Europe can succeed if it acts collectively, as a Union. We need a strategy to help us come out stronger from the crisis and turn the EU into a smart, sustainable and inclusive economy delivering high levels of employment, productivity and social cohesion. Europe 2020 sets out a vision of Europe's social market economy for the 21st century. (European Commission, 2010: 3)

The Communication 'EUROPE 2020 – A strategy for smart, sustainable and inclusive growth' was not, however, 'only' a recovery plan to handle the immediate economic crisis, but also a strategy to identify and resolve what the Commission argued to be Europe's structural weaknesses. The Commission declared that Europe's economy had had challenges long before the economic crisis burst out and added that such structural challenges included (among others) a relatively low average growth rate compared to other regions around the world, low levels of investments in research and development, limited implementation of information and communications technologies, cultural reluctance to prioritize and embrace innovations, and a weakened business environment as well as existing obstacles to finding risk capital and entering new markets. Europe's economic structural weaknesses were especially alarming with the fast-developing global competitiveness from other economic regions around the world. The Commission pointed out that China and India, as economically dynamic actors with high levels of investments in research and technology and therefore competitors, were also potential markets for European investment and economic expansion. In addition, the remarkable economic progress showed by the G-20 has come to symbolize a new, fast-developing global economic order.

A second potential hindrance identified by scholars is the limited functions of EU governance. The way for Europe to handle growing global economic competition is to act together within the EU to solve shared problems, and by acting together, adding extra value to the global economy. As stated, 'The EU will influence global policy decisions only if it acts jointly. Stronger external representation will need to go hand in hand with stronger internal co-ordination' (European Commission, 2010: 6). The Communication clearly stated the importance of stronger cohesiveness within the Union to act as one global and regional actor. It stated the importance of multiple actors working towards a greater Europe of prosperity and democracy and how such efforts required strengthened internal coordination. In political science, the EU call for internal coordination has been referred to as European governance. European governance has been defined as a distinct form of political steering of European politics embedding networks of public and private actors that, in cooperation and competition, promote public policies towards common objectives. European governance has been defined as something very different from the traditional perspective on government with hierarchical steering based on centralized authority. The many references to the EU as governance is also present in Europe 2020. The agenda from the Commission calls upon all of Europe – European institutions, EU member states, regional and local authorities, as well as private actors and the civil society – to implement Europe 2020. The Commission also declares that all EU policies, instruments, judicial and financial instruments have to be mobilized to meet all the objectives set out in Europe 2020. It was stated that the Single Market is a vital instrument to promote the implementation of Europe 2020 and to ensure a future Europe of growth, job opportunities and prosperity.

One potential hindrance within Europe 2020 has been on the one hand the important role of the EU member states to implement policies to reach the objectives, and on the other hand the limited legitimacy and capacity of the Commission to convince all member states that embedded flagships and objectives are the most important ones. There seems to be a lack of member state commitment to Europe 2020 and an unwillingness to provide the Commission with authority to promote European objectives from a supranational level in favour of a strengthened and more active European Council (Becker et al., 2016: 1011–12). Based on experience from the Lisbon Strategy, the open method of coordination (OMC) has proven to be a fragile method due to the implied voluntary cooperation from member states and the non-existence of competences on the EU level. Different European member states have had different kinds of economic and social challenges to be tackled by other means than perhaps mentioned in Europe 2020. Some scholars have therefore argued that Europe 2020 requires an improved Annual Growth Survey by the Commission that more specifically points out national progress made and progress kept strictly related to the Europe 2020 targets. What has also been argued to be missing is a regional and local priority, with more resources and focus on subnational possibilities and problems rather than the three overall EU targets in smart, sustainable and socially inclusive growth. One such approach would be to break down overall EU objectives to subnational settings. As stated,

> the belief that one central strategy can fit the entire European Union, with 27 disparate economies of different profiles and reform requirements, borders on a central-planning mentality that can only damage economic growth. Too

often European policy-makers fall victim to the view that Europe is a uniform economy and that its member economies all behave in the same way. (Erixon, 2010: 31)

There has been reluctance among richer states to assist or bail out weaker states from their economic hardships. There are disparities in fundamental socioeconomic standards with imbalances between member states regarding resources, know-how and productivity, with a wide range of diversity on when and where to begin reforms to meet future targets (Fura et al., 2017: 976–7). All this has raised a debate on poor governance within the EU or on the fact that individual member states primarily seek their own interests and safeguard their own national policies (see Zaucha et al., 2014). The Europe 2020 initiative has therefore lacked real owner-ship on those levels where the targets were to be met through successful implementation. Stronger governance would be required between the EU, member states and subnational regions to address Europe 2020's targets rather than promoting a 'one-size-fits-all' policy (Pagliacci, 2017: 601–604, 615; Renda, 2014: 1-3; Budd, 2013: 284–6; Armstrong, 2012: 295–7; Walburn, 2010: 702; Warleigh-Lack, 2010: 299–300; Erixon, 2010: 29–37; Walden, 2010: 2). As stated,

> Put simply, the governance of Europe 2020 is broken since member states have *de facto* and *de jure* no incentive to align their agendas to the target set by the strategy. This is confirmed by the absence of any reference to the agenda in the overwhelming majority of government plans at national and regional levels in the EU28. (Renda, 2014: 11)

A third potential obstacle for the implementation of Europe 2020 has been the lack of evaluation of why the preceding strategy failed and of the practical quality of the 2020 strategy. The Lisbon strategy had a limited effect on European economic growth and prosperity. It has been stated that not a single target was achieved in 2010, and regardless of the great economic crisis of 2008, many have argued that such targets would never have been reached without the economic crisis. Although there is no need to focus on the Lisbon Strategy, it has been argued that some of the targets in it have been reflected in the new Europe 2020 without any critical assessments of why such targets should be kept in a new strategy when the previous ones failed to be reached (Walburn, 2010: 700). Some previously failed targets have concerned public investments, research and development and the quality of jobs created. As argued by scholars,

> The Europe 2020 Strategy is about improving EU competitiveness and achiev-ing sustainable growth. It builds on the revised Lisbon Strategy with some

reinforcement of economic policy cooperation but within the same governance framework. Yet the reformed Lisbon Strategy of 2005 did not produce results in terms of undoing the large persisting differences between member states in the implementation of Lisbon goals. (Bongardt and Torres, 2010: 140)

In addition, critical arguments have also exposed how the flagship initiatives have been implemented in isolation from each other, missing out on significant synergies between, for instance, a greener economy and new products, digitalization and new jobs, education and social inclusion, and so on, leaving Europe 2020 more a group of fragmented initiatives rather than a comprehensive, integrated framework of reforms. It has also been pointed out how EU policies have too often missed out on referring to the targets set out in Europe 2020 and/or have had limited ties to such targets, leaving the different initiatives as set out in Europe 2020 marginalized from the EU policy process. For instance, there has been a lack of critical assessments and recommendations on how to tackle the tension between promoting economic growth for prosperity and social cohesion and a sustainable, greener economy with reduced greenhouse gas emissions. Europe 2020 states the importance of smart growth, but it has been argued that this concept has been poorly defined; in addition, how Europe is to decouple growth from emissions needs to be addressed. It has also been argued that the flagships have been far too limited in scope to address the real challenges in building smart, sustainable and socially inclusive growth in Europe. While some flagships have already been fully implemented, the Europe 2020 targets have not been reached and challenges remain. This has been argued to be a major symbol of imperfect (or at least inadequate) measures to solve existing problems (see Daly, 2012).

STRUCTURE OF THE STUDY

This study explores the Europe 2020 strategy and the role of European political entrepreneurship in debating, shaping and implementing it within the EU. The main idea is to explore the content of, conditions for and consequences of Europe 2020 by analysing the strategy for a future prosperous EU economy. The main focus is on European political entrepreneurship and how the strategy has been debated, decided on and implemented from a European governance perspective. The overall objective of this chapter has been to introduce the 2020 strategy to readers to become a platform for the chapters to come on analysing Europe 2020 and smart, sustainable and inclusive growth.

The Europe 2020 strategy called for major reforms on smart, sustainable and socially inclusive growth. The strategy also called for European leadership and new, bold, innovative and ambitious ideas on political entrepreneurship to help Europe become economically and socially great again. In contrast to other studies on European entrepreneurship, this study embeds a focus on potential and existing European political entre-preneurship aiming for growth and employment in Europe. It addresses the political entrepreneurial activities beyond day-to-day activities that challenge and change traditional institutions to favour entrepreneurship for smart, sustainable and socially inclusive growth. The first part of the book addresses the context and content of Europe 2020, with a focus on European governance and political entrepreneurship. It also sheds light upon what the EU wants to pursue through Europe 2020 in a social-economic model for the 21st century (see Chapter 2). The first part is followed by Part II, which addresses core European actors to implement the initiative by the Commission on Europe 2020 in the European Council, the Council of the EU, the European Parliament, local and regional actors as well as EU agencies. Part III focuses on policies on smart, sustainable and socially inclusive growth by discussing competitiveness and industrial policies, research and innovation, gender equality policy, asylum and migration policy, and environmental and climate policy. The final part, Part IV, concludes and discusses the state of the EU and Europe beyond 2020.

REFERENCES

Armstrong, K.A. (2012). 'EU social policy and the governance architecture of Europe 2020'. *Transfer*, **18**(3): 285–300.

Barbier, J.C. (2011). *Changes in Political Discourse from the Lisbon Strategy to Europe 2020: Tracing the Fate of 'Social Policy'*. European Trade Union Institute (ETUI). Brussels: ETUI.

Barroso, J.M. (2010). 'Preface' in *Com 2020. Communication from the Commission: Europe 2020: A Strategy for Smart, Sustainable and Inclusive Growth*. Brussels, 3.3.2010. Brussels: European Commission.

Baumol, W.J. (1990). 'Entrepreneurship: productive, unproductive and destruc-tive'. *Journal of Political Economy*, **98**(5): 893–921.

Becker, S., M.W. Bauer, S. Connolly and H. Kassim (2016). 'The Commission: boxed in and constrained, but still an engine of integration'. *West European Politics*, **39**(5): 1011–31.

Bongardt, A. and F. Torres (2010). 'Europe 2020 – a promising strategy?' *Intereconomics*, **2010**(3): 136–41.

Borghetto, E. and F. Franchino (2010). 'The role of subnational authorities in the implementation of EU directives'. *Journal of European Public Policy*, **17**(6): 759–80.

Borzaga, C., G. Galera and R. Nogales (eds) (2008). *Social Enterprise: A New*

Model for Poverty Reduction and Employment Generation – An Examination of the Concept and Practice in Europe and the Commonwealth of Independent States. UNDP Regional Bureau for Europe and the Commonwealth of Independent States.

Boyett, I. (1996). 'The public sector entrepreneur – a definition'. *International Journal of Public Sector Management*, **9**(2): 36–51.

Brickerhoff, P.C. (2000). *Social Entrepreneurship – The Art of Mission-Based Venture Development.* New York: John Wiley and Sons.

Budd, L. (2013). 'EUROPE 2020: a strategy in search of a regional policy rationale?' *Policy Studies*, **34**(3): 274–90.

Carroll, J.J. (2017). 'Failure is an option: the entrepreneurial governance framework'. *Journal of Entrepreneurship and Public Policy*, **6**(1): 108–26.

Casson, M.C. (1995). *Entrepreneurship and Business Culture.* Aldershot, UK and Brookfield, VT, USA: Edward Elgar Publishing.

Chung, H., S. Bekker and H. Houwing (2012). 'Young people and the post-recession labour market in the context of Europe 2020'. *Transfer*, **18**(3): 301–17.

Cross, D.M.K. (2017). *The Politics of Crisis in Europe.* Cambridge: Cambridge University Press.

Dahl, R.A. (1974). *Who Governs? Democracy and Power in an American City.* New Haven: Yale University Press.

Daly, M. (2012). 'Paradigm in EU social policy: a critical account of Europe 2020'. *Transfer*, **18**(3): 273–84.

Erixon, F. (2010). 'The Europe 2020 strategy: time for Europe to think again'. *European View*, **9**(June): 29–37.

EUR-Lex: Distribution of Competences (2018). Accessed 8 May 2018 at https://eur-lex.europa.eu/summary/glossary/competences.html?locale=en.

EUR-Lex: OMC (Open Method of Coordination) (2018). Accessed 8 May 2018 at https://eur-lex.europa.eu/summary/glossary/open_method_coordination.html.

European Commission (2010). *Communication from the Commission: Europe 2020: A Strategy for Smart, Sustainable and Inclusive Growth.* Brussels, 3.3.2010. Brussels: European Commission.

European Commission, The European Semester (2018). Accessed 2 February 2018 at https://ec.europa.eu/info/business-economy-euro/economic-and-fiscal-policy-coordination/eu-economic-governance-monitoring-prevention-correcti on/european-semester_en.

Eurostat (2017). *Smarter, Greener, More Inclusive? Indicators to Support the Europe 2020 Strategy: 2017 edn.* Luxembourg: Publications Office of the European Union.

Eurostat (2018a). *Smarter, Greener, More Inclusive? Indicators to Support the Europe 2020 Strategy: 2018 edn.* Luxembourg: Publications Office of the European Union.

Eurostat (2018b). Europe 2020 indicators: Poverty and social exclusion. Accessed January 2019 at https://ec.europa.eu/eurostat/statistics-explained/index.php/ Europe_2020_indicators_-_poverty_and_social_exclusion.

Finnemore, M. and K. Sikkink (1998). 'International norm dynamics and political change'. *International Organizations*, **52**(4): 887–917.

Fura, B., J. Wojnar and B. Kasprzyk (2017). 'Ranking and classification of EU countries regarding their levels of implementation of the Europe 2020 strategy'. *Journal of Cleaner Production*, **165**: 968–79.

Gawell, M., B. Johannisson and M. Lundqvist (2009). *Samhällets Entreprenörer*

– *En Forskarantologi om Samhällsentreprenörskap* [Social Entrepreneurs – A Research Anthology on Social Entrepreneurship]. Stockholm: KK-stiftelsen.

Gros, D. and F. Roth (2012). *The Europe 2020 Strategy – Can it Maintain the EU's Competitiveness in the World?*. Brussels: Centre for European Policy Studies (CEPS).

Hix, S. and K.H. Goetz (2000). 'Introduction: European integration and national political systems'. *West European Politics*, **23**(4): 52–72.

Hoedl, E. (2011). 'Europe 2020 strategy and European recovery'. *Problems of Sustainable Development*, **6**(2): 11–18.

Holcombe, R.G. (2002). 'Political entrepreneurship and the democratic allocation of economic resources'. *The Review of Austrian Economics*, **15**(2/3): 143–59.

Hudrliková, L. (2013). 'Composite indicators as a useful tool for international comparison: the Europe 2020 example'. *Prague Economic Papers*, **4**: 459–73.

Istvan, L., D. Eva and N.T. Orsolya (2016). 'Competitiveness – higher education'. *Studia Universitatis Economics Series*, **26**(1): 11–25.

Jones, P. (1978). 'The appeal of the political entrepreneur'. *British Journal of Political Science*, **8**(4): 498–504.

Kaiser, C.P. (1990). 'Entrepreneurship and resource allocation'. *Eastern Economic Journal*, **16**(1): 9–20.

Karlsson, C., C. Silander and D. Silander (eds) (2016). *Political Entrepreneurship for Regional Growth and Entrepreneurial Diversity: the Case of Sweden*. Cheltenham, UK and Northampton, MA, USA: Edward Elgar Publishing.

Karlsson, C., C. Silander and D. Silander (eds) (2018). *Governance and Political Entrepreneurship in Europe: Promoting Growth and Welfare in Times of Crisis*. Cheltenham, UK and Northampton, MA, USA: Edward Elgar Publishing.

Kingdon, J. (1995). *Agendas, Alternatives, and Public Policies*. New York: HarperCollins.

Kotz, H.H. (2005). 'The Lisbon Agenda. On getting Europe back on track', in R. Caesar, K. Lammers and H-E. Scharrer (eds), *Europa auf dem Weg zum Wettbewerbsfähigsten und Dynamischsten Wirtschaftsraum der Welt?*, No. 76. Baden-Baden: HWWA Studies.

Liobikienè, G. and M. Butkus (2017). 'The European Union possibilities to achieve targets of Europe 2020 and Paris agreement climate policy', *Renewable Energy*, **106**: 298–309.

Lisbon Treaty (2009). Accessed 8 May 2018 at http://www.lisbon-treaty.org/wcm/the-lisbon-treaty.html.

Makarovič, M., J. Šušteršič and B. Rončević (2014). 'Is Europe 2020 set to fail? The cultural political economy of the EU grand strategies'. *European Planning Studies*, **22**(3): 610–26.

McCaffrey, M. and J.T. Salerno (2011). 'A theory of political entrepreneurship'. *Modern Economy*, **2**(4): 552–60.

Moreno, B. and M.T. García-Álvarez (2018). 'Measuring the progress towards a resource-efficient European Union under the Europe 2020 strategy'. *Journal of Cleaner Production*, **170**: 991–1005.

Morgan, G. (1986). *Images of Organizations*. Los Angeles: Sage Publications.

Nakamura, R.T. and F. Smallwood (1980). *The Politics of Policy Implementation*. New York: St Martin's Press.

North, D.C. (1990). *Institutions, Institutional Change and Economic Performance*. Cambridge: Cambridge University Press.

Osborne, D. and P. Plastrik (1993). *Reinventing Government: How the Entrepreneurial Spirit Is Transforming the Public Sector*. New York: Penguin Books.
Ostrom, E. (1965). *Public Entrepreneurship: A Case Study in Ground Water Basin Management*. Los Angeles: University of California, Los Angeles (UCLA).
Pagliacci, F. (2017). 'Regional paths towards Europe 2020 targets: a spatial approach'. *European Planning Studies*, **25**(4): 601–19.
Prijon, L. (2012). 'Clientelism and Slovenian public administration reform'. *Polish Sociological Review*, **180**(4): 545–60.
Putnam, R. (1993). *Making Democracy Work – Civic Traditions in Modern Italy*. Princeton, NJ: Princeton University Press.
Renda, A. (2014). *The Review of the Europe 2020 Strategy: From Austerity to Prosperity?* CEPS Policy Brief, No. 322: 1–13.
Roberts, N.C. and P.J. King (1991). 'Policy entrepreneurs: their activity structure and function in the policy process'. *Journal of Public Administration Research and Theory*, **1**(2): 147–75.
Salerno, J.T. (2008). 'The entrepreneur: real and imagined'. *Quarterly Journal of Austrian Economics*, **11**(3): 188–207.
Scheingate, A.D. (2003). 'Political entrepreneurship, institutional change and American political development'. *Studies in American Political Development*, **17**(2): 185–203.
Schneider, M. and P. Teske (1992). 'Toward a theory of the political entrepreneur: evidence from local government'. *American Political Science Review*, **86**(3): 737–47.
Schumpeter, J.A. (1934). *The Theory of Economic Development: An Inquiry into Profits, Capital, Credit, Interest, and the Business Cycle*. Cambridge: Harvard University Press.
Silander, D. (2016). 'The political entrepreneur', in C. Karlsson, C. Silander and D. Silander (eds), *Political Entrepreneurship: Regional Growth and Entrepreneurial Diversity in Sweden*. Cheltenham, UK and Northampton, MA, USA: Edward Elgar Publishing, pp. 7–20.
Silander, D. (2018). 'European governance and political entrepreneurship in times of economic crisis', in C. Karlsson, C. Silander and D. Silander (eds), *Governance and Political Entrepreneurship in Europe: Promoting Growth and Welfare in Times of Crisis*. Cheltenham, UK and Northampton, MA, USA: Edward Elgar Publishing, pp. 3–24.
Silander, D. and C. Silander (eds) (2015). *Politiskt Entreprenörskap – Den Offentliga Sektorns Sätt att Skapa Bättre Förutsättningar för Entreprenörskap Lokalt, Regional och Nationellt* [Political Entrepreneurship – The Public Sector and Measurements to Improve Conditions for Entrepreneurship on Local, Regional and National Level]. Stockholm: Santérus förlag.
Simmons, R.T., R.M. Yonk and D.W. Thomas (2011). 'Bootleggers, baptists, and political entrepreneurs – key players in the rational game and morality play of regulatory politics'. *The Independent Review*, **15**(3): 367–81.
Stec, M. and M. Grzebyk (2018). 'The implementation of the Strategy Europe 2020 objectives in European Union countries: the concept analysis and statistical evaluation'. *Quality & Quantity*, **52**(1): 119–33.
Theodoropoulou, S. (2010). 'Skills and education for growth and well-being in Europe 2020: are we on the right path?' *EPC Issue* Paper No. 61: 5–31. European Political Economy Programme.

Tilford, S. and P. Whyte (2010). *The Lisbon Scorecard X*. Brussels: Centre for Economic Reform.

Tusińska, M. (2016). 'Competitiveness of the European Union – expectations, reality and challenges towards 2020'. *Horizons of Politics*, **7**(21): 185–204.

Walburn, D. (2010). 'Europe 2020'. *Local Economy*, **25**(8): 699–702.

Walden, W. (2010). 'Europe 2020 and beyond'. *European View*, **9**: 1–3.

Wandel, J. (2016). 'The role of government and markets in the strategy "Europe 2020" of the European Union: a robust political economy analysis'. *International Journal of Management and Economics*, **49**(January–March): 7–33.

Warleigh-Lack, A. (2010). 'Greening the European Union for legitimacy? A cautionary reading of Europe 2020'. *Innovation – The European Journal of Social Science Research*, **23**(4): 297–311.

Zaucha, J., T. Komornicki, K. Böhme, D. Swiatek and P. Zuber (2014). 'Territorial keys for bringing closer the territorial agenda of the EU and Europe 2020'. *European Planning Studies*, **22**(2): 246–67.

Zeitlin, J. and B. Vanhercke (2014). 'Socializing the European semester? Economic governance and social policy coordination in Europe 2020'. Brown University, The Watson Institute for International Studies Research Paper No. 2014-17.

2. EU, Europe 2020 and a social market economy

Daniel Silander

The Europe 2020 Strategy (see Chapter 1) was a communication from the Commission pointing out the grave danger of an economic recession in Europe. It also served as a roadmap for a prosperous Europe in the future based on smart, sustainable and socially inclusive growth. The economic recession had challenged years of economic and social developments, and Europe 2020 addressed how it was time for European actors to set out countermeasures as one coherent European Union (EU). It was further argued that Europe could become the most competitive, dynamic and knowledge-driven economy in the world based on a strong industrial production, a dynamic service sector, a high quality agricultural sector, a great maritime tradition and an established single market and common currency, making the EU the largest trading bloc in the world. To become a global competitor, the EU called for the dual capacities to advance in export for growth and to provide for growth efficiency based on existing resources (European Commission, 2010; see also Krugman, 1994).

The overall objective in the Europe 2020 Strategy, however, was also to promote 'a vision of Europe's social market economy for the 21st century' (European Commission, 2010: 5). It required confronting emergent challenges in growing unemployment, social exclusion, poverty and limited education through the creation of new jobs, research and innovations, that is, smart and sustainable growth to provide for social growth (European Commission, 2010: 9). As stated, 'We need a strategy to help us come out stronger from the crisis and turn the EU into a smart, sustainable and inclusive economy delivering high levels of employment, productivity and social cohesion. Europe 2020 sets out a vision of Europe's social market economy for the 21st century' (European Commission, 2010: 5).

This chapter discusses the Europe 2020 Strategy implications of building a European social market economic model for the 21st century. The overall question is the following: What does a European social market economy model mean and what are the historical, political and entrepreneurial visions behind such a model? It is argued that the European project has embedded an international, unique kind of European political entrepreneurship in which Europe has been founded on norms and values providing for a European liberal order of international collaboration, common institutions, democratic governance and a social market economy. This chapter is divided into four sections, including the introductory note. While the second section discusses previous research on the EU as a normative actor, the third section explores the meanings of a social market economic model in the context of the Europe 2020 Strategy. The fourth section concludes the main ideas presented in the chapter.

EUROPE AS A POLITICAL COMMUNITY

How Europe is defined has been a question for generations of scholars to debate. For decades, Europe was often defined in terms of geographic proximity, as determined by landmarks providing for fixed national identities of us as Europeans and the others. The Cold War European order was a consequence of the outcome of World War II. The victory powers divided Europe into east and west, guiding European states politically, economically and militarily. The institutionalization of the east and west occurred in political and economic organizations (Huntington, 1991: 92–3). The founding step to the norms and values within the contemporary EU occurred with the customs union established by the Benelux states in 1948, the European Coal and Steel Community (ECSC) of 1950, the Treaty of Rome in 1957, the European Economic Community (EEC) and the European Atomic Energy (EURATOM). Later on, the Single European Act (1986), the Maastricht Treaty (1993), the Amsterdam Treaty (1997), the Nice Treaty (2000) and the Lisbon Treaty (2007) established an ever closer union of European norms and values shared by a significantly increased number of member states. Over the decades, the re-institutionalization process in Europe included the dissemination of Western norms and values and an international socialization process by the Western government eastward. With governments and organizations, the West provided socialization activities towards the former Eastern Europe where Western integration wielded powerful and persuasive influence on the neighbouring states by symbolizing shared norms and values (Ikenberry, 2001: 3–49).

In the 1990s and forward, Europe was debated and defined more commonly in terms of European norms and values based on the regional organizational membership of the EU. It was argued that political entrepreneurship, in initiating and consolidating political ideas among leaders and people, led to established shared norms and values. These European norms and values had changed over time, providing for a transforming European regional integration (Schimmelfennig, 2001). The shared norms set out the standards of behaviour that were accepted and expected by the member states and that defined us as Europeans from the others. The result was a constitutional, liberal order in which democratic governance, market economy, solidarity and peace were cornerstones institutionalized in national governments and common institutions (see Finnemore and Sikkink, 1998; Ikenberry, 2001).

Rooted in a somewhat limited discussion in the 1970s, on the nature of the European community of norms and values, scholars in the 1990s and forward explored the notions of Europe by discussing Europe's cohesiveness, actorness, capacity and international role (Sjöstedt, 1977; Hill, 1993). One debate concerned what kind of political entity the EU is: a sovereign entity, a hybrid or an emerging federation. Some scholars argued that the EU lacked actorness. Other scholars counter-argued that states were also heterogeneous, with a myriad of different interests within the government, opposition, political parties and regional and local actors. This scholarly debate included disagreement on how to perceive Europe in international politics. Another scholarly disagreement concerned the assessment of European capacities to implement policies as an international actor. This debate referred mostly to the EU as a possible foreign policy maker by discussing the nature of the Common Foreign and Security Policy (CFSP) and the lack of a military edge in EU foreign policymaking. The debate on EU actorness and capacity to act internationally sprung out of a critical approach on Europe provided by Hedley Bull. Bull argued against Europe as one political actor and stated how 'Europe is not an actor in international affairs, and does not seem likely to become one' (Bull, 1982: 151). Bull's main argument was that Europe lacked actorness in international affairs due to its hybrid character and limited military capacity (Bull, 1982). Bull's criticism received support from others (Hill, 1993; Kagan, 2003), focusing on Europe's limited actorness and foreign policy capacities and how Europe's ambition to speak with one voice was more rhetorical than European practice.

In the early 1970s, François Duchêne argued to the contrary in favour of Europe as a political entity and presented counterarguments to the above-mentioned criticism. He explicitly stressed that Europe was a civilian power (Duchêne, 1972; 1973) by focusing on existing political and economic capacities among European states. Europe's civilian power was argued to be something different and unique in international politics, that is, *sui generis*, that required scholarly attention. As a consequence, a growing number of scholars have argued that Europe is a civilian power, stating how Europe, despite limited military resources, had other essential

capacities to be used. Based on such civilian capacities, in political, economic and diplomatic ones, Europe could develop into a new type of actor
with a civilian identity among like-minded European states (Smith, 2000;
Zielonka, 1998; Whitman, 1998). Europe, it was argued, had a unique
history in the development of a regional community (ECC and EU) with
constitutional order of treaties, institutions, legal commitments and so on.
In short, these scholars stressed how Europe symbolized a post-Cold War
entity beyond Cold War power politics (Van Vooren, 2012; Ikenberry,
2001).

In the late 1990s and onwards, articles written by Ian Manners
strengthened the notion of Europe as *sui generis* in international politics.
Manners argued that Europe is a normative power under development
(Manners, 2002; see also Rosecrance, 1998). Based on Duchêne's idea of a
civilian power, Manners stressed how Europe could become an *idée force*
in international politics in a post-Cold War context (Manners, 2002: 239;
see also Pace, 2007: 1042). The end of the Cold War and the collapse of
the communist Eastern bloc provided for Western European norms and
values to flourish and to symbolize a new European era without dividing
lines (Bosse, 2009: 215; Dannreuther, 2006). Manners argued how a
European normative power included the '[a]bility to shape conceptions of
"normal"' (Manners, 2002: 240). As stated, 'Thus the notion of a normative power Europe is located in a discussion of the "power over opinion",
"*idée force*", or "ideological power", and the desire to move beyond the
debate over state-like features through an understanding of the EU's
international identity' (Manners, 2002: 239).

First, Manners stressed how Europe was a unique international actor
in the world. The European project of European collaboration and
integration eventually resulted in the EU as a hybrid regime of governance
with multilevel authorities rather than a traditional vertical, hierarchical
government (Manners, 2002: 240–41). The EU did not only symbolize a
post-Cold War constitutional order of international institutions, treaties
and policies but also a post-Westphalia order of supranational institutions, treaties and policies (Manners, 2002: 253; see also Hubel, 2004).
As stated by Manners, 'This combination of historical context, hybrid
polity and legal constitution has, in the post-cold war period, accelerated
a commitment to placing universal norms and principles at the centre of
its relations with its Member States and the world' (Manners, 2002: 241).

Second, Manners also argued how Europe's normative power was
not only based on the development of a European identity and hybrid
structures but also on how such a European order was based on specific
norms and values (see also Pace, 2007: 1045), which were five in number:
peace, liberty, democracy, the rule of law and human rights. Europe's

normative power was based on a founding norm in peace, as stated in the European Coal and Steel Treaty (1951) and the TEC (1957). Other norms were liberty (TEC and TEU of 1991); democracy, rule of law and human rights as founding ideas in the TEU; the development cooperation policy of TEC (Article 177); the common foreign and security provisions of the TEC (Article 11); and the enlargement criteria (membership requirements of 1993 from the European Summit in Copenhagen) (Manners, 2002: 242). Guided by the idea of pursuing European peace, major European states, through political entrepreneurship, collaborated in increasing the number of policy areas to construct a peaceful, constitutional European order. As expressed by Michelle Pace, 'The EU explicitly refers to the constitutive norms of the Western community and defines the promotion and protection of liberal democracy, the democratic peace and multilateralism collaboration as its basic purpose' (Pace, 2007: 1045; see also Rosecrance, 1998; Whitman, 1998). The post-Cold War EU project was fostered on the idea of Europe being a potential normative 'force for the good' (Scheipers and Sicurelli, 2007: 437; see also Tocci, 2008: I; Sjursen, 2006: 235–6). Over the last two decades, a growing number of studies have explored Europe's normative power by assessing real actions. Such studies have in various ways focused on Ian Manners' originally stated substantive norms with particular focus on peace, democracy, human rights, rule of law and good governance (see Manners, 2006; 2008).

Europe as a Democratic Community

There has been half a century of European political entrepreneurship behind the growing number of consolidated European democracies. There is a solid scholarly tradition focusing on European democracies and regional peace. The EU member states have obliged themselves to promote and consolidate democratic governance (see Reform Treaty, Articles 8 and 10a). The issue of democracy protection and promotion gained scholarly attention out of the ashes of World War II and was further focused on in the Cold War context of authoritarian states. Western Europe and the US alliance saw the promotion of democracy as a political vaccine for a better world and as a foreign policy strategy for security. The institutionalization of EU democracy promotion was based on the activities of the OSCE, UN and the Council of Europe, and it was rooted in the Universal Declaration of 1948 and the development of the International Covenants of 1966. The democratic norm was explicitly stressed in Article 237 of the Rome Treaty and further specified in the 1962 Birkelbach Report of the political committee of the European Parliament. Over the decades, the democracy norm set the dividing lines between Europe and the others, that is, towards

Greece in the late 1960s and Portugal and Spain in the 1970s. The EC membership for Greece in 1981, followed by Portugal and Spain in 1986, was a result of years of political convergence towards the democracy norm (Pridham, 1991).

Europe's democratic community was further strengthened with the collapse of communism in the late 1980s and early 1990s (Pridham, 1994). The end of the Cold War resulted in the vision of a widened European democratic community of a reunited east and west. In 1992, in a report to the Lisbon European Council, the EU Commission restressed four criteria to become a member state of the EU. These requirements were to pursue a European identity, be ruled by a democratic government, provide solid protection of human rights and include and implement the community system. These membership requirements were fully institutionalized at the Copenhagen Summit by the European Council in 1993. All EU member states agreed that the EU was a solid democratic community. Any new possible member state had to show stability of institutions guaranteeing democracy, the rule of law, human rights and the respect for and protection of minorities. In addition, also demanded were a functioning market economy, economic strength and competitiveness to cope with pressure and market forces within the Union and the ability to take on the obligations of membership, including adherence to the aims of the monetary union. Based on the Copenhagen Summit, the Maastricht Treaty of 1 November 1993 stressed human rights and democratic principles as the core European norms within the EU and in external relations by providing for new budget posts and initiatives. In 1995, a new democracy clause was agreed upon that stressed the suspension of aid and trade provisions in third states with democratic setbacks. In addition, the Amsterdam Treaty further recognized democracy and other fundamental EU norms by updating Article 237 of the Rome Treaty. Article 6 of the Amsterdam Treaty stated that the EU 'is founded on the principles of liberty, democracy, respect for human rights and fundamental freedoms, and the rule of law, principles which are common to the member States'.

The enlargement success of 2004 and 2007 symbolized a successful European democratic model. The EU had deepened in state relations and widened to include new member states. As a result, a growing number of studies assessed the consequences of the enlargement procedures but also acknowledged the European Neighbourhood Policy (ENP) initiative by the Commission as an alternative strategy to future enlargement. The ENP became a new policy towards new neighbouring states in the east and south after the EU was widened to promote good relationships. The ENP has aimed to build a ring of friends through specific partnerships rather than membership; the Eastern Partnership (EaP) was launched in spring

2009 to create a ring of countries sharing the common European norms and values. The ENP has therefore not been about enlargement but rather a tool to promote a commitment to common values in democracy, human rights, rule of law, market economy principles, good governance and so on (see Silander and Nilsson, 2013; 2014; 2016).

A EUROPEAN SOCIAL COMMUNITY

The political entrepreneurial idea of the EU as a normative power embedding norms in democracy, rule of law, human rights and peace has been one dimension of European integration. However, the notion of a European normative power also embeds a too-often-forgotten dimension in a European social market economy model. Ian Manners strongly argued for such a dimension, including social freedom, equality, solidarity and sustainability as core norms of European normative power.

First, by *social freedom*, Manners referred to a Union of freedom, security and justice without internal borders. Social freedom included the free movement of persons, goods, services, capital and establishment as well as fundamental freedoms in democratic rights and liberties (the Charter of Fundamental Rights).

Second, *social equality* referred to taking countermeasures to social exclusion, discrimination and social injustices. Social equality especially focused on discrimination or exclusion due to sex, race, colour, ethnic or social origin, genetic features, language, religion or belief, political or any other opinion, national minority, property, birth, disability, age or sexual orientation.

Third, *social solidarity* as a European norm linked economic growth, in a competitive market economy and a functioning single European market, to a social dimension of full employment, social cohesion and progress and eradication of poverty, that is, a balanced economic growth.

Fourth and finally, Ian Manners also stressed the importance of *sustainable development* as a core European norm. Sustainable development referred to the objective to promote improved quality of the environment, sustainable management of global natural resources and a greener economic growth.

The roots to building a European social market economic model began in the ashes of World War II. The Treaty of Rome did provide for ECC legislation to foster economic development and the creation of the European Social Fund (ESF) for industrial conversion and training (Fernandez, 2016: 1). In addition, the Treaty of the European Community (TEC) emphasized the cornerstones of a future Social Europe in 'the promotion of employment, improved living and working conditions . . . proper social protection, dialogue between management and labour, the development of human resources with a view to lasting high employment and the combating of exclusion.' The overall vision was to build a post-war Europe in peace and stability based on social and economic progress, with the main priorities being societal solidarity and social inclusion and cohesion. Economic growth and prosperity had to embed the promotion of social prosperity for all nations and people throughout Europe. As argued by Walby,

> The suite of concepts of social cohesion, social inclusion, and social exclusion is important in EU institutions and policy. These concepts represent a compromise after a historical series of political contestations over the nature of the economy, polity, and society. They are not only a form of ideological political legitimation, but are given effectivity in the institutional structure and practices of the EU. This historical compromise is embedded within social, economic, and political institutions and policy frameworks. (Walby, 2004: 13)

The dominating political idea in the 1950s and 1960s was, however, market oriented. Member states agreed on the perception that free trade and competition would bring not only European growth and prosperity but also welfare and social equality. In the 1970s, the European debate concerned how market forces would not provide for social development in Europe. A growing number of member states within the European community and an assessment of social development led to a stronger European voice on the importance of social development for a healthy European order. The founding idea of free movement of labour forced member states to explore the working conditions within European states. It resulted in a stronger interest in the treaty articles that did focus on social development: Article 118 on training, employment, labour law, work conditions and social security; Article 119 on the equal pay principle; Article 121 on social security for migrant workers; and Article 123 on the ESF with a focus on employment and re-employment and the mobility of workers (for extended analysis of social development, see Hantrais, 2007: 2–24).

In 1974, the Council of Ministers presented a resolution on a social action programme stressing how social progress had to be accounted for when promoting economic growth. The resolution focused on the social dimension of economics by highlighting challenges in working environments and the importance of full and improved employment, improved living and working conditions and increased engagement of management and labour in socio-economic decisions. In the 1980s, further ideas on social development were argued for where social development was stressed to be a prerequisite to economic integration. The Single European Act (SEA), dated to 1986, and the added Article 118a to the EEC Treaty included the importance of an improved working environment, specifically with regard to health and safety issues for workers (Hantrais, 2007: 6–7).

The institutionalization of the SEA embedded new social aspects to the ongoing and escalating economic integration in Europe. Some social areas came to be decided by a quality majority vote, and the European social dialogue was approved as a procedure within the EEC. As a core objective, the EEC also stated that it would promote socio-economic cohesion with an increased budget for the cohesion funds of the late 1980s and forward. The SEA was soon followed by the Community Charter of Fundamental Social Rights of Workers in 1989 and the Social Policy Protocol. The Social Policy Protocol stressed the importance of the harmonization of social systems within member states and the importance for the Commission to monitor, support and facilitate social progress and coordination. It was then explicitly stressed how social development was as important as economic development. These social reforms, institutionalized within the EU, were the beginning of a greater EU concern for social and employment issues, although disagreement remained between member states on the idea to develop a common social policy (Hantrais, 2007: 7–8).

In the early 1990s, the Commission presented two documents highlighting the importance of a European social policy. The green (1993) and white (1994) papers on European social policy identified objectives that needed to be met and multiple actors that had to be considered within areas such as the labour market, social protection and equal opportunities. These papers were followed up by social action programmes, and in 1997 the Treaty of Amsterdam included social policies and stressed the importance of the institutionalization of social development for further European integration. The Social Protection Committee was meant to oversee social development and conduct reports on the progress made. In the Charter of Fundamental Rights of the European Union of 2000, social policy referred not only to rights and safety issues at the workplace but also to family life, the protection of children and the elderly, preventive health care, housing assistance and so on.

In the Treaty of Lisbon of 2007, the EU decided on new intervention methods and called upon member states to coordinate their national policies based on the Open Method of Coordination (OMC). Member states were asked to cooperate on social policies by identifying common objectives, provide assessments of progress made in national action plans and exchange information and best practice advice. These progress reports have frequently been used when it comes to social policy areas related to the Single European Market (SEM) and the relation between free trade and competition to provide for welfare and prosperity (Fernandez, 2016: 1; see also Grosse, 2016: 106–107). The Commission was again the driving engine and political entrepreneur to see social developments in member states and was behind evaluations and presentations on the national developments made. Within a few years, the OMC included social protection systems, education and research, immigration, pensions and health. In the early 2000s, the Commission had successfully, through years of political entrepreneurship, managed to set social issues on the official agenda and pushed for social developments within member states. Social progress and economic progress have in the last decade been viewed as integrated processes and as prerequisites to each other. Economic growth and full employment have been cornerstones in the Commission's statements on economic progress in Europe but are strongly tied to social inclusiveness, cohesion, equality and non-discrimination (Hantrais, 2007: 20–21; Fernandez, 2016: 2).

Although social policies have traditionally been a concern for member states' governments, with traditional limited EU competences (see Chapter 1) to influence national policymaking (Grosse, 2016: 105), the EU has received a gradually increased empowerment through the ongoing economic integration and the establishment of the Single European Market (SEM). It has required new legislation and coordination of social security systems and measures against discrimination to provide for the free movement of labour. This has led to shared competences between individual member states and the EU regarding issues of working environments, discrimination, equality, coordination of social security issues for migrating labour and support of the free movement on the SEM. The ESF and the European Regional Development Fund are two instruments to promote social cohesiveness and inclusion throughout the EU. In addition, through the OMC, the EU may also influence individual member states through reports, assessments and best-practice policies.

The European social market economic model has embedded a political vision of fostering economic growth with high social living and working standards. Such socio-economic development has included a political commitment to full employment, tighter (compared to China and the US) distribution of earnings and a visible egalitarian distribution of the benefits of growth, public companies serving broader public interest, expanded labour rights and active trade unions. In addition, socioeconomic development has also referred to social protection and inclusion through pensions and insurance schemes, compulsory and free primary education and subsidized higher education, universal, free or subsidized health treatment, welfare programmes regarding unemployment insurances, public housing, care for dependents and aid policies for less favoured collectives (Hyman, 2005; Sapir, 2005). As stated,

> The Welfare State, in its role of re-distribution has embodied the maturity of the European countries. The approach, which has been more egalitarian than elsewhere, has not been limited just to companies but has found its place in terms of social goods, such as education and healthcare. In spite of its imperfections this approach has proven effective and has clearly helped towards growth. (Foundation of Robert Schuman, 2012: 3)

Today, we may identify five different European social models: (1) the Nordic Model; (2) the Continental Model; (3) the Anglo-Saxon Model; (4) the Mediterranean Model; and (5) the Post-Communist Model (see Sapir, 2005; Barr, 2004).

1. The Nordic Model (e.g. Denmark, Finland, Norway, Iceland and Sweden) is characterized by high taxes to support a universal provision of social services and protection. The Nordic Model has also symbolized fair access to social provisions, proactive labour market policies, a large share of public employment, a high level of female participation in the workforce, labour rights and active trade unions, low income dispersion and ambitions to foster fair income distribution for social inclusion.
2. The Continental Model (e.g. Austria, Belgium, France, Germany and Luxembourg) has similarities to the Nordic Model, although public expenditures are focused on pensions and subsidies, with a strong participation of trade unions providing for collective agreements.
3. The Anglo-Saxon model differs from the Nordic Model, with its low levels of taxes and public spending, low-wage employments, subsidies to working-age populations rather than on pensions, higher socio-economic inequalities, limited social security networks often tied to employability, higher costs for social services and lower costs for companies and entrepreneurs (e.g. Ireland, Switzerland, the UK).
4. The Mediterranean Model was developed late compared to the Nordic and continental European states, with a lower share of public expenditures, a low level of social assistance, early retirement and focus on pensions, strong judicial employment protection and active trade unions, a higher level of unemployment and a low level of women in the labour force.
5. The Post-Communist Model, as an Eastern European version, has embedded an egalitarian system, lower economic growth and lower confidence in the public system.

Different European states have embedded different welfare aspects into their national settings. The European welfare models have shared some important commonalities based on 'interventions organised by the state which are aimed at guaranteeing the provision of a minimum level of services to the population via a system of social protection' (Learn Europe, 2018). This has allowed the European Commission to act as a political entrepreneur to push for social development and some degree of harmonization.

EUROPE 2020'S FLAGSHIPS FOR A SOCIAL MARKET ECONOMY

The EU Commission has called upon member states to promote an improved socio-economic market model for the 21st century. The Europe 2020 Strategy has been the European growth strategy of the last decade. The overall objective of such a strategy has been to promote smart, sustainable and socially inclusive growth. The strategy is focused on employment, innovation, climate and energy policy and poverty reduction and social inclusiveness. By initiating suggestions of reforms from the Commission to EU member states, the EU, as a regional and supranational identity, would become strong, competitive and prosperous in a global economic setting. The EU backbone has been stressed to be the European SEM, and the ambition has been to externalize the 'Market Power Europe' externally through policies and regulations (Stec and Grzebyk, 2018: 120). As stated by Stec and Grzebyk:

> From the start of the Union, it was not intended to build Europe at a single stroke, but by setting in motion a true solidarity among the countries through concrete actions to reduce asymmetries among the European Union's (EU's) countries in order to increase social and economic cohesion within its borders. (Stec and Grzebyk, 2018: 120)

As stated in Chapter 1, Europe's social market economy was to be built upon smart, sustainable and social growth. While smart growth referred to promoting an economy based on knowledge and innovation, and sustainable growth referred to resource efficiency and a greener economy, the social dimension of the Europe 2020 Strategy highlighted the importance of 'fostering a high-employment economy delivering economic, social and territorial cohesion' (European Commission, 2010: 10).

Headline targets included the following: (1) increase employment to target 75 per cent of the population aged 20–64 who are employed; (2) decrease the number of early school leavers to lower than 10 per cent; and

(3) with at least 40 per cent of the younger generation, obtain a tertiary degree and finally reduce the number of people at risk of poverty to 20 million (European Commission, 2010: 5). In addition, social inclusive growth 'means empowering people through high levels of employment, investing in skills, fighting poverty and modernising labour markets, training and social protection systems so as to help anticipate and manage change, and build a cohesive society' (European Commission, 2010: 17). Social inclusive growth was based on economic growth and the diffusion of growth to all parts of the EU to consolidate territorial cohesion. It also required social inclusiveness of all groups of society; an improved employment rate among the working-age population to deal with demographic changes; gender equality to improve women's employment rate; and access to education and the labour market for the young generation to avoid socio-economic marginalization, poverty and health challenges.

The Europe 2020 Strategy initiated seven flagships to meet objectives, two dealing with social growth in 'An agenda for new skills and jobs' and 'European platform against poverty'. The main objectives of the flagships were to increase the employment rate by modernizing the labour market and to ensure a sustainable European social model. The initiative focused on empowering people to acquire new know-how and skills and the ability to access new types of jobs. The Commission declared its ambition to promote a modernized, strengthened employment of education and training policies, as well as for the overall social protection systems. It required increasing the employment rate; increasing labour participation from all societal groups by dismantling structural hindrances; demanding increased corporate social responsibility in the economic sector; and promoting a healthy and active ageing population to facilitate social inclusion and economic growth. In addition, the flagships also aimed to promote socio-economic and territorial cohesion by combating social and economic marginalization and poverty and increasing the awareness of existing rights for a life of dignity and societal participation (European Commission, 2010: 18–19). Some of the most important aspects of the flagships are summarized in Table 2.1.

To promote and implement the flagships identified in the Europe 2020 Strategy, the EU Commission has focused on reforms of the European single market. There is a need to fight signs of economic nationalism and protectionism and to improve the single market. Such efforts should focus on dealing with member states' different legal systems to ease all kinds of transborder transactions for companies. The Commission also identified the importance of a single market for services; improved access for SMEs; simplification of company law for entrepreneurship; strengthened consumer ability to buy cross-border and online; and implementation

Table 2.1   *Flagships: an agenda for new skills and jobs, and European*
platform against poverty (summary)

An agenda for new skills and jobs	European platform against poverty
1. Manage economic transitions and fight unemployment 2. Promote intra-EU labour mobility 3. Match labour supply with demand with structural funds 4. Strengthen cooperation between labour market institutions 5. Cooperation in education and training and implementation of lifelong principles 6. Reduce labour market segmentation 7. Review efficiency of tax and benefit systems 8. Promote new forms of work–life balance 9. Increase gender equality 10. Promote necessary competences for labour market	1. Reduce social exclusion 2. Promote social innovation, in education, training and employment opportunities, for deprived communities 3. Fight discrimination 4. Develop new agenda for migrants' integration 5. Assess adequacy of social protection and pension systems 6. Improve access to health care systems 7. Combat poverty 8. Implement specific measures such as income support and access to health care for groups at major risk (one-parent families, elderly women, minorities, Roma, people with disabilities and the homeless)

of the competition policy to ensure anticompetitive agreements between companies and market abuse. However, a single European market could also allow for negative competition in the sense of 'race to the bottom' where member states with the lowest social protection become the most cost-effective markets, resulting in economic growth and social degradation (Fernandez, 2016: 2). Therefore, the Commission also called for socio-economic and territorial cohesion based on a cohesion policy with structural funds and by coordinating European businesses and governments to collaborate on investments and innovation projects in a strengthened private–public partnership. Such efforts had to be backed up by the European Investment Bank and the European Investment Fund (European Commission, 2010: 20–22).

It has been argued that the EU social model to growth is very much about social cohesion. It has also been stated that, in contrast to the US, social cohesion has embedded state and EU measures against social exclusion, social inequality and social disadvantages to promote a better life but also to enhance the conditions for an 'efficient, productive, and

globally competitive economy' (see Walby, 2004: 13). From an EU point
of view, social exclusion is not only harmful to livelihood and wealth but
is also a challenge to economic growth and development. For instance,
poverty and homelessness risk individual well-being as well as productivity through employment; discrimination harms engagement in the labour
market, and therefore economic growth and structural socio-economic
imbalances may cause social unrest, criminality and political stress. As
stated by Walby on the social–economic nexus, 'Social inclusion involves
both the social and economic conditions necessary for the effective human
functioning that makes for an efficient economy and also a process of
inclusion in the political decision-making process to ensure social and
political stability' (Walby, 2004: 13).

CONCLUDING REMARKS

As stated by Stec and Grzebyk, 'From the start of the Union, it was not
intended to build Europe at a single stroke, but by setting in motion a
true solidarity among the countries through concrete actions to reduce
asymmetries among the EU's countries in order to increase social
and economic cohesion within its borders' (Stec and Grzebyk, 2018:
120). The path toward a social market economy of the 21st century
has embedded decades of European political entrepreneurship. As
has been stressed in this chapter, European integration has embedded
the institutionalization of European collaboration based on shared
European norms and values. Such European norms and values have
been about promoting integration, cooperation, peace, prosperity and
social cohesiveness and solidarity among like-minded, democratically
governed European states.

Europe is a contemporary realization of Immanuel Kant's 'perpetual
peace'. European integration is founded in a liberal tradition of seeking
peace and prosperity through common European laws and regulation,
institutions and policies instead of traditional power politics among rivalry
states (Kant, 1795; Kagan, 2003: 3). In close collaboration with and protection by the US, post-World War Europe was determined to build peace
and prosperity by becoming one political, economic and social entity
institutionalized in what is today referred to as the EU. The scholarly and
political debate on Europe's actorness and capacities has to a large extent
described decades of a European lack of military growth and unity in
favour of soft power developments in a social-economic market model,
democratic governance and European laws and institutions (Kagan, 2003:
57). The European social market model among democratic member states

is not, however, determined only by European measures within the EU. The progress of the European single market is expected to attract global actors as the largest trading bloc in the world. The EU Commission has stressed the importance of building strategic relationships with developing economies around the world to attract companies and investments to the European market and to promote global free trade to ensure market access for EU businesses (European Commission, 2010: 22–3).

REFERENCES

Amsterdam Treaty (1997). Accessed 10 October 2018 at http://www.europarl. europa.eu/about-parliament/en/in-the-past/the-parliament-and-the-treaties/tre aty-of-amsterdam.

Barr, N. (2004). *Economics of the Welfare State*. New York: Oxford University Press.

Bosse, G. (2009). 'Challenges for EU governance through neighbourhood policy and eastern partnership: the values/security nexus in EU–Belarus relations', *Contemporary Politics*, **15**(2): 215–27.

Bull, H. (1982). 'Civilian power Europe: a contradiction in terms?' *Journal of Common Market Studies*, **21**(2): 149–64.

Dannreuther, R. (2006). 'Developing the alternative to enlargement: the European neighborhood policy', *European Foreign Affairs Review*, **11**: 187–95.

Duchêne, F. (1972). 'Europe's role in world peace'. In R. Mayne (ed.), *Europe Tomorrow: Sixteen Europeans Look Ahead*. London: Fontana, pp. 32–47.

Duchêne, F. (1973). 'The European community and the uncertainties of interdependence'. In M. Kohnstamm and W. Hager (eds), *A Nation Writ Large? Foreign Policy Problems Before the European Community*. Basingstoke: Macmillan, pp. 1–21.

European Commission (2010). *Communication from the Commission: Europe 2020: A Strategy for Smart, Sustainable and Inclusive Growth*. Brussels, 3.3.2010. Brussels: European Commission.

Fernandez, S. (2016). *Is There Such a Thing as 'Social Europe'?* Berlin: Notre Europe: Jacques Delors Institute.

Finnemore, M. and K. Sikkink (1998). 'International norm dynamics and political change'. *International Organization*, **52**(4): 897–917.

Foundation of Robert Schuman (2012). 'The emerging European Social Model – an advantage in the face of the crisis'. No. 248, accessed 11 April 2018 at https://www.robert-schuman.eu/en/european-issues/0248-the-emerging-european-social-model-an-advantage-in-the-face-of-the-crisis.

Grosse, I. (2016). 'Social politik – om den ökande betydelsen av EU:s indirekta effecter'. In D. Silander and Mats Öhlén (eds), *Svensk Politik och EU – Hur Svensk Politik har Förändrats av Medlemsskapet i EU*. Stockholm: Santérus förlag.

Hantrais, L. (2007). *Social Policy in the European Union*. Basingstoke: Palgrave Macmillan.

Hill, C. (1993). 'The capability–expectations gap, or conceptualizing Europe's international role'. *Journal of Common Market Studies*, **31**(3): 305–28.

Hubel, H. (2004). 'The EU's three-level game in dealing with neighbors'. *European Foreign Affairs Review*, **9**(3): 347–62.

Huntington, S.P. (1991). *The Third Wave: Democratization in the Late Twentieth Century*. Norman: University of Oklahoma Press.

Hyman, R. (2005). 'Trade unions and the politics of the European social model'. *Economic and Industrial Democracy*, **26**(1): 9–40.

Ikenberry, J. (2001). *After Victory – Institutions, Strategic Restraint, and the Rebuilding of Order after Major Wars*. Princeton, NJ, USA and Oxford, UK: Princeton University Press.

Kagan, R. (2003). *Of Paradise and Power: America and Europe in the New World Order*. New York: A.A. Knopf.

Kant, I. (1795). *Perpetual Peace: A Philosophic Essay*, Montreal: LibriVox, accessed 15 October 2018 at https://librivox.org/perpetual-peace-by-immanuel-kant/.

Krugman, P. (1994). 'Competitiveness: a dangerous obsession'. *Foreign Affairs*, March/April, accessed 21 March 2018 at https://www.foreignaffairs.com/arti cles/1994-03-01/competitiveness-dangerous-obsession.

Learn Europe (2018). 'Models of the welfare state in Europe', accessed 1 April 2018 at www.learneruope.eu/index.php?cID=300.

Maastricht Treaty (1993). Accessed 10 October 2018 at http://www.europarl. europa.eu/about-parliament/en/in-the-past/the-parliament-and-the-treaties/ma astricht-treaty.

Manners, I. (2002). 'Normative power Europe: a contradiction in terms?' *Journal of Common Market Studies*, **40**(2): 235–58.

Manners, I. (2006). 'Normative power Europe reconsidered: beyond the cross-roads'. *Journal of European Public Policy*, **13**(2): 182–99.

Manners, I. (2008). 'The normative ethics of the European Union'. *International Affairs*, **82**(1): 45–60.

Pace, M. (2007). 'The construction of EU normative power'. *Journal of Common Market Studies*, **45**(5): 1041–5.

Pridham, G. (1991). 'International influences and democratic transition: problems of theory and practice in linkage politics'. In G. Pridham (ed.), *Encouraging Democracy: The International Context of Regime Transition in Southern Europe*. Leicester: Leicester University Press, pp. 1–28.

Pridham, G. (1994). 'The international dimension of democratization: theory, prac-tice, and inter-regional comparisons'. In G. Pridham, E. Herring and G. Sanford (eds), *Building Democracy? The International Dimension of Democratization in Eastern Europe*. New York: St Martin's Press, pp. 7–31.

Rosecrance, R. (1998). 'The European Union: a new type of international actor'. In J. Zielonka (ed.), *Paradoxes of European Foreign Policy*. The Hague: Kluwer Law International, pp. 15–24.

Sapir, A. (2005). *Globalisation and the Reform of European Social Models*. Brussels: Bruegel Policy Contribution.

Scheipers, S. and D. Sicurelli (2007). 'Normative power Europe: a credible utopia?' *Journal of Common Market Studies*, **45**(2): 435–57.

Schimmelfennig, F. (2001). 'The community trap: liberal norms, rhetorical action, and the eastern enlargement of the European Union'. *International Organization*, **55**(1): 47–80.

Silander, D. and M. Nilsson (2013). 'Democratization without enlargement? The European neighborhood policy on post-communist transitions'. *Contemporary Politics*, **19**(4): 441–58.

Silander, D. and M. Nilsson (2014). 'Protecting and promoting Europe: the ENP and the democracy–security nexus in partner states'. *Journal of Applied Security Research*, **9**(4): 460–77.

Silander, D. and M. Nilsson (2016). 'Democracy and security in the EU's Eastern neighborhood? Assessing the ENP in Georgia, Moldova and Ukraine'. *Democracy and Security*, **12**(1): 44–61.

Sjöstedt, G. (1977). *The External Role of the European Community.* Westmead: Saxon House, Swedish Institute of International Affairs.

Sjursen, H. (2006). 'The EU as a "normative" power: how can this be?' *Journal of European Public Policy*, **13**(2): 235–51.

Smith, K. (2000). 'The end of civilian power EU: a welcome demise or cause for concern?' *International Spectator*, **23**(2): 11–28.

Stec, M. and M. Grzebyk (2018). 'The implementation of the Strategy Europe 2020 objectives in European Union countries: the concept analysis and statistical evaluation'. *Quality & Quantity*, **52**(1): 119–33.

Tocci, N. (ed.) (2008). *Who is a Normative Foreign Policy Actor – the European Union and its Global Partners.* Brussels: Centre for European Policy Studies.

Van Vooren, B. (2012). *EU External Relations Law and the European Neighbourhood Policy: a Paradigm for Coherence.* London and New York: Taylor and Francis.

Walby, Sylvia (2004). 'The European Union and gender equality: emergent varieties of gender regime'. *Social Politics*, **11**(1): 4–29.

Whitman, R. (1998). *From Civilian Power to Superpower? The International Identity of the European Union.* Basingstoke: Palgrave Macmillan.

Zielonka, J. (1998). *Explaining Euro-Paralysis: Why Europe Is Unable to Act in International Politics.* Basingstoke: Palgrave Macmillan.

PART II

Core actors on Europe 2020

3. Policy-making in the European Council and the Council of the EU on Europe 2020: the presidency effect

Brigitte Pircher

The European Council endorsed the overall aims, headline targets, and national targets of the Europe 2020 strategy in March 2010 (European Commission, 2010). After several discussions in the Council of the EU (the Council) and following an opinion by the European Parliament, the European Council finally adopted the strategy in June 2010 (European Council, 2010a). The new strategy entails a complex governance architecture that involves all levels of governance: the EU level as well as the national, and local and regional levels.

At the EU level, the European Council is the main body that develops and strengthens the strategy. It sets the main priorities and headline targets and steers the strategy. Moreover, the European Council ensures the integration of the various policy areas and guarantees both interinstitutional cooperation and cooperation between the EU and the national level. The European Council therefore developed various specifically focused policy areas and provided the necessary impulses and guidelines during the formulation of the strategy. The Council, on the other hand, is responsible for involving all the relevant Council formations in order to pursue the objectives of Europe 2020. Moreover, the Council provides a platform for an exchange of views among all member states.

After the onset of the financial crisis in 2008, new institutional changes favouring intergovernmental agreements and intergovernmental institutions, such as the European Council and the Council, were introduced (Fabbrini, 2013; Puetter, 2012). As Bickerton et al. (2015) point out, instead of competencies being transferred from the member states to the supranational level, policy coordination became the common method of policy-making. The Europe 2020 strategy is a prime example of these developments. The European Council was granted extensive powers in formulating the headline targets and in setting up and adopting the strategy. Moreover, the Council and its various formations constituted an important platform for debating and enhancing the strategy.

Despite the fact that both these councils were major actors as far as Europe 2020 is concerned, little is known about how the strategy was actually debated in these institutions and – more importantly – who the decisive actors were in promoting the strategy. Therefore, this chapter asks: To what extent has the European Council and the Council shaped the Europe 2020 strategy? Who were the political entrepreneurs involved in developing and enhancing the strategy? And in which way did they promote the strategy?

The chapter provides insights into the decision-making process while adopting the Europe 2020 strategy and therefore contributes to our understanding of EU policy-making within the European Council and the Council and the different positions and perceptions in adopting the strategy. Moreover, it contributes to the conceptual framework of political entrepreneurship by investigating possible entrepreneurial potential in intergovernmental EU institutions and by identifying actors that serve as political entrepreneurs in this process. By analysing EU Council debates, the chapter demonstrates that the presidencies in both intergovernmental institutions behaved like political entrepreneurs by advocating a certain policy favourable to the strategy that was ultimately adopted. This entrepreneurial role of the presidencies was achievable in view of a lack of consensus among member states.

The next section of the chapter discusses the concept of political entrepreneurship in relation to intergovernmental institutions. This is followed by an analysis of the debates in the European Council and the Council, which includes certain highly controversial policy areas such as the common agriculture policy. The chapter focuses on the actors that were able to shape and assert their policies, i.e. the political entrepreneurs. The final section of the chapter examines those entrepreneurs who were most successful in adopting the strategy.

POLITICAL ENTREPRENEURSHIP AND INTERGOVERNMENTAL EU INSTITUTIONS

With regard to the EU, it is primarily the European Commission that scholars have examined as a potential policy or political entrepreneur (Copeland and James, 2014; Laffan, 1997; Pollack, 1997; Schön-Quinlivan and Scipioni, 2017; Steinebach and Knill, 2017). This relates, *inter alia*, to the fact that the Commission is a supranational institution that has gained an increasing level of power over time. This supranational influence seems to be most pervasive 'where belief in European and democratic ideals is strongest' and where supranational officials are regarded as more legitimate (Moravcsik, 1999: 280). Whereas some researchers regard the entrepreneurial power of the Commission as exaggerated (Moravcsik, 1999), others stress the Commission's role as a key policy entrepreneur (Copeland and James, 2014; Schön-Quinlivan and Scipioni, 2017).

Copeland and James (2014) demonstrate that three policy streams combined at the beginning of the Europe 2020 process, and that this was what made it possible for the Commission to initiate and formulate the strategy successfully. Other studies confirm this outcome by demonstrating how the Commission served as a policy or political entrepreneur by successfully drafting and placing certain policies first at the agenda-setting stage and subsequently at the adoption stage (Schön-Quinlivan and Scipioni, 2017; Steinebach and Knill, 2017). The Commission's power as a political entrepreneur is often traced back to the right to initiate and draft policies and proposals. It is therefore not surprising that only a few researchers have thus far focused on intergovernmental institutions as possible political entrepreneurs.

Nevertheless, research hints at the fact that under certain conditions, intergovernmental institutions as a whole – or parts of them (for example the Council Secretariat) – also have the potential to act as political entrepreneurs (Juncos and Pomorska, 2010; Pircher, 2018a; 2018b). Juncos and Pomorska (2010: 19) demonstrate that officials in the Council Secretariat have emphasised their role in drafting and shaping legislation and policies and in agenda-setting, while working closely together with the presidency. This close cooperation has been regarded as a 'source of influence' for the whole Secretariat. This study also demonstrated that the power and role of the Council Secretariat in acting as a policy entrepreneur was highly dependent on the presidency in place, and was more relevant in policy areas in which the Commission had restricted power (Juncos and Pomorska, 2010: 19). Pircher (2018b) demonstrates that the Council was able to utilise a crisis-induced window of opportunity in order to introduce ready-made plans at the agenda-setting and decision-making stages. However, this was only achievable in the light of broad consensus in the Council and a common understanding of the need for reforms as a result of a crisis situation that pressured politicians into taking swift action. The study also reveals that a lack of consensus between member states, as well as their diverging interests, may also have the contrary effect and constrain entrepreneurial policies (Pircher, 2018b).

In intergovernmental institutions such as the European Council and the Council, it is theoretically possible to observe four different kinds of entrepreneurs: policy, bureaucratic, traditional political and political entrepreneurs, as defined in this book (see Table 1.1, Chapter 1).[1] A policy entrepreneur is an actor, normally placed outside of the legislative policy-making, who seeks to introduce and implement new ideas into the public sector. Policy entrepreneurs are focused on the development of public goods or on their own individual profit (Kingdon, 2011: 122–80). Successful policy entrepreneurs are often experts who are taken seriously and have the necessary reputation, political network, and skills to advocate certain policies (Capano, 2009: 19–25; Kingdon, 2011: 165). This role of policy entrepreneur applies to many experts working in the Council behind the scenes, such as the experts and officials in the General Secretariat, the experts and officials from each member state in the preparatory bodies (working groups, parties and committees) and experts and national officials involved in the presidency work. The concept of the policy entrepreneur within intergovernmental institutions overlaps with that of the bureaucratic entrepreneur, which refers to actors that influence the policy process and the public sector by gaining power from the policy-makers. This applies to public servants who drive policy change due to their relevant influence in the policy process. Bureaucratic entrepreneurs are more reluctant to adopt new policy ideas, but advocate stronger proposals that prove to be workable (Teske and Schneider, 1994: 338).

By contrast, political entrepreneurs can be politicians driven either by their individual profit-seeking from the political system or by the common good (Dahl, 1974; McCaffrey and Salerno, 2011). In the case of intergovernmental EU institutions, this refers to the president and the heads of state or government of the member states in the European Council. Moreover, it refers to the presidency, represented by national politicians, and the various ministers in the Council.

This study adopts a broader definition of the term 'political entrepreneur' to include actors and institutions within the public sector that make use of innovative approaches to promote entrepreneurship or businesses. In contrast to other definitions, however, we limit the scope by including the overarching goal in terms of which political entrepreneurs act. This goal is growth and employment for the common good (see Chapter 1). This includes politicians, bureaucrats, officers, and even institutions or parts of institutions that challenge traditional institutions, strategies, policies or laws in order to create favourable conditions for entrepreneurial activities and growth and employment (Silander, 2016; 2018).

---

[1] It might be argued that the concept of the public entrepreneur is suitable as well, but public entrepreneurs are actors within municipal and public corporations. This definition does not apply to the EU level.

When this definition is applied to the intergovernmental EU institutions, it involves policy, bureaucratic, and political entrepreneurs. In addition to this focus on the policy outcome, we define it in terms of the process in which political entrepreneurs often do not operate in terms of the official and traditional ways, but rather use innovative and creative channels and networks to improve the conditions for entrepreneurs (see Chapter 1).

In order to identify possible types of entrepreneurs in the European Council and the Council, this chapter evaluates the debates held within the two institutions in the process of drafting and adopting the Europe 2020 strategy. As this is the most relevant EU strategy in terms of economic governance in recent years and sets out guidelines and policy objectives for a longer time period, it seems suitable for identifying various entrepreneurs within the intergovernmental EU institutions. Therefore, the study contributes to our understanding of entrepreneurial actors and behaviours within EU institutions, and the mechanisms that lead to entrepreneurial approaches at the EU level.

ANALYSING DEBATES WITHIN EU INSTITUTIONS

This chapter analyses the debates in the European Council and the Council on the Europe 2020 strategy. In order to answer the research questions, the study focuses on current research on political entrepreneurship and combines this with research on EU institutions, and specifically intergovernmental institutions. This combination makes it possible to examine the potential of political entrepreneurs in intergovernmental institutions and then to compare it with the actual debates in the institutions during the adoption of the Europe 2020 strategy. This provides the basis for identifying political entrepreneurs and analysing their behaviour during the launch of the strategy.

As a starting point, the study includes government documents on the Europe 2020 strategy from the different official EU websites and sources. These encompass primary sources such as the strategy itself, reports of the Commission, conclusions and decisions of the European Council, and conclusions, background notes and minutes of the Council. As these documents are more representative of the outcomes of the various debates than the controversial discussions that took place, press releases and newspaper articles are also taken into account.

In addition to press releases from the European Council and the Council, the analysis of the institutional discussions is built primarily on an analysis of newspaper articles from *Agence Europe*, a daily newspaper that presents the latest news on EU governance. *Agence Europe* articles from March 2010 until June 2012 were analysed. This time period was chosen as it covers the crucial time of the development and the adoption of Europe 2020. All articles in this period relating to Europe 2020 were collected, reviewed, analysed and qualitatively evaluated by means of a content analysis. Analysing the debates on political entrepreneurship within EU institutions via *Agence Europe* constitutes an approach that has already proved to be adequate (Pircher, 2018a, 2018b).

The analysis of the debates is presented in chronological order, beginning with the starting point of the strategy until its adoption. The sections are divided into the various headline areas of growth (smart, sustainable and inclusive growth) and into various policy areas. The analysis covers all relevant topics that were discussed during this process.

Initial Debates on the Europe 2020 Strategy

In 2008, the European Council invited the Commission and the Council to start renewing the Lisbon strategy and to find further commitments to structural reforms, sustainable development, and social cohesion (Council of the EU, 2008). These attempts soon came to a halt and were followed up only in late 2009 and 2010. Copeland and James (2014: 7) argue that the trigger for the relaunch was a specific focusing event, namely increasing speculation about a Greek sovereignty default. This coincided with the fact that in late 2009, when the Lisbon Treaty came into effect, Herman Van Rompuy was elected as president of the European Council, and his aim was to push the strategy through. In his first speech, he announced that overcoming the economic crisis was a priority objective (General Secretariat of the Council, 2009). Van Rompuy and the newly elected Commission president José Manuel Barroso rapidly allied after the former's election and decided on a plan to launch a new strategy for Europe. The presidencies' efforts were successful and resulted in the start of the Europe 2020 process. This demonstrates that the presidencies of both the European Council and the Commission played a crucial role in initiating Europe 2020.

Sustainable growth
The task of the Council was to discuss the strategy in all the various Council formations, beginning with the environment policy area. After the Commission's presentation of the strategy in March 2010, the main question was how European energy policy could contribute to stronger economic growth and the creation of jobs in Europe (Council of the EU, 2010a: 14–15). Günther Öttinger, representing the Commission, promised

to assist member states to achieve the green targets and even to exceed them (*Agence Europe*, 2010v). While the environmental ministers supported the objectives in the area of climate change and energy and welcomed the inclusion of sustainability as a priority objective, some delegations held the view that too much attention was focused on the green dimension in this approach. Therefore, the French proposal to allow state aid for green growth in order to achieve the environmental targets was refused (*Agence Europe,* 2010w).

In addition to the environment, the strengthening of the internal market in order to overcome the economic crisis became a crucial question. The Council conclusions therefore state that the strategy 'outlines an adequate framework for the European Union and Member States for exiting the crisis and addressing the structural weaknesses of the European economy and the macroeconomic challenges that have increased with the crisis' (Council of the EU, 2010b: 7). The conclusions further stress the Council's practical support for full utilisation of the internal market and cross-border activities with a view to strengthening the external economic agenda and improving the financing instruments of the strategy. As the strategy would contribute to safeguarding the European social market models[2] (Council of the EU, 2010b: 7–9), medium- and long-term reforms were discussed.

The presidencies of the EU institutions were decisive actors in promoting the single market. The draft conclusions were compiled by the European Council's president Herman Van Rompuy, together with the Spanish presidency in the Council, represented by José Luis Zapatero (Spanish Prime Minister at the time) and the Commission's president José Manuel Barroso. The main topics were the strengthening of the internal market to boost Europe's competitiveness, with a strong emphasis on opening markets at a global level, national targets, and national reform programmes set out by the various member states in dialogue with the Commission (*Agence Europe*, 2010g), as well as the introduction of a governance architecture involving all levels of governance (EU, national, local and regional) (*Agence Europe*, 2010g).

Inclusive and smart growth

Despite consensus that the objective of the strategy was to overcome the crisis situation, two main areas caused controversial discussion: employment and poverty. Germany and a number of other delegations stated that several targets – for example, reducing the number of people at risk

---

[2] For a definition and discussion of the term, please see Chapter 2.

of falling below the poverty line by 20 million – were the competence of the member states and not the EU. Moreover, certain countries believed that the target of investing 3 per cent of EU GDP in the area of research and development was too ambitious, while other delegations criticised the simultaneous submission of the 2020 strategy reports with the Stability and Growth Pact reports (*Agence Europe*, 2010n).

During these controversies – and still under the Spanish presidency – the president of the European Council, Herman Van Rompuy, played a decisive role and met the employment ministers of the trio presidency – consisting of Spain, Belgium and Hungary (Trio 3) at the time – represented in the meeting by Celestino Corbacho (Spain), Joëlle Milquet (Belgium), and Laszlo Herczog (Hungary). The aim was to discuss the linkage between economic growth and the creation of (green) jobs, in particular for young people. They further demanded a strengthened employment strategy. Moreover, Spain's territorial policy minister, Manuel Chaves, demanded an enhanced EU governance system in which EU institutions, countries, regions, local authorities and municipalities work closer together (*Agence Europe*, 2010u). This demonstrates that the presidencies of both institutions soon adopted leading roles not only in initiating, but also in discussions on the Europe 2020 strategy.

Critical concerns were voiced by BusinessEurope, the confederation of European businesses. It stressed three main topics that should receive closer attention after the failure of the Lisbon strategy: concrete actions for the sustainability of public financing and structural reforms, flexicurity as key for reducing unemployment, and a reliable governance system (*Agence Europe*, 2010o).

Shortcomings

The Europe 2020 strategy and its headline targets were approved during the 25 and 26 March 2010 summit of the European Council (European Council, 2010b). Unresolved topics included the failure of meeting national targets by member states and the definition of poverty. Once again, the presidencies of both the European Council and the Council played a leading role in finding consensus and agreement. In the discussions, Herman Van Rompuy stressed the need for the internal market to be enshrined at the global level, too, as well as the need to maintain and strengthen a social market economy, accompanied by an environmental dimension (*Agence Europe*, 2010aa). Moreover, special attention was given to the educational targets and the various competitiveness conditions among the member states (*Agence Europe*, 2010x). José Manuel Barroso highlighted the need to focus on economic growth in view of the economic crisis and lauded the excellent cooperation between the European Council and the Council.

Spain's Prime Minister, José Luis Zapatero, regarded the strategy as a major step towards the recovery of the European economy and the creation of jobs, and he emphasised the importance of coordinated economic governance at the various levels. The Council presidency was able to achieve a broad consensus, and Zapatero mentioned that two main topics were pivotal in that regard: the aim of lifting the EU out of the crisis while maintaining the European social model, and strengthening the Euro for greater security (*Agence Europe*, 2010y).

Despite close cooperation between the European Council and the Council and agreement on certain policy objectives, the European Parliament, in particular, was critical. Members argued that greater emphasis should have been placed on addressing unemployment (*Agence Europe*, 2010b) and combating poverty (*Agence Europe*, 2010f). However, the president of the Commission, together with the president of the European Council and the Council's presidency, defended the approach adopted. The only critical voice was raised by the European Council's president with regard to the establishment of a poverty indicator. Nicolas Sarkozy, the French president at the time, and Angela Merkel, the German Chancellor, therefore announced new proposals on the poverty indicator. Further criticism was raised by some delegations since certain policy areas had not been included – agriculture, in particular. A number of missing areas were therefore included at a basic level, and it was stated that these policies should support the strategy. Moreover, it was stated that '[A] sustainable, productive and competitive agricultural sector will make an important contribution to the new strategy, considering the growth and employment potential of rural areas while ensuring fair competition' (European Council, 2010b: 4). Sarkozy highlighted the fact that Europe was the world's second largest farm product exporter, which was why he could not imagine or support a 2020 Agenda that did not include agriculture. He regarded agriculture as key for the economic power of the EU, and an area in which several reforms would be needed (*Agence Europe*, 2010aa).

THE COMMON AGRICULTURAL POLICY

Agricultural policy has always been at the heart of the evolution and development of the EU. As one of the largest economic sectors in the EU, agriculture provides 44 million jobs in the food sector and accounts for a workforce of 22 million, working either as farmers or agricultural workers (European Commission, 2018). In 2017, the EU achieved peak agro-food exports valued at €137.9 billion (European Commission, 2017). The

Common Agricultural Policy (CAP), its future plans and improvements relating to the food supply chain and milk and dairy markets, as well as the role of agriculture policy in realising the objectives of the Europe 2020 strategy were debated in the Council in March 2010 (*Agence Europe*, 2010h).

Yet again, the Council presidency took a leading position. Due to a lack of consensus on the improved functioning of the food supply chain, the conclusions formulated by the presidency were taken over as common Council conclusions. However, these conclusions represented only the opinion of the trio presidency and not that of the individual member states. The United Kingdom (UK), Denmark, Switzerland and the Czech Republic opposed these provisions, as they were against the relaxation of competition rules that allow for the reinforcement of competitiveness in this area (*Agence Europe*, 2010l). Five main sectors were included in the text: first, the strengthening of the agro-food sector by improving its structure and consolidation and by integrating all relevant suppliers in the food supply chain and simplifying the rules; second, increasing transparency in the food chain; third, combating unfair trading practices; fourth, encouraging self-regulated initiatives; and fifth, finding a balance between the CAP and competition policy (*Agence Europe*, 2010l).

The post-2013 conclusions were a second example of the presidency succeeding in gaining support for its proposals. Even though the conclusions were supported by a majority of delegations, certain countries such as Germany, Sweden, Denmark, the UK, the Netherlands and Estonia supported a more market-oriented policy and therefore opposed the text (*Agence Europe*, 2010k). The lack of consensus again led to the fact that the important conclusions of the trio-presidency (Spain, Belgium and Hungary) were taken into account, not those of the individual member states. Once again, these conclusions represented only the view of the presidency on this issue (*Agence Europe*, 2010h).

In general, the ministers believed that agriculture did not receive sufficient prominence in the strategy, given its importance for realising the Europe 2020 objectives. They regarded agriculture and the agro-food industry as major promoters of economic growth and employment (Council of the EU, 2010c: 9). France and Germany drafted a paper in which agriculture featured more prominently. The UK called for the CAP to be revised entirely, while Germany held the view that the strategy should not interfere with the CAP budget. France – backed by Austria, Cyprus, Greece, Hungary, Ireland and Lithuania – believed that high levels of funding should continue to be granted after 2013. France and Germany announced that they would produce a joint contribution on these agricultural issues before the European Council meeting in June

2010 (*Agence Europe*, 2010i). Moreover, Sarkozy criticised the fact that the strategy would exclude farming, even though it accounted for an important part of the European economy. That is why he even threatened the non-participation of France in the Council meetings as had happened in the 1960s during the 'empty chair crisis'.[3] Yet again, this issue was subject to intervention at the highest political level, with France and Germany striving for a common solution for a sustainable CAP (*Agence Europe*, 2010ac). The European Parliament also criticised the non-inclusion of agriculture, adopting the joint resolution in this regard at its plenary session (*Agence Europe*, 2010a).

An agreement on the CAP was achieved in June 2010. Agriculture was granted a crucial role in meeting the Europe 2020 targets, but major divergences among the member states arose with regard to how to achieve this goal. While a large number of countries, such as France, Ireland, Italy, Spain, Portugal, Greece, Luxembourg, Poland and Hungary, were in favour of establishing market-regulating instruments and supporting farmers, other – more liberal – countries, namely the UK, Denmark and Sweden, demanded a consistent withdrawal of direct aid and the introduction of new instruments based on research and innovation to promote competitiveness. At the same time, discussions were held on spending on agriculture. While a majority of member states supported the maintenance of a strong CAP after 2013 – for example Germany, France, Italy, Ireland, Greece, Spain, Poland, *inter alia* – once again the UK, Sweden and Denmark demanded a reduction in expenditure. While France and Germany followed a similar approach with respect to the budget, they differed with regard to the degree or extent of market regulation. Germany made it very clear that it did not support a return to market regulation. Several delegations from the so-called new member states wanted to keep a strong CAP in its current form and supported a redistribution in their favour (*Agence Europe*, 2010j).

DEVELOPING EUROPE 2020

In addition to agriculture, the realisation of the targets in the fields of poverty and education was the topic of heated discussion (*Agence Europe*, 2010e; 2010z). The Education Council debated education targets, the rate reduction of early school leavers to 10 per cent, and increasing the

---

[3] After a Commission proposal on financing the CAP in 1965, which France opposed, France no longer attended the Council meetings. This was the first major decision-making gridlock crisis in the EU, referred to as the 'empty chair crisis'.

share of the population with a tertiary education to 40 per cent (*Agence Europe*, 2010r; European Commission, 2010), in order to derive unanimity on quantified targets (*Agence Europe*, 2010p). However, the Council failed to reach consensus, which would have been an important message to the heads of state and government. Due to the results of the UK general election, the UK delegation opposed common quantified targets. As a consequence, the conclusions were forwarded from the Spanish presidency and not from the Education Council (*Agence Europe*, 2010q). This is a further example of the presidency assuming a leading role and its conclusions being presented as the final outcome. Moreover, the Spanish presidency enabled a quick adoption of the strategy and announced that it would be adopted at the European Council summit in June 2010 due to the urgency of overcoming the crisis situation and promoting economic growth (*Agence Europe*, 2010d). This was done against the background of the European Parliament having beforehand called for the adoption to be postponed due to a lack of time to examine the proposals (*Agence Europe*, 2010c).

In addition to an enhanced role of the presidency in the Council, the president of the European Council also strengthened its position. A special task force chaired by Herman Van Rompuy and made up of representatives of all EU member states was established with a view to tightening budgetary discipline under the stability and growth pact, reducing the divergences in competitiveness among member states, and ensuring macroeconomic surveillance and effective crisis management (European Council, 2010c).

Further debates related to national targets for investment in research and development (Council of the EU, 2010d), the creation of a digital single market (Council of the EU, 2010e), and guidelines for member states' employment strategies with regard to social protection and social inclusion (*Agence Europe*, 2010t). Shortly before the European Council summit on 17 June 2010, the Council adopted its conclusions on the Europe 2020 strategy, which included all the various conclusions from the Council formations that were discussed before, such as the headline targets, integrated guidelines, the main areas for sustainable growth, and enhanced economic policy coordination (Council of the EU, 2010f).

Adoption of the Strategy

The European Council finally adopted the Europe 2020 strategy and its objectives on 17 June 2010. It thereby approved the integrated guidelines for economic and employment policies, including national recommendations from the Council to the EU countries, and approved the specific targets in the areas of energy, competitiveness, research and innovation, a digital agenda, education, social inclusion, poverty reduction, and a strategy on how to implement these policies at member-state level. In addition, the European Council announced that further flagship initiatives and a follow-up by December 2010 could be expected (European Council, 2010a).

After the adoption, the presidencies maintained their important role. Herman Van Rompuy and José Manuel Barroso welcomed the finalisation of the strategy as a key factor in promoting economic growth. The Spanish presidency stressed the importance of the strategy in the creation of jobs. The forthcoming Belgian presidency demanded the inclusion of specific targets for industrial policy, in order to stimulate the economy. These demands were taken up by the European Council (*Agence Europe*, 2010ab). By the end of June 2010, the Council had agreed to incorporate transport in the Europe 2020 strategy by improving the competitiveness of the European transport sector (Council of the EU, 2010g). In the second half of 2010, the Belgian presidency pursued the further development of the strategy and included integrated guidelines for the implementation of economic policies in terms of which member states need to formulate their national reform programmes (*Agence Europe*, 2010m), as well as cultural and audio-visual dimensions in the digital agenda (Council of the EU, 2010h: 11).

Employment and social affairs
The Council debates in late 2010 and 2011 were focused on the areas of employment and social affairs. The presidency again took the most relevant initiatives. The Belgian presidency and its successors Hungary and Poland met European social partners and trade unions and agreed on creating a sustainable employment strategy by boosting employment demand as well as job supply. Ministers further stressed the urgent need to protect the European social and pension systems. However, criticism was raised by trade unions that the recommendations were not far-reaching enough, and that employment as such was no guarantee against poverty, as the quality of work also needed to be taken into consideration (*Agence Europe*, 2010s). After debating employment, the Council adopted its conclusions on this topic in June 2011, and finalised the European Semester, an instrument to ensure proper implementation of the 2020 Agenda. For the first time, the recommendations represented a combination of employment and economic aspects (Council of the EU, 2010i: 11). Reservations were raised by three member states in relation to the retirement age and wage negotiations, as training and wage matters are issues where member states have sovereignty. Belgium criticised the fact that the employment

ministers were not able to provide their views on euro area issues. Cyprus called for a greater inclusion of social partners in the pension debate, while Malta expressed its reservations on technical constraints in the retirement system. As Germany and France pressed for a common solution to these issues, a trialogue with the above three member states and the Commission was established with a view to reaching an agreement. France also stressed the need to fully include social partners in this debate and the need to address unemployment, working poverty, and low salary traps. Italy called for a greater inclusion of cohesion policy as a guarantor in overcoming the crisis situation. Austria and Luxembourg demanded a more active growth strategy than the defensive strategy at this time. The UK appealed for the time frame to be extended, while Slovenia demanded the inclusion of the different Council formations and their recommendations in the process (*Agence Europe*, 2011).

In the autumn of 2011, the ministers decided to integrate the European Social Fund into the strategy more extensively. In addition to combating social exclusion and the reduction of poverty, strategies for helping young people to integrate into labour markets were agreed upon by a broad consensus (Council of the EU, 2011a: 8–9). Both debates in the Council that took place in October and December and its formulated conclusions were preceded by a presidency background note. The conclusions related to increasing employment and social cohesion, the need for structural reform (for example, the benefit and pensions systems, as already debated), and the combining of education and training (Council of the EU, 2011b). In a follow-up in June 2012, the employment ministers decided to introduce further measures to create jobs, combat youth unemployment and labour market segmentation, increase access to labour markets, and strengthen the role of social partners (Council of the EU, 2012: 8–9).

CONCLUDING REMARKS

When Herman Van Rompuy was elected president of the European Council in late 2009, together with the newly elected Commission president José Manuel Barroso he rapidly launched a plan for a new strategy for Europe, and advocated specific policies and programmes. He challenged the formal institutions via new and innovative approaches and acted in an entrepreneurial manner in order to achieve a long-term strategy for Europe. If we revert to the definitions of the various types of entrepreneur referred to earlier in this book, this behaviour can be identified as that of the political entrepreneur. The fact that the two presidents allied so quickly, has been referred to as 'pivotal in unlocking the political process and creating the conditions for effective policy entrepreneurship' by Copeland and James (2014: 9). In fact, this was the starting point for drafting and adopting the Europe 2020 strategy. This means that the presidencies were decisive in placing the strategy on the agenda and in assigning it such high priority, especially against the background that the debates on the strategy had already come to a halt. As the analysis of the debates demonstrates, the leading role of the European Council president remained consistent and was even enhanced during the policy process. For example, Herman Van Rompuy also established a special task force to strengthen economic measures and governance.

When we focus our attention on identifying possible entrepreneurs in EU intergovernmental institutions, it is clear that with regard to Europe 2020 it was primarily political entrepreneurs – in this case the presidencies of the EU Councils – who were decisive in formulating and adopting the strategy. This confirms previous studies on the Council which demonstrated that only parts of the institutions are able to serve successfully as political entrepreneurs (Juncos and Pomorska, 2010). In addition to Herman Van Rompuy, the role of the presidency and the trio presidency in the Council of the EU were crucial in adopting the strategy. Moreover, when the first major controversies in the field of employment and social inclusion began, it was the two presidencies of both Councils that pursued certain policies and broad agreement on those policies.

In the controversial policy area of agriculture, the improved functioning of the food supply chain and the post-2013 conclusions are examples where the presidency increased its political power. Due to a lack of consensus among the member states, it was the presidency's conclusions, and not normal Council conclusions, that were published and passed on to the European Council. The same happened shortly thereafter with regard to education, where ministers were once again unable to reach an agreement. In this respect, the presidency played an increasingly important role and was able to strengthen its power in the decision-making process. This situation remained stable after the adoption of the strategy and after the change from the Spanish to the Belgian presidency.

We define political entrepreneurs as actors or institutions – for example politicians, bureaucrats, officers and institutions within the publicly funded sector – that make use of innovative approaches to encourage entrepreneurship, where the goals are growth and employment. The presidencies represented by politicians served as political entrepreneurs. In his role as president of the European Council, Herman Van Rompuy acted as a political entrepreneur, as the term is traditionally used to describe politicians driven by the common good or individual profit from the political system. As the main goal in this context was to create growth and employment, he can also be described as a political entrepreneur as defined in this book.

The analysis of the debates in the Council of the EU revealed that the presidency played the most relevant role in drafting, adopting and agreeing on the Europe 2020 strategy. Even though various actors (prime minister, ministers, national officials and so on) are included from one main member state and two supporting member states from the previous and future presidencies, we are able to observe political entrepreneurship as defined and explained in terms of the presidency effect. It might therefore be argued that the presidency can be regarded as an institution that challenged existing institutional structure via innovative approaches with a view to achieving growth and employment. Interestingly, this study has found stronger evidence for political entrepreneurs within the EU Council than for policy or bureaucratic entrepreneurs. This has to do with the fact that both councils are organised in an intergovernmental manner and that it is primarily politicians that drive the policy process. This is in contrast to a supranational institution such as the Commission, for example, where experts and bureaucrats play a more decisive role and shape policies.

REFERENCES

Agence Europe (2010a). (EU) EP/2020 STRATEGY: EP calls for ambitious social agenda and enhanced economic governance, without forgetting agriculture, Brussels, 10/03/2010, AE 10095, 11.3.2010.

Agence Europe (2010b). (EU) EP/BUDGET 2011: Giving greater substance to EU 2020 strategy and priority to young people, economic recovery and innovation, Brussels, AE 10106, 26.3.2010.

Agence Europe (2010c). (EU) EP/COMPETITIVENESS: Adoption of the EU 2020 strategy delayed until autumn?, Brussels, 23/04/2010, AE 10125, 24.4.2010.

Agence Europe (2010d). (EU) EP/EU 2020 STRATEGY: Final adoption of strategy by June summit, says Diego Lopez Garrido – José Manuel Barroso speaks of coordinated reform – Political groups uncertain about success of strategy, Brussels, 06/05/2010, AE 10134, 7.5.2010.

Agence Europe (2010e). (EU) EP/EUROPEAN COUNCIL: MEPs reiterate expectations for economic governance and 2020 strategy objectives, Brussels, 07/04/2010, AE 10113, 8.4.2010.

Agence Europe (2010f). (EU) EP/POVERTY: European fourth World Committee calls for fight against poverty to be given pride of place in EU priorities – Letter to Van Rompuy, Barroso and Buzek, Brussels, 25/03/2010, AE 10106, 26.3.2010.

Agence Europe (2010g). (EU) EU/2020 STRATEGY: General Affairs Council examines conclusions on new strategy, Brussels, 22/03/2010, AE 10103, 23.3.2010.

Agence Europe (2010h). (EU) EU/AGRICULTURE COUNCIL: Monday's meeting to discuss future of Common Agricultural Policy, EU 2020 strategy, climate change and dairy market, Brussels, 26/03/2010, AE 10107, 27.3.2010.

Agence Europe (2010i). (EU) EU/AGRICULTURE: Agriculture's clear contribution to 2020 strategy – Franco-German paper before June, Brussels, 30/03/2010, AE 10109, 31.3.2010.

Agence Europe (2010j). (EU) EU/AGRICULTURE: Divergences over future CAP agendas and funding, Brussels, 02/06/2010, AE 10151, 3.6.2010.

Agence Europe (2010k). (EU) EU/AGRICULTURE: Need to keep market measures in future supported by majority of countries, Brussels, 29/03/2010, AE 10108, 30.3.2018.

Agence Europe (2010l). (EU) EU/AGRICULTURE: No consensus at Council on ways of making food supply chain more efficient, Brussels, 29/03/2010, AE 10108, 30.3.2010.

Agence Europe (2010m). (EU) EU/ECOFIN COUNCIL: Broad economic policy guidelines adopted, Brussels, 13/07/2010, AE 10180, 14.7.2010.

Agence Europe (2010n). (EU) EU/ECOFIN COUNCIL: Tuesday's meeting to discuss Greek public deficit, draft compromise on hedge funds and 2020 Strategy, Brussels, 12/03/2010, AE 10097, 13.3.2010.

Agence Europe (2010o). (EU) EU/ECONOMY: Improved access to finance, more flexicurity and credible governance are BusinessEurope's priorities for 2020 strategy, Brussels, 23/03/2010, AE 10104, 24.3.2010.

Agence Europe (2010p). (EU) EU/EDUCATION-YOUTH-CULTURE COUNCIL: Ministers seek unanimity on quantified education objectives for EU 2020 strategy – First formal discussions on sport, Brussels, 06/05/2010, AE 10134, 7.5.2010.

Agence Europe (2010q). (EU) EU/EDUCATION COUNCIL: UK will not countenance quantified objectives and prevents unanimous message to European Council, Brussels, 11/05/2010, AE 10138, 12.5.2010.

Agence Europe (2010r). (EU) EU/EDUCATION: Reducing school drop out rate and increasing number of higher qualifications remain goals to be achieved in 2020, says Spanish EU Presidency in Madrid, Brussels, 14/04/2010, AE 10118, 15.4.2010.

Agence Europe (2010s). (EU) EU/EMPLOYMENT-SOCIAL AFFAIRS COUNCIL: Employment and social dimension must play essential role in EU 2020 strategy, Brussels, 08/07/2010, AE 10177, 9.7.2010.

Agence Europe (2010t). (EU) EU/EMPLOYMENT COUNCIL: Social inclusion indicators, health and pension inequalities and social security on Council agenda for 7 June, Brussels, 02/06/2010, AE, 3.6.2010.

Agence Europe (2010u). (EU) EU/EMPLOYMENT: Rotating presidency trio's employment ministers meet with President of European Council, Herman Van Rompuy, Brussels, 18/03/2010, AE 10101, 19.3.2010.

Agence Europe (2010v). (EU) EU/ENERGY: EU on track to meet 20% renewables target by 2020, Brussels, 11/03/2010, AE 10096, 12.3.2010.

Agence Europe (2010w). (EU) EU/ENVIRONMENT COUNCIL: Member states highlight positive benefits of environmental policies to green growth recommended in EU2020 strategy, Brussels, 17/03/2010, AE 10100, 18.3.2010.

Agence Europe (2010x). (EU) EU/EUROPEAN COUNCIL: EU27 urged to endorse aid mechanism for Greece, Brussels, 24/03/2010, AE 10105, 25.3.2010.

Agence Europe (2010y). (EU) EU/SOCIAL: European aid to Greece dominates tripartite social summit – European social partners' agreement on inclusive labour markets, Brussels, 25/03/2010, AE 10106, 26.3.2010.

Agence Europe (2010z). (EU) EU/YOUTH: Youth organisations say EU2020 strategy doomed to failure if it rules out stricter criteria on education and eradicating poverty, Brussels, 01/04/2010, AE 10111, 2.4.2010.

Agence Europe (2010aa). (EU) EUROPEAN COUNCIL: EU 2020 strategy is approved – José Luis Zapatero says the great idea underpinning this strategy is coordination, i.e. a Union moving towards coordinated economic governance, Brussels, 26/03/2010, AE 10107, 27.3.2010.

Agence Europe (2010ab). (EU) EUROPEAN COUNCIL: Targets set for EU2020 Strategy, Brussels, 17/06/2010, AE 10162, 18.6.2010.

Agence Europe (2010ac). A Look Behind The News, by Ferdinando Riccardi: Agriculture: future debate on CAP enters institutional phase – Divergence at Council, role of European Parliament, Brussels, AE 10110, 1.4.2010.

Agence Europe (2011). (AE) EU/EMPLOYMENT: National programmes – Belgian, Cypriot and Maltese reservations, Brussels, 17/06/2011, AE 10400, 18.6.2011.

Bickerton, C.J., D. Hodson and U. Puetter (2015), 'The new intergovernmentalism: European integration in the post-Maastricht era', *Journal of Common Market Studies*, **53**(4), 703–22.

Capano, G. (2009). 'Understanding policy change as an epistemological and theoretical problem'. *Journal of Comparative Policy Analysis Research and Practice*, **11**(1), 7–31.

Copeland, P. and S. James (2014). 'Policy windows, ambiguity and Commission entrepreneurship: explaining the relaunch of the European Union's economic reform agenda'. *Journal of European Public Policy*, **21**(1), 1–19.

Council of the EU (2008). Presidency Conclusions 7652/1/08, REV 1, CONCL 1, Brussels European Council, 13/14 March 2008, Brussels, 20 May 2008.

Council of the EU (2010a). Press Release, 7332/10 (Presse 55), 3001st Council meeting, Transport, Telecommunications and Energy, Brussels, 11–12 March 2010.

Council of the EU (2010b). Press Release, 7498/10 (Presse 63), 3003rd Council meeting, Economic and Financial Affairs, Brussels, 16 March 2010.

Council of the EU (2010c). Press Release, 8099/10 (Presse 78), 3006th Council meeting, Agriculture and Fisheries, Brussels, 29 March 2010.

Council of the EU (2010d). Press Release, 10123/10, PRESSE 136, 3016th Council meeting, Competitiveness (Internal Market, Industry and Research), Brussels, 25 and 26 May 2010.

Council of the EU (2010e). Press Release, 10418/10, PRESSE 146, 3017th Council meeting, Transport, Telecommunications and Energy, Brussels, 31 May 2010.

Council of the EU (2010f). Press Release, 10689/10, PRESSE 162, PR CO 7, 3020th Council meeting, Economic and Financial Affairs, Luxembourg, 8 June 2010.

Council of the EU (2010g). Press Release, 11442/10, PRESSE 191, PR CO 6, 3024th Council meeting, Transport, Telecommunications and Energy, Luxembourg, 24 June 2010.

Council of the EU (2010h). Press Release, 16500/10, PRESSE 304, PR CO 36, 3046th Council meeting, Education, Youth, Culture and Sport, Brussels, 18 and 19 November 2010.

Council of the EU (2010i). Press Release, PRESSE 176, PR CO 40, 3099th Council meeting, Employment, Social Policy, Health and Consumer Affairs, Employment and Social Policy, Luxembourg, 17 June 2011.

Council of the EU (2011a). Press Release, 14730/11, PRESSE 332, PR CO 56, 3114th Council meeting, Employment, Social Policy, Health and Consumer Affairs, Luxembourg, 3 October 2011.

Council of the EU (2011b). Press Release, 17943/1/11 REV 1, PRESSE 471, PR CO 75, 3131st Council meeting, Employment, Social Policy, Health and Consumer Affairs, Brussels, 1 and 2 December 2011.

Council of the EU (2012). Press Release, 11386/12, PRESSE 266, PR CO 39, 3177th Council meeting, Employment, Social Policy, Health and Consumer Affairs, Luxembourg, 21 and 22 June 2012.

Dahl, R.A. (1974). *Who Governs? Democracy and Power in an American City*. New Haven: Yale University Press.

European Commission (2010). *EUROPE 2020. A strategy for smart, sustainable and inclusive growth, Brussels, 3.3.2010, COM(2010) 2020 final*.

European Commission (2017). Monitoring EU Agri-Food Trade: Development in 2017, accessed 10 October 2018 at https://ec.europa.eu/agriculture/trade-analysis/monitoring-agri-food-trade_en.

European Commission (2018). Agriculture and Rural Development, CAP at a glance, accessed 17 October 2018 at https://ec.europa.eu/agriculture/cap-overview_en.

European Council (2010a). European Council, 17 June 2010, Conclusions, Brussels, 17 June 2010, EUCO 13/10, CO EUR 9, CONCL 2.

European Council (2010b). European Council, 25/26 March 2010 Conclusions, Brussels, 26 March 2010, EUCO 7/10, CO EUR 4, CONCL 1.

European Council (2010c). The President, Remarks by Herman Van Rompuy, President of the European Council, following the first meeting of the task force on economic governance, Brussels, 21 May 2010, PCE 102/10.

Fabbrini, S. (2013). 'Intergovernmentalism and its limits: assessing the European Union's answer to the euro crisis'. *Comparative Political Studies*, **46**(9), 1003–29.

General Secretariat of the Council (2009). Intervention by Herman Van Rompuy, President of the European Council at the ceremony on the occasion of the entry into force of the Lisbon Treaty, Brussels, 1 December 2009, PCE 02/09, Lisbon, 1 December 2009.

Juncos, A.E. and K. Pomorska (2010). 'Secretariat, facilitator or policy entrepreneur? Role perceptions of officials of the council secretariat'. In S. Vanhoonacker, H. Dijkstra and H. Maurer (eds), *Understanding the Role of Bureaucracy in the European Security and Defence Policy*, Special Issue, European Integration online Papers (EIoP), **14**(7): 1–26.

Kingdon, J.W. (2011). *Agendas, Alternatives, and Public Policies* (updated 2nd edn). Harlow: Pearson.

Laffan, B. (1997). 'From policy entrepreneur to policy manager: the challenge facing the European Commission'. *Journal of European Public Policy*, **4**(3), 422–38.

McCaffrey, M. and J.T. Salerno (2011). 'A theory of political entrepreneurship'. *Modern Economy*, **2**(4), 552–60.

Moravcsik, A. (1999). 'New statecraft? Supranational entrepreneurs and international cooperation'. *International Organization*, **53**(3), 267–306.

Pircher, B. (2018a). 'Debating the economic crisis in the European Parliament: enriching the discourse'. In C. Karlsson, C. Silander and D. Silander (eds), *Governance and Political Entrepreneurship in Europe: Promoting Growth and Welfare in Times of Crisis*. Cheltenham, UK and Northampton, MA, USA: Edward Elgar Publishing, pp. 100–119.

Pircher, B. (2018b). 'Entrepreneurship policy in the Council of the EU: reaching consensus among member states?' In C. Karlsson, C. Silander and D. Silander (eds), *Governance and Political Entrepreneurship in Europe: Promoting Growth and Welfare in Times of Crisis*. Cheltenham, UK and Northampton, MA, USA: Edward Elgar Publishing, pp. 82–99.

Pollack, M.A. (1997). 'Delegation, agency and agenda setting in the European Community'. *International Organization*, **51**(1), 99–135.

Puetter, U. (2012). 'Europe's deliberative intergovernmentalism: the role of the Council and European Council in EU economic governance'. *Journal of European Public Policy*, **19**(2), 161–78.

Schön-Quinlivan, E. and M. Scipioni (2017). 'The Commission as policy entrepreneur in European economic governance: a comparative multiple stream analysis of the 2005 and 2011 reform of the Stability and Growth Pact'. *Journal of European Public Policy*, **24**(8), 1172–90.

Silander, D. (2016). 'The political entrepreneur'. In C. Karlsson, C. Silander and D. Silander (eds), *Political Entrepreneurship: Regional Growth and Entrepreneurial Diversity in Sweden*. Cheltenham, UK and Northampton, MA, USA: Edward Elgar Publishing, pp. 7–20.

Silander, D. (2018). 'European governance and political entrepreneurship in times of economic crisis'. In C. Karlsson, C. Silander and D. Silander (eds), *Governance and Political Entrepreneurship in Europe: Promoting Growth and Welfare in Times of Crisis*. Cheltenham, UK and Northampton, MA, USA: Edward Elgar Publishing, pp. 3–24.

Steinebach, Y. and C. Knill (2017). 'Still an entrepreneur? The changing role of the European Commission in EU environmental policy-making'. *Journal of European Public Policy*, **24**(3), 429–46.

Teske, P. and M. Schneider (1994). 'The bureaucratic entrepreneur: the case of city managers'. *Public Administration Review*, **54**(4), 331–40.

4. The European Parliament and the Europe 2020 strategy: an arena for public debate or political entrepreneurship?

Mats Öhlén

INTRODUCTION

The European Parliament (EP) is the only directly elected European Union (EU) institution and with its role as the main arena for public debate at the EU level, it is central for the democratic legitimacy of the EU (Bache et al., 2011: 69; Burns, 2013: 160; Warleigh, 2003: 77–8). In light of the criticism concerning the Lisbon strategy with lack of insight and democratic accountability (see Büchs, 2008), the EP has therefore a potentially important role for the legitimacy of the Europe 2020 strategy. However, at the same time, the EP does not have the same powerful position that national parliaments usually have. It is one of several institutional actors in the EU system where the Council and the Commission have powerful roles. Moreover, the Europe 2020 strategy concerns areas where the EP has little or no formal influence. Therefore, the EP is not only an arena for public debate, but also an actor in itself seeking to enhance its role in the decision-making process. Here there is often room for pragmatism among the political groups and here there is also potential for political entrepreneurship.

This combination between on the one hand a source of democratic legitimacy and on the other hand an actor in the EU system is the point of departure of this chapter. The aim is to examine how the Europe 2020 strategy has been debated in the EP with regard to issue-specific themes and conflicts. A second aim is to assess the degree and type of political entrepreneurship within the EP in the context of the Europe 2020 strategy, that is, attempts to influence the process of shaping and implementing the strategy with innovative ideas on how to stimulate growth and entrepreneurship. This may take place at the individual level, that is, specific members of the EP (MEPs) or at the institutional level, that is, the EP acts strategically. Departing from the overarching focus of this book – *to analyse the Europe 2020 strategy and the role of European political entrepreneurship in debating, shaping and implementing the strategy* – this chapter will focus on the EP's specific role in this context. The following questions will steer the analysis:

- In what way has the Europe 2020 strategy been debated in the EP? Which concrete views and ideas have been delivered and from which political groups? Which are the main conflict dimensions of the debate and to what degree is the debate politicised, that is, steered by ideological arguments in contrast to discussions on technicalities?
- To what extent can we identify elements of political entrepreneurship in the EP with regard to the Europe 2020 strategy? Are there any examples of political entrepreneurship in the debate regarding individual MEPs and political groups? Are there any examples of political entrepreneurship regarding the EP as an institution in this context?

The main data used for this analysis consist of two plenary debates in the European Parliament concerning Europe 2020. The first took place in February 2010 shortly after the European Council had presented a draft version of the strategy. The second was held in October 2015 and concerned the mid-term review of the Europe 2020 strategy. When it comes to political entrepreneurship, the analysis will depart from the two plenary debates mentioned above but also resolutions and reports from the EP regarding Europe 2020. As the aim here is to identify patterns of the debate and in written resolutions from the EP, the main methodological technique will be content analysis where the core themes will be pinpointed and discussed.

THE EUROPEAN PARLIAMENT'S ROLE IN THE FRAMEWORK OF THE EUROPE 2020 STRATEGY

Just like its predecessor, the Lisbon strategy, the Europe 2020 strategy is mainly concerned with policy areas outside EU legislation competence, for example employment, education and social policy. Therefore, the main policy method applied has been coordination of member states' policies rather than binding EU legislation. The Lisbon strategy, which was adopted in March 2000, explicitly identified this strategy as distinctive policy method: the 'open method of coordination' (OMC). The main institutional actors in this policy method are the Commission, the Council and sometimes the European Council. The Commission has a certain role in putting together various networks of experts and other actors which may contribute in the deliberative process. Thereafter, high-level national experts and sometimes ministers meet in the Council to discuss possible goals as a framework for coordination (Wallace and Reh, 2015: 107–108). Even though some initially welcomed the OMC as novel and creative (Scott and Trubek, 2002), several voices have raised doubts about its efficiency due to lack of control mechanisms but also regarding democratic legitimacy due to lack of transparency and weak political accountability (Szyszczak, 2006). In particular the EP has been concerned about the legitimacy of this policy method as it is practically excluded from the decision-making process (European Parliament, 2014a). The EP is involved to a certain extent through a structured dialogue between the involved experts and ministers and the specialist EP committees (Wallace and Reh, 2015: 107) but that is not enough. As the EU's sole directly elected institution, it has pledged to become more involved in the process of OMC in order to make it more democratic (European Parliament, 2003).

In the light of the fact that the OMC situates the EP in a weaker position, it is reasonable to ask whether the EP has the possibility to act as a political entrepreneur at all. In the academic debate, it is primarily the Commission that is analysed as a policy entrepreneur (see for example Copeland and James, 2014; Laffan, 1997). This is natural as it has the legislative initiative in most areas of EU decision-making. Furthermore, as illustrated in Brigitte Pircher's chapter (Chapter 3 in this volume), the European Council and the Council of the EU have a strong potential for political entrepreneurship. In fact, the economic crisis increased the power of the Commission and especially the European Council while at the same time the role of the EP was rather weak (Bauer and Becker, 2014). Important measures such as the European Semester and the Euro-Plus Pact were adopted with minimal impact from the EP (Pircher, 2018: 102). Yet the EP has some tools for influence even for these circumstances. First, it has a certain role in the policy formulation process as draft legislation is sent to the responsible EP committee. Here, the EP may exercise legislative power by shaping the legislative acts in a way that strengthens economic surveillance and democratic commitments (Fasone, 2013). Secondly, the EP may apply institutional bargaining pressure, that is, in order to adopt a legislative act in one area through co-decision, the EP demands greater influence in a related area where it lacks formal influence (Rittberger, 2014). Thirdly, the EP may apply flexible policy-influencing rather than traditional policy-making instruments. These instruments include different types of initiatives such as resolutions, reports, opinions, public hearings and open debates. They also had the function to influence the values among various civil society organisations. This strategy of flexible policy-influencing was especially frequent in the context of the economic crisis (Pircher, 2018: 103).

THE POLITICAL GROUPS OF THE EUROPEAN PARLIAMENT

Why is it necessary to focus on transnational political groups in the EP when analysing the debate on the Europe 2020 strategy? The answer lies in the fact that it is the only institution in the EU system which can claim direct democratic legitimacy. If the Commission and European Council want the Europe 2020 strategy to be viewed as legitimate, they will have to listen to the EP's opinion. Yet it is easily forgotten that this legitimacy is based on the existence of political parties which play a central role in modern representative democracies. By offering a limited set of political alternatives built on long-term ideological visions of society, parties are crucial for linking citizens to the government (Dalton and Wattenberg, 2000). Although party politics in the traditional form is weak in the EU political system, with its lack of a clear government opposition, all high-profile politicians in the EU are party politicians; they have been recruited, trained and formed within their respective political parties at the national level (Hix and Høyland, 2011; Hix and Lord, 1997). The EP is the institution where this is most noticeable as it is built on transnational political groups, which can be described as the 'democratic backbone' of the EU. They take part in EP debates and legislation processes, they debate and adopt the EU budget and scrutinise the Commission's work. Furthermore, most of them are part of transnational European-level party families, which all have member parties from various member states in the EU. In this sense they constitute the most important link between the citizens and the EU level.

Table 4.1 presents the political groups which have been present in the EP during the timeframe of this study. It is clear from the table that two groups dominate: the Christian democratic European People's Party (EPP) and the social democratic Progressive Alliance of Socialists and Democrats (S&D). These two groups are, together with the liberal Alliance of Liberals and Democrats in Europe (ALDE), the most institutionalised with well organised European-level parties (Öhlén, 2013: 120–21). Focusing on the ideological spectrum of the EP, there are two dimensions of conflict (Hix

Table 4.1   The political groups in the European Parliament 2009–14 and 2014–19

Political group	Ideology	EU-integration	Seats 2009–14	Seats 2014–19
EPP (European People's Party)	Christian democratic	Pro-integration	274 (36%)	219 (29%)
S&D (Progressive Alliance of Socialists and Democrats)	Social democratic	Pro-integration	195 (25%)	189 (25%)
ALDE (Alliance of Liberals and Democrats in Europe)	Liberal	Pro-integration	85 (11%)	68 (9%)
ECR (European Conservatives and Reformists)	Conservative	Soft EU-sceptic	56 (7%)	73 (10%)
Greens–EFA (Greens–European Free Alliance)	Green–regionalist	Pro-integration	58 (8%)	52 (7%)
GUE–NGL (European United Left–Nordic Green Left)	Socialist/Communist	Soft EU-sceptic	35 (5%)	51 (7%)
EFDD (Europe of Freedom and Direct Democracy)	Right-wing populist	EU-sceptic	33 (4%)	43 (6%)
ENF (Europe of Nations and Freedom)	Nationalist	Hard EU-sceptic	–	35 (5%)
NI (Non-Inscrits)			30 (4%)	21 (3%)
Total			766 (100%)	751 (100%)

Source: Developed with help from the following sources: European Parliament (2018); Bache et al. (2011: 306).

and Lord, 1997). First, we have the traditional Left–Right dimension, which is mainly economic but has over time included the environmentalist and to some degree conservative versus liberal issues. To the right, we find the European Conservatives and Reformists (ECR), the Europe of Freedom and Direct Democracy (EFDD) and the Europe of Nations and Freedom (ENF). The EPP and ALDE are also positioned to the right but close to the centre. To the left, we find the European United Left–Nordic Green Left (GUE-NGL) and the centre-left consists of the S&D and the Greens–European Free Alliance (Greens-EFA).

Secondly, there is the 'integration dimension', which divides the groups into for versus against EU integration. As illustrated in the table, the two dominating groups of the EP are both pro-integration. The EPP and the S&D have earlier been rather equal in size, but since the early 2000s, the EPP has been the biggest group. In fact, it remained the strongest group after it was split in 2009 when the new EU-sceptic ECR was formed (*The Telegraph*, 2009). It must finally be underlined that there is some pragmatic cooperation between the EPP and S&D in so-called 'grand coalitions'. Even if Left–Right voting has increasingly dominated, this does not stop the EPP and S&D from creating grand coalitions from time to time (Kreppel and Hix, 2003).

TWO DEBATES IN THE EUROPEAN PARLIAMENT ON THE EUROPE 2020 STRATEGY

The Plenary Debate 24 February 2010[1]

The main issue of this debate was the informal Council conclusions that had been presented on the Europe 2020 strategy. The atmosphere could be described as somewhat solemn as two prominent guests were present: the recently appointed president of the European Council Herman van Rompuy and the recently re-appointed president of the European Commission José Manuel Barroso. Both were there to present the main points of the Europe 2020 strategy and listen to the reactions of the Parliament. After two introductory speeches by Mr Van Rompuy and Mr Barroso, each political group gave a short speech, which in turn was followed by a more ad hoc speech order.

So what characterised this debate? First, the allocation of speeches for each political group demonstrates that the two largest groups, the EPP and the S&D, dominated the scene. The EPP had 16 contributions (of which six were written) and the S&D had 15 contributions (five were written). This can be compared with five contributions from the Greens–EFA and four from ALDE and GUE–NGL respectively. The ECR, as the third largest group, had only three contributions and this says something about their small interest in the issue. Secondly, the context is important. The treaty of Lisbon came into effect on 1 December 2009, which was less than three months before this debate. This treaty made the EP equal co-legislator with the Council in most issues. This was moreover the first time that a senior representative from the European Council attended a plenary session after this new treaty and several MEPs made remarks about this. One example was the opening statement of the EPP group-leader Joseph Daul, who welcomed Mr Van Rompuy's presence but reminded him that 'we are now equal decision makers, and this has not only legal consequences but political ones as well' (European Parliament, 2010a).

---

[1]   All references in the text relating to the plenary debate on 24 February 2010 are based on a protocol from the debate retrieved from the homepage of the European Parliament. See European Parliament (2010a).

What were the main topics of the debate? Here again, the context played a certain role. Greece was in the midst of a financial and social crisis with rapidly rising unemployment, and several speeches were dominated by the ongoing crisis. Yet they spoke of the crisis in different ways. The EPP spoke about the Greek crisis as an example warning of the consequences of a weak and slow EU economic policy. In contrast, the S&D and the GUE–NGL focused more on the failure of the strict focus on financial austerity as a way out of the crisis. The ALDE and the Greens–EFA focused almost entirely on the Greek crisis. The ALDE group leader, Guy Verhovstadt, even called for the EU to issue euro obligations in order to solve the Greek debt crisis. Related to the discussions of the Greek crisis, there seemed to be a general frustration and concern across party lines about the lack of focus and efficiency in the strategy. Several MEPs from ALDE and Greens–EFA called for fewer targets which were measurable. The same critique was directed towards the OMC as an inefficient process without clear accountability. Some MEPs from EPP and Greens–EFA indirectly criticised the inefficiency of the OMC by proposing stronger EU-coordination of economic policy and the abandonment of sovereignty in some areas. MEPs from the ALDE went further: Lena Ek even argued that the OMC should be entirely abandoned as it lacks transparency and 'has turned into a closed collusion and open humiliation' (European Parliament, 2010a).

When it comes to ideological conflict, the debate was no doubt filled with strong statements, clearly dominated by the economic Left–Right and EU-integration dimensions and to a certain extent a Green critique of the strategy. The Left–Right conflict was most visible in statements from the S&D, the GUE–NGL and to some extent the Greens–EFA. While the S&D and Greens–EFA speakers took a rather polite and constructive tone in their critique, the GUE–NGL rhetoric could rather be described as radically anti-market. While S&D's Stephen Hughes spoke about the need to focus on bringing down unemployment and focusing on the people who are affected by the crisis, Nikolaos Chountis from the GUE–NGL assumed a more aggressive tone: 'You are treating Greece as a scapegoat, dictating measures against the workers, who are not to blame for the crisis' (European Parliament, 2010a).

As we can see, the main critique from the left concerns the policy of budgetary austerity. Somewhat surprisingly, there is not the same strong rhetoric from the EPP. Perhaps this is so because they belong to the same European-level party as the creators of the strategy and that it already reflects their views. The clearest pro-market statements were delivered by the conservative ECR. Timothy Kirkhope for example argued that we must 'recognize that government do not create productive jobs or raise living standards. Only competitive business and successful entrepreneurs can do that' (European Parliament, 2010a). The green perspectives in the debate were (not surprisingly) mainly delivered by the Greens–EFA. The main point here was that the target of reducing CO_2 by 20 per cent is far from ambitious. Instead, they called for a target of around 40 per cent as more reasonable. They also argued that the issue is not only about climate but also about resource efficiency and availability. The environmental perspective was raised to a certain extent also by the S&D and then linked to a potential for new jobs in the emerging green sector.

Finally, the debate was clearly influenced by the EU integration issue. The EPP and ALDE can be seen here as the main pro-integration propagators proposing stronger EU coordination in economic policy. The EPP aired the idea of abandoning national sovereignty 'in some areas', while the ALDE called for euro obligations to be introduced. Similar but less radical pro-integration arguments could be seen among the S&D and Green–EFA groups. The GUE–NGL was very critical of the EU 2020 strategy due to its focus on growth but never criticised the EU project as such. In fact, they proposed that an EU minimum wage should be introduced together with a harmonisation of tax. On the anti-integration camp, the most clear example was the EU-sceptic EFDD group. Its group leader Nigel Farage made a spectacular and provocative speech, where he accused the European Council President of being the 'quiet assassin' of the nation state.

The Plenary Debate 28 October 2015[2]

The theme of this debate was 'Perspectives and review of the EU 2020 strategy' and the atmosphere of this debate was clearly less ceremonial and more of a working session. No political group leader took part in the debate this time and instead of the President of the Commission and European Council, the newly appointed 'Commissioner for Economic and Monetary Affairs and the Euro', Valdis Dombrovskis represented the Commission. The number of participants in the debate was also clearly smaller, with 23 contributions compared to 64 contributions in the 2010 debate. Yet the fact that this debate was smaller and less formal may at the same time have made conditions better for influencing the Commission.

In general, the 2015 debate could be characterised as somewhat more 'technical' and more focused on practical issues. This is to some degree

---

[2] All references in the text relating to the plenary debate of 28 October 2015 are based on a protocol from the debate retrieved from the homepage of the European Parliament. See European Parliament (2015a).

natural as the focus of the debate concerned a review of the strategy and how it could be improved. The tone was generally critical, with the main message that all was not well with the strategy, especially in terms of how it had been implemented. This was not only stated by the overall critical groups such as the ECR, the EFDD and the GUE–NGL. Also the more pro-EU groups of the political centre expressed concern. Several MEPs from the S&D group stated rather bluntly that it was a failure. Carlos Zorrinho from the S&D argued that 'it is clear . . . that the first five years of the implementation of the Europe 2020 strategy have failed' (European Parliament, 2015a) and another S&D MEP, Sergiu Gaetanu, stated '[W]e must say frankly that the experience we have had in the past five years, relating to the Europe 2020 strategy, has been unsuccessful' (European Parliament, 2015a). The same critique came from the ALDE group where Pavel Telička depicted the Europe 2020 strategy as a missed opportunity with a weak compromise as a result where everybody had to be satisfied. It is noteworthy that even the EPP, despite its link to the Commission and European Council leaderships, expressed criticism although in a more polite manner, by for example stating that the Europe 2020 targets tend to be somewhat forgotten in the daily legislative work.

If we look into the various ideas and proposals raised by MEPs, it is clear that they are pragmatic, non-ideological and sometimes rather innovative, which we will come back to in the next section on political entrepreneurship. Most constructive ideas came from the two dominating groups in the EP: the EPP and the S&D. Several MEPs from the EPP raised the need for a stronger focus on the targets, which are actually measurable. The 3 per cent target for investment in research and development was mentioned as especially important for a revival of the strategy. Lambert van Nistelrooij from the EPP pointed out the risk that the Europe 2020 strategy may miss its objectives due to its highly top-down approach. The S&D group raised several problems with the strategy. The central challenge according to S&D was the focus on budget austerity. In a rather lengthy speech, Maria João Rodrigues raised the problem of a growing lack of coherence between the Europe 2020 strategy and the European Semester and she recommended that the Commission reintegrate the 2020 targets in the upcoming semester cycle. Rodrigues is often referred to as the 'mother of the Lisbon strategy' and is highly respected for her knowledge and experience. Therefore it can be assumed that the Commission listened extra carefully to her opinions. Other ideas from S&D focused on sustainability issues, for example the idea of a circular economy and the proposal to combine the energy union with the digital union. It is interesting that the S&D was most active in proposals relating to environmentalist concerns and that the Greens–EFA were quite passive.

Even if the ideological dimension was somewhat toned down in this debate, it was definitely not absent. The ideological positions were more or less the same compared to the debate in 2010. One difference is that the domination of the Left–Right dimension was even more prominent in this debate, very much thanks to the fact that the social democratic S&D was most active of all groups, with 40 per cent of the contributions. The S&D as well as the GUE–NGL noticeably criticised the narrow focus on austerity measures and neglect of employment and social issues in the first five years of the strategy. They were also critical of the lack of action when it comes to poverty and social inequality. Agnes Jongerius from S&D especially warned of the long-term consequences once families are threatened by poverty and stated that 'poverty reduction has actually become, just like the Europe 2020 strategy, a neglected child' (European Parliament, 2015a).

The other dimensions of country-specific issues, EU integration and green issues were present but clearly less visible in this debate. The green dimension was raised in three contributions from the Greens–EFA and from PES, which argued for more attention to sustainable development and the circular economy. The country-specific issues concerned almost exclusively Greece and the economic hardships the country was going through. In general, South-European MEPs independently of group affiliation tended to focus more on the issue of poverty and inequality, which indicates a North–South divide in the debate.

Summarising the Two Debates

It is quite clear that the main conflict in the debate on the Europe 2020 strategy touches both the traditional Left–Right dimension, including green perspectives and the EU integration dimension. The Left–Right dimension is mainly seen in the critical remarks from the S&D against the tough budget austerity measures and the need for more focus on employment, social equality and poverty reduction. This is also supported by the GUE–NGL and to some degree the Greens–EFA. Partly integrated into the Left–Right dimension is also a 'North–South' dimension in the debate where South European and in particular Greek MEPs tended to focus on the grim consequences of the economic crisis in the home countries. The EU integration dimension was clearly visible in the 2010 debate with heated arguments but disappeared almost entirely in the 2015 debate. This is somewhat puzzling as the EU-sceptic groups had grown in strength after the 2014 elections. One explanation might be that the debate in 2015 was clearly more low-key in its atmosphere and tone. There was hardly any participation at all from the EU-sceptic groups, which indicates a lack of interest in the issue as such. Reflecting on the relative strength of the political groups in the debate, it is clear that the EPP has a very strong position in the EU system. It has leading positions in the Commission, in the European Council and is the strongest group in the EP. This gives the EPP as a party in the broader sense a certain responsibility regarding the Europe 2020 strategy (see Martens, 2010). This has repercussions for its role in the EP debates. By its share size, it dominated the debates and tended to take the role of something similar to a cheering squad, supporting their party colleagues from the Commission and European Council that attended the EP debate. But at the same time, as a party they refrain to a certain extent from making critical points. The S&D, on the other hand, has the driving role in the debates since they are the most influential opposition group, raising critical remarks.

When it comes to the character of the debate, there were elements of both ideological conflict and issue-specific themes. This mirrors in a way the double role of the EP as arena for public debate as well as a forum for deliberation and issue-specific pragmatic discussions. The issue-specific themes related mostly to the targets of the strategy. In most cases they were seen as too modest. The 2015 debate, which was more about reviewing an existing strategy than shaping a new one, was clearly less ideological and more oriented towards issue-specific themes. Finally, there was a sense of frustration among several MEPs across party lines in both analysed debates regarding how the Europe 2020 strategy has been put forward with little opportunity for proper scrutiny. This was most clear in the 2015 debate as there was disappointment on how the European Council tried to hasten the process of adopting the strategy, giving the EP too little time for scrutiny. The statement from Jean Lambert (MEP for Greens–EFA) that the EP 'had to fight to find a way into [having] any sort of sense of ownership with it' (European Parliament 2015a) is an illustrating point of this disappointment.

ELEMENTS OF POLITICAL ENTREPRENEURSHIP IN THE EP REGARDING THE EUROPE 2020 STRATEGY

Before reviewing the degree of and character of political entrepreneurship in the EP, it is necessary to reflect on the very concept of 'political entrepreneur'. The definition used in this book is stated in Chapter 1: 'Actors and institutions (politicians/bureaucrats/officers/institutions) within the public funded sector that with innovative approaches encourage entrepreneurship/business and where the goal is growth and employment for the common good'. First, it is important to clarify that this definition is not outcome-oriented, that is, the political entrepreneur does not have to actually create growth and employment. Thus, it is the intention of the actor that is central in our understanding of the concept, not the result. Secondly, the modus operandi of the actor is essential in the definition used in this book: 'The political entrepreneur operates beyond traditional and routinized procedures and is innovative and creative in using formal and informal institutions and networks to improve the public sector's activities towards entrepreneurs and entrepreneurship by developing and promoting new norms that have not been embedded in traditional day-to-day public activities' (Silander, 2016: 10). Accordingly, a political entrepreneur has a certain *intention* (encourage entrepreneurship and stimulate jobs/growth) and a certain *modus operandi* (innovative and creative in finding ways forward using both institutions and networks). When it comes to the EP, it has already been mentioned that it does not have the same agenda-setting role as the Commission or European Council with regard to the Europe 2020 strategy and therefore clear-cut examples with both intention and modus operandi are not easily identified. Yet, there are ingredients of political entrepreneurship which will be discussed below.

First of all, there are several cases in the debate where MEPs argue in terms of 'possibilities' and 'opportunities' in ways that can be related to a successful political entrepreneur according to Kingdon's view of using windows of opportunity (2011: 165). One illustrating example is EPP's Maurio Mauro who applied a football analogy to make his point. He described the role of Van Rompuy as a 'midfielder who has the job of bringing order to the game' where it is harder to score goals, and that it is up to the EP to 'risk more than the other players, to be a striker who continually reinvents the game, taking inspiration from new rules so as to strengthen the team's attacking ability and to put our hypothetical centre forward – the Barroso Commission – in a position to score' (European Parliament, 2010a). Without drawing too much relevance from football tactics, it is interesting that the EP is here seen as a potential ally with the presidents of the Commission and European Council in a situation when they have an opportunity to create a new momentum in EU integration. This is in a time of economic crisis and difficult quarrels and power struggles between member states. The same kind of 'using the window of opportunity' rhetoric is used by ALDE's Pavel Telička, who argued that the preparations of a new long-term vision raised an important opportunity and 'this time we cannot afford to miss the opportunity' (European Parliament, 2015a). He continued arguing that the European Council had gained too much ownership of the strategy, implying that the EP and the Commission should cooperate to even out the scores.

Secondly, many concrete ideas were raised in the debate. Most are rather uncontroversial, but some are 'innovative' to a certain extent. One example is EPP's Lambert van Nistelrooij, who argues that the strategy must change from a top-down to a bottom-up approach that would 'connect industrial regions, cities and knowledge institutes with citizens and provide a platform for specific projects' (European Parliament, 2015a). He also mentions that two other Commissioners have already committed themselves to this idea. Van Nistelrooij has moreover a leading role in the platform 'knowledge4Innovation', which arranges regular seminars in the EP. He has in this context written articles where he presents ideas for more growth and synergies (see for example Van Nistelrooij, 2017). As such, he is a typical example of a political entrepreneur: he raises innovative ideas on how to create more growth and he is active in networks that in turn have contacts with high-profile figures such as Commissioners. Another example comes from the social democratic S&D group, which argues that the 'green sector' has a strong potential for new jobs. MEP Marita Ulvskog argues, 'The first society to get away from our dependence on fossil fuels, for example, will take the lead in the creation of new green jobs' (European Parliament, 2010a). Several S&D MEPs follow this argumentation and some also add the concept of the 'circular economy' which is also seen as a new potential for jobs.

When it comes to political entrepreneurship in the EP as an institution, the most clear-cut example is partly connected to the S&D ideas of 'new green jobs'. This concerns a viewpoint on growth and entrepreneurship, which seems to differ somewhat from that of the Commission and the Council. In the analysed debates as well as in various reports and resolutions, the EP advocates a stronger focus on labour law and social aspects. In relation to economic growth, 'sustainability' seems to be the key concept for the EP. The main argument is that although deregulation of the labour market combined with strict budget austerity may lead to increased economic growth in the short-term perspective, the long-term consequences are socially and environmentally unsustainable societies through a downward spiral with wage-dumping, undeclared work, deteriorating working conditions and so on. Instead, social equality, gender equality, and social security on the labour market provide a basic security for people, which in turn makes them feel safer. This means more productive employees and people daring to take risks, which can lead to starting an enterprise. Moreover, the argument is that gender equality will lead to higher employment and the new green sector will also provide new jobs. In short, a stronger focus on social equality and the environment will in the long term lead to more growth. This alternative view adds another dimension to economic growth, which is to some degree innovative in seeing new potential in previously ignored areas (such as the green sector) or neglected groups (such as employees, women and immigrants).

The debates include frequent ingredients of these arguments, mainly from the S&D group. For example, Stephen Hughes argued that concern for the people, especially the most vulnerable, must be 'at the heart of the European project' and that public spending in key areas would create millions of new jobs and that 'this will demand a political leap in thinking with regard to Europe's – and in particular, the Eurozone's – economic governance' (European Parliament, 2010a). In the same line of innovative thinking, S&D advocated ecological leadership as a tool for new jobs and growth. What is perhaps most interesting here is that the EPP never explicitly argued against these critical statements. This indicates a certain consensus that the social dimension should be strengthened. This brings us to the question whether the EP as an institution has behaved as a political entrepreneur in this context.

The EP has to a large extent used resolutions as a means to influence the Commission and the European Council when it comes to the Europe 2020 strategy. Resolutions are non-binding recommendations, suggesting a political desire to act in a certain area and to suggest guidelines. As the EP has limited formal power regarding Europe 2020, it is a reasonable strategy. However, what is interesting is that the EP as an arena for political battle has produced a range of resolutions regarding the strategy, which all more or less point in the same direction: they criticise the Commission and European Council for neglecting social equality perspectives, the need for more labour market regulations, gender equality and the environment. In 2010, the three main groups in the EP (EPP, S&D and ALDE) put forward a joint resolution, which called for more focus on social issues in the strategy (see European Parliament, 2010b). This is clearly a sign of pragmatism and strategic behaviour; it sends a clear signal to the Commission and the European Council that the EP is (more or less) unified in its critique. Several EP resolutions reveal the same critical remarks as mentioned above (European Parliament, 2010c; 2014b; 2015b; 2016). Another example of how the EP may operate beyond routinized procedures in order to gain influence took place in April 2010 when the EP's 'Conference of Presidents' appealed to the European Council to postpone the adoption of the EU 2020 strategy to allow the EP time to examine the proposals (*Agence Europe*, 2010a). The Conference of Presidents consists of the EP president and the chairman for each political group. This is, again, a pragmatic/innovative initiative including all political groups, which gives the appeal a certain legitimacy. In the same context, the Employment and Social Affairs Committee adopted a resolution that argued that high employment and job quality must be key aims of the strategy. As the EP has the legal right to be consulted on employment issues, it could threaten to delay the adoption strategy if it was not satisfied with its content (*Agence Europe*, 2010b).

CONCLUDING REMARKS

The two debates illustrate that the EP is both a forum for strong ideological debate and a forum for a more toned down, pragmatic, issue-specific discussion. The ideological debate has elements of the Left–Right dimension, the EU-integration dimension and to some degree environmentalist dimension. But overall it has been dominated by the Left–Right dimension and it becomes increasingly clear that we have a situation in the EP where the EPP is a part of a European political party which steers the EU through its leadership in the Commission, in the European Council and in the Council. It has executive power in the EU institutions and this has a certain limiting effect on its MEPs. Despite being the largest political group, it is another group that is more visible with its constant critique of the current policy: the S&D. Consequently, the EP is increasingly reminiscent of a national parliament where there is a government and an opposition. In this sense, it has fulfilled its traditional role as an arena for democratic debate among elected officials but at the same time it has been pragmatic in several cases with constructive proposals from MEPs and cross-party cooperation with resolutions and reports on the strategy. However, this bright picture does not really mirror the atmosphere of the two debates. In the midst of the ideological conflict, there was a general frustration among several MEPs across party lines on how the Europe 2020 strategy had been prepared. The EP had more or less been excluded from the agenda-setting and policy-formulation phases and (many felt) was only used to claim the democratic legitimacy needed. This frustration was felt even more in the 2015 debate as many MEPs bluntly stated that the strategy had failed. The debate in itself was perhaps an indication of some stagnation. No high-profile representatives from the Commission or European Council were present. No political group leaders took part in the debate. Both the Commission and the European Council had new presidents appointed, perhaps with new priorities, the 'Juncker plan' for example or the refugee crisis. It is easy to think that the Europe 2020 strategy had already faded into the background in 2015, or as one MEP from S&D stated in relation to poverty reduction: the strategy had actually become a 'neglected child'.

When it comes to political entrepreneurship, there are definitely ingredients in the EP with regard to the Europe 2020 strategy. A number of innovative and constructive proposals from individual MEPs were delivered, some very concrete and others rather visionary, even with football tactics involved. The EP has also demonstrated that it is ready to lay ideological conflicts aside and cooperate in order to attain influence on the strategy through resolutions, reports and sometimes by putting real pressure on the European Council. However, how much these really produced in terms of real changes in the strategy is difficult to judge. After all, the EP has weak formal competences in these areas and it has mostly focused on the so-called flexible, policy-influencing instruments to influence. Moreover, as Pircher (2018: 115) argues, it is not self-evident to what degree the EP's actions can be defined as political entrepreneurship or merely the daily working life of the EP. The EU system is in fact in itself very much a system of negotiations with a number of networks, which in a way integrate an expectation of individual and institutional entrepreneurship.

REFERENCES

Agence Europe (2010a), (EU) EP/COMPETITIVENESS: Adoption of the EU 2020 strategy delayed until autumn?, Brussels, 23/04/2010, AE 10125, 23.04.2010.
Agence Europe (2010b), (EU) EP/EMPLOYMENT: High employment and job quality must be key aims of EU 2020 strategy, Brussels 30/04/2010, AE 10130, 01.05.2010.
Bache, I., S. George and S. Bulmer (2011), *Politics in the European Union*, 3rd edn. Oxford: Oxford University Press.
Bauer, M.W. and S. Becker (2014), 'The unexpected winner of the crisis: the European Commission's strengthened role in economic governance'. *Journal of European Integration*, **36** (3), 213–29.
Büchs, M. (2008), 'How legitimate is the Open Method of Co-ordination?' *Journal of Common Market Studies*, **46** (4), 765–86.
Burns, C. (2013), 'The European Parliament', in Michelle Cini and Nieves Pérez-Solórzano Borragán (eds), *European Union Politics*, 4th edn. Oxford: Oxford University Press.
Copeland, P. and S. James (2014), 'Policy windows, ambiguity and Commission entrepreneurship: explaining the relaunch of the European Union's economic reform agenda'. *Journal of European Public Policy*, **21** (1), 1–19.
Dalton, R. and M. Wattenberg (2000), 'Unthinkable democracy: political change in advanced industrial democracies', in Russell Dalton and Martin Wattenberg (eds), *Parties Without Partisans: Political Chance in Advanced Industrial Democracies*. Oxford: Oxford University Press, pp. 3–16.
European Parliament (2003), Resolution on the application of the open method of coordination. Accessed 1 September 2018 at https://eur-lex.europa.eu/legal-content/EN/TXT/PDF/?uri=CELEX:52003IP0268&rid=1.
European Parliament (2010a), Minutes from the debate 24 February 2010. Accessed 5 May 2018 at http://www.europarl.europa.eu/sides/getDoc.do?type=CRE&reference=20100224&secondRef=ITEM-013&language=EN.
European Parliament (2010b), Resolution of 10 March 2010 on EU 2020. Accessed

12 October 2018 at http://www.europarl.europa.eu/sides/getDoc.do?pubRef=-//
EP//TEXT+TA+P7-TA-2010-0053+0+DOC+XML+V0//EN.

European Parliament (2010c), Resolution of 16 June 2010 on economic governance. Accessed 1 September 2018 at https://eur-lex.europa.eu/legal-content/EN/
TXT/HTML/?uri=CELEX:52010IP0224&rid=14.

European Parliament (2014a), 'The open method of coordination'. European parliamentary research service. Accessed 1 September 2018 at http://www.europarl.
europa.eu/EPRS/EPRS-AaG-542142-Open-Method-of-Coordination-FINAL.
pdf.

European Parliament (2014b), Resolution of 25 November 2014 on employment
and social aspects of the Europe 2020 strategy. Accessed 12 October 2018 at
http://www.europarl.europa.eu/sides/getDoc.do?type=TA&reference=P8-TA-
2014-0060&language=EN.

European Parliament (2015a), Minutes from the debate 28 October 2015. Accessed
5 September 2018 at http://www.europarl.europa.eu/sides/getDoc.do?type=CR
E&reference=20151028&secondRef=ITEM-017&language=EN.

European Parliament (2015b). Resolution of 28 October on cohesion policy and
the review of the Europe 2020 strategy. Accessed 12 October 2018 at http://
www.europarl.europa.eu/sides/getDoc.do?type=TA&language=EN&reference=
P8-TA-2015-0384.

European Parliament (2016), Resolution of 26 October on the European Semester for
economic policy coordination: implementation of the 2016 priorities. Accessed 12
October 2018 at http://www.europarl.europa.eu/sides/getDoc.do?type=TA&ref
erence=P8-TA-2016-0416&language=EN.

European Parliament (2018), MEPs by Member State and political group. Accessed
3 September 2018 at http://www.europarl.europa.eu/meps/en/crosstable.html.

Fasone, C. (2013), 'European economic governance and parliamentary representation. What place for the European Parliament?' *European Law Journal*, **20** (2),
164–85.

Hix, S. and B. Høyland (2011), *The Political System of the European Union*.
Basingstoke: Palgrave Macmillan.

Hix, S. and C. Lord (1997), *Political Parties in the European Union*. London:
Macmillan.

Kingdon, J.W. (2011), *Agendas, Alternatives and Public Policies*, 2nd edn. Boston,
MA: Pearson.

Kreppel, A. and S. Hix (2003), 'From "Grand Coalition" to Left–Right confronta-
tion: explaining the shifting structure of party competition in the European
Parliament'. *Comparative Political Studies*, **36** (1–2), 75–96.

Laffan, B. (1997), 'From policy entrepreneur to policy manager: the challenge
facing the European Commission'. *Journal of European Public Policy*, **4** (3),
422–38.

Martens, W. (2010), 'Europe 2020 and beyond'. *European Studies*, **9** (1).

Öhlén, M. (2013), *The Eastward Enlargement of European Parties: Party Adaptation
in the Light of EU-enlargement*. Örebro: Örebro Studies in Political Science 31.

Pircher, B. (2018), 'Debating the economic crisis in the European Parliament:
enriching the discourse', in C. Karlsson, C. Silander and D. Silander (eds),
*Governance and Political Entrepreneurship in Europe: Promoting Growth and
Welfare in Times of Crisis*. Cheltenham, UK and Northampton, MA, USA:
Edward Elgar Publishing, pp. 100–119.

Rittberger, B. (2014), 'Integration without representation? The European

Parliament and the reform of the economic governance in the EU'. *Journal of Common Market Studies*, **52** (6), 1174–83.

Scott, J. and D. Trubek (2002), 'Mind the gap: law and new approaches to governance in the European Union'. *European Law Journal*, **8** (1), 1–8.

Silander, D. (2016), 'The political entrepreneur', in C. Karlsson, C. Silander and D. Silander (eds), *Political Entrepreneurship: Regional Growth and Entrepreneurial Diversity in Sweden*. Cheltenham, UK and Northampton, MA, USA: Edward Elgar Publishing, pp. 7–20.

Szyszczak, E. (2006), 'Experimental governance: the Open Method of Coordination'. *European Law Journal*, **12** (4), 485–502.

The Telegraph (2009), 'Conservative MEPs form new "anti-federalist" group in the European Parliament', 22 June 2009. Accessed 3 September 2018 at https://www.telegraph.co.uk/news/politics/conservative/5602509/Conservative-MEPs-form-new-anti-federalist-group-in-the-European-Parliament.html.

Van Nistelrooij, L. (2017), 'Cohesion funds can stop Europe from moving at different speeds', EURACTIV 23 November 2017. Accessed 13 October 2018 at https://www.euractiv.com/section/economy-jobs/opinion/cohesion-funds-can-stop-eur ope-from-moving-at-different-speeds/.

Wallace, H. and C. Reh (2015), 'An institutional anatomy and five policy modes', in Helen Wallace, Mark A. Pollack and Alasdair R. Young (eds), *Policy-making in the European Union*, 7th edn. Oxford: Oxford University Press, pp. 72–112.

Warleigh, A. (2003), *Democracy in the European Union. Theory, Practice and Reform*. London: Sage Publications.

5. Local and regional involvement in Europe 2020: a success story?

Brigitte Pircher

The success of policy strategies within a multilevel governance system such as the EU is dependent on the interplay between the various levels of governance, *inter alia*. In order to ensure the realisation of such a strategy, various actors at EU, national and regional level need to cooperate and jointly pursue the strategy's targets. Therefore, the EU has often focused on the idea of partnership. Partnership has been a prominent EU policy instrument since 1989. It originated from the area of regional policy where decisions on the spending of funds have to be made collaboratively by state and non-state actors from supranational, national and regional level (Bache, 2010). This notion has been taken up and modified within Europe 2020 in order to ensure the implementation and realisation of the strategy: 'This partnership approach should extend to EU committees, to national parliaments and national, local and regional authorities, to social partners and to stakeholders and civil society so that everyone is involved in delivering on the vision' (European Commission, 2010: 4).

With a view to achieving this goal, the European Commission established a specific governance system and an enhanced strategy for partnership that is characterised by actions and programmes at all levels, including the EU and national and regional levels (European Commission, 2010). For example, each member state adopts national targets and national programmes in the specific policy areas in order to meet the Europe 2020 strategy headline targets. National reform programmes as well as territorial pacts – a tool to identify the specific partners' commitments at all levels – were also adopted (Committee of the Regions, 2010).

This special governance system was also established to overcome the shortcomings of the former Lisbon strategy that was characterised by a weak governance architecture and led to the failure of the strategy (Copeland, 2012: 229). The Europe 2020 strategy therefore provides a complex multilevel structure that is characterised by specific rules and provisions at all levels. It is a basic principle of the EU that in addition to hard law, with its binding character, soft law also needs to be implemented and applied at member state level. This is vital for successful policy outcomes and the success of the strategy as a whole. Indeed, it is important to the legitimation of the entire system. At the different levels of governance it is possible to identify various potential political entrepreneurs who shape the policy outcomes.

Existing research has focused primarily on the EU institutions, in particular the European Commission, as possible policy or political entrepreneurs in initiating and developing the Europe 2020 strategy. To date, there has been surprisingly little analysis of the role of potential political entrepreneurs at regional and local level who could have a significant influence on the policy outcomes in the last phase of this policy process. While extensive statistical data are gathered by the European Commission and Eurostat in order to assess the national performance of the Europe 2020 strategy (see Chapter 1), little is known about the constraining and enabling effects that influence the implementation of the strategy at regional and local level.

This chapter therefore poses the following questions: What characterises the governance architecture of the Europe 2020 strategy and to what extent are local and regional authorities (LRA) involved in the implementation of the strategy? Does their involvement really matter in terms of policy outcome (that is, better performance)? Do we find room and potential for political entrepreneurs to shape policy outcomes at regional level?

In answering these questions, the chapter provides an overall picture of the concrete cycle of the implementation of the Europe 2020 strategy in a multilevel governance system. It focuses on the role of regions and their involvement in the process and impact on the policy outcome. In the process it identifies the potential for political entrepreneurs at regional and local level. In analysing the practical implementation at the lowest level of policy-making, the chapter also assesses whether the involvement of LRA leads to the strategy as a whole being more successful. EU strategies can only be successful if they are implemented and applied at national and regional level.

The results demonstrate that the degree of LRA involvement varies considerably between member states. Most interestingly, their involvement always contributes to a better national performance. This is a strong indication that LRA have to be included in the realisation of the headline targets in order for these targets to be met.

The next section of the chapter discusses the theoretical framework of multilevel governance and how the concept of partnership is realised in the Europe 2020 strategy. This is followed by an examination of the implementation of the Europe 2020 strategy at national and regional level, including the involvement of LRA within the strategy and their impact on the policy outcome. The chapter concludes by identifying the potential for political entrepreneurs at local and regional level.

MULTILEVEL GOVERNANCE AND THE EUROPE 2020 STRATEGY

Governance in the EU is characterised by various territorial levels beyond the national state, including multiple actors (both public and private) who make policy via informal and formal channels at all levels (Hooghe and Marks, 2001; Marks et al., 1996). In contrast to other international organisations, such as specific actor constellations, the interdependency among actors at all levels, and a different form of governance are unique to the EU and one of the reasons why the organisation is referred to as a political system *sui generis* (Knodt, 1998; Marks, 1993). These complex interactions between public actors and an increasing number of private actors determine the decision-making processes and enhance integration within the EU (Knodt and Große Hültmann, 2010: 192). As the competencies in the various policy areas are vested in the EU as well as the member states, both supranational and intergovernmental forms of cooperation have been developed. Multilevel governance describes the various forms of cooperation at all levels, including the EU, national, regional and local levels and their authorities. This means that it involves participation and coordination at all government levels in the decision-making and implementation processes, marked by two different interaction dimensions: vertical (between the different levels) and horizontal (within the same level) (Hooghe and Marks, 2001).

Multilevel approaches were developed as a result of criticism of the intergovernmentalist assumption that only national governments and their national preferences are decisive and constitute the main actors in the EU policy-making process. The multilevel theory emphasises that there are also direct interactions between EU actors and regional and local ones, interactions that bypass the central governments. This has led to national governments losing their monopolistic position (Hooghe and Marks, 2001), as multi-actors moved to the centre of decision-making (Piattoni, 2010).

There are four main stages of decision-making within this multilevel system: the policy initiation, decision-making, implementation, and adjudication. EU institutions are individual actors in this policy process and not only execution actors (agents) of the member states (principals) (Knodt and Große Hültmann, 2010: 191–2). This is reminiscent of Kingdon's policy process (2011), which distinguishes between three main streams: the problem stream, the policy stream, and the politics stream in relation to policy entrepreneurs. However, the difference is that the multilevel governance approach focuses more on the implementation stage. This is of utmost importance when analysing whether a certain policy is successful or not. Various kinds of policy networks prevail in the implementation phase. For example, as independent actors in this process, local and regional municipalities represent territorial interests at the EU level (Christiansen, 2016: 101), but they also play an important role in the implementation and application of EU legislation. In this context, regional and transnational cooperation became important and non-state actors such as civil society or economic and social partners are integrated into the decision-making process. In this phase, the European Commission has direct contact with LRA, which relativize the importance of the central state (Knodt and Große Hültmann, 2010: 194). The implementation of EU policies therefore requires effective cooperation and contact between the various levels (Marks, 1993). As a result, a new governance design was created that is characterised by interconnected competencies, flexible institutional designs, different levels of actions, and new forms of cooperation that led to a form of 'regional authority' (Hooghe et al., 2010).

In this regard, the Treaty of Lisbon was an important step in strengthening the role and influence of LRA by enhancing the role of national and regional parliaments and the Committee of the Regions. The Commission's 2001 White Paper, the 2009 White Paper of the Committee of the Regions and the 2014 Charter for Multilevel Governance of the Committee of the Regions gave more prominence to the partnership principle that was enshrined in the EU regional policy by granting LRA the right to participate in the policy process as legitimate actors (Committee of the Regions, 2009; 2014b; European Commission, 2001). This also provides the opportunity for political entrepreneurs at local and regional level to shape policies in a certain manner.

The involvement of the regional level was already recognised as important during the discussions on the Europe 2020 strategy within the EU institutions in March 2010. When formulating the Council conclusions, Commissioner Johannes Hahn stressed the importance of the Europe 2020 strategy for the implementation of regional policies (*Agence Europe*, 2010a). Prior to the European Council summit in June 2010, and after broad consultation conducted by the Committee of the Regions, a large number of regions and cities criticised the fact that the Europe 2020 strategy and its plans were not sufficient to deliver growth. Moreover, they raised the criticism that the regions would suffer from coordination problems in attempting to implement the strategy efficiently (*Agence Europe*, 2010b).

Consequently, the partnership principle was also incorporated into the Europe 2020 strategy. This approach was extended to the EU committees, to national parliaments and LRA, to social partners, and to stakeholders and civil society. It was achieved through the establishment of a permanent dialogue between the various levels of government. The former Lisbon strategy with its 'one-size-fits-all' policy lacked a specific focus on the disparities between the member states. Therefore, the Commission proposed to translate the EU policy objectives into national targets and trajectories, including a large number of actions at all levels. The seven flagship initiatives involve both the EU and the member-states levels. Two pillars were developed: first, integrated guidelines at the EU level to set up the priorities and second, a thematic approach that includes country reporting by member states in order to implement the strategy. As an instrument of effective implementation, the Commission may issue policy warnings in case of inadequate responses (European Commission, 2010: 3–4). National aims and actions were formulated for every flagship initiative in the Europe 2020 strategy. Furthermore, all member states need to report their implementation status in National Reform Programmes (NRP) on a yearly basis. Territorial pacts may be voluntarily adopted by member states to identify the partner's commitments at national and regional level. Moreover, policy recommendations were addressed to member states to ensure proper implementation (Committee of the Regions, 2010: 4; European Commission, 2010). The LRA involvement in this process is dependent on the member states and varies significantly between the EU countries.

Against this background, the following section analyses the extent to which LRA are involved in the implementation of the Europe 2020 strategy and whether their involvement contributes to improved policy outcomes and thereby to the success of the strategy as a whole. A further question relates to how much room or potential that political entrepreneurs have at regional and local level to engage in policy-making and in shaping the implementation of the strategy.

METHODS

In analysing the governance architecture of the Europe 2020 strategy and the LRA involvement in the strategy, the chapter relies primarily on official EU documents. This includes a wide variety of different sources: the Europe 2020 strategy, Commission documents, monitoring reports of the Committee of the Regions, documents, reports, and surveys of the Europe 2020 Monitoring Platform, and newspaper articles from *Agence Europe*, a daily newspaper on EU governance.

After assessing the LRA involvement in the strategy, based on the reports of the Committee of the Regions, the chapter examines whether this involvement is correlated with the performance of the EU member states in various policy areas. With a view to establishing this, correlation analyses are conducted between the LRA involvement in all 28 countries and the performance of member states in certain policy fields within the main categories of the Europe 2020 strategy. One policy field is covered in respect of each category of growth, namely smart growth, sustainable growth and inclusive growth. The correlation is done between the involvement and the areas of employment (inclusive growth), research and development (smart growth), and environmental issues (sustainable growth). Data relating to the performance of member states are taken from Eurostat (2018).

Based on correlation models, the chapter assesses whether the LRA involvement contributes to improved performance by member states in the areas concerned and to an improved implementation of the strategy's headline targets. By analysing the practical implementation of the headline targets at regional level, the chapter also addresses the question of whether the LRA involvement led to a more successful implementation of the strategy as a whole.

Based on this involvement in the policy process and on the correlation between LRA involvement and the performance of member states, the chapter further identifies opportunities for political entrepreneurs at local and regional level.

LOCAL AND REGIONAL AUTHORITIES' INVOLVEMENT IN THE EUROPE 2020 STRATEGY

In preparation for the National Reform Programmes (NRPs), local and regional authorities (LRA) were involved in only nine member states until November 2010. Their involvement ranged from an active observation function (Austria), being involved in public consultations (Cyprus, Romania, Slovakia, Lithuania, Sweden), and participating in specific events (Cyprus, Romania and Sweden) to participating in working groups and meetings in the case of France and Italy, and providing comments or documents in the case of Slovakia and Italy. Until the final submission of the NRPs in April 2011, LRA were systematically involved in federal states such as Austria, Germany and Belgium, but also in other member states such as Italy, Spain, Greece and France. However, the involvement of LRA went beyond consultation in only a few cases, namely Austria, Belgium, Germany, Italy and Spain, where legal and political provisions were also set up. For example, Poland and Portugal regarded this first phase of the NRP as a purely national issue (Committee of the Regions, 2010: 5–18).

The Committee of the Regions monitoring reports on Europe 2020 demonstrate that LRA are involved in this policy process in the various member states in very different ways. Although the LRA indicated in the Europe 2020 Monitoring Platform surveys that they regarded their involvement in the strategy and flagship initiatives as an opportunity to shape policies, the reports indicate a 'partnership gap' in the EU, where Europe 2020 governance fails to include the regional level as extensively as it should (Committee of the Regions, 2011: 8–10). As at the end of 2011, 18 member states had included their LRA in the national programmes in some way or other – ranging from consultation, the submission of written texts, or occasional participation in meetings. However, in only five cases (Austria, Czech Republic, Germany, Italy and Latvia) were representatives of LRA part of certain permanent working groups (Committee of the Regions, 2011: 19–20).

This trend of significant differences in levels of LRA involvement in the various EU countries remained stable over the years. Nevertheless, it remained a policy objective to achieve greater involvement of LRA and to meet their needs more effectively. On the basis of surveys called 'What's happening on the ground', the Europe 2020 Monitoring Platform and the Committee of the Regions gathered data on the constraining and enabling effects for the involvement of LRA. The surveys and reports reveal that LRA are becoming increasingly familiar with the strategy. The national targets are also regarded, to some extent, as appropriate for their territories, and cooperation and coordination in this multilevel governance system is consistently improving, particularly in the field of cohesion policy. However, the reports also stress severe constraints. LRA face financial constraints due to the economic crisis and the austerity measures that have been put in place. Public expenditure is focused primarily on short-term interventions. This policy approach often obstructs long-term planning. Another shortcoming has always been the cooperation and coordination between all levels of governance and the strategy's failure to address territorial differentiations. The reports state that national programmes are still decided primarily by national governments, despite the increasing involvement of LRA. They also indicate that LRA are involved primarily in the implementation and not in the design or governance of the strategy (Committee of the Regions, 2012; 2013; 2014a; 2015; 2016).

Today, significant differences remain in the level of LRA involvement in the various member states. It is only if LRA are involved at national level that local and regional political entrepreneurs will enjoy the room and

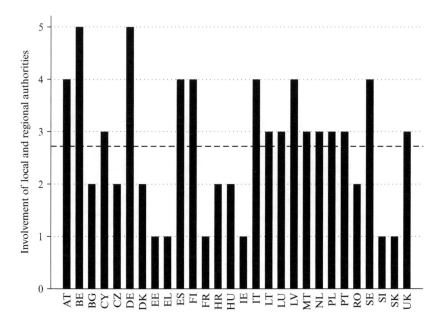

Source: Author's compilation based on Committee of the Regions (2017: 10); involvement
scores are classified into five categories.

Figure 5.1   LRA involvement by member states and mean value

opportunity to shape policies. Again, this relates to the mere possibility of
local and regional actors engaging in policy-making and having an actual
impact on the policy process. The greater this possibility is, the higher the
potential is for actors to influence policy outcomes. The most recent scores
relating to LRA involvement (2017) illustrate that this involvement – and
thus the potential for political entrepreneurs – differs significantly among
the various member states.

Figure 5.1 presents the level of LRA involvement in the 28 EU member
states. It is clear that there is a higher level of LRA involvement in
certain Northern and Central European states with a tradition of regional
self-government. This applies especially to states with federal structures
(Austria, Belgium and Germany) and to the Netherlands and Sweden,
where LRA have extensive powers. By contrast, there is a lower level of
LRA involvement in Mediterranean and Central and Eastern European
states, with the exception of Italy, Spain and Latvia. However, in the case
of Spain, previous reports point to a lower level of involvement, suggesting
that this is a new development or an exception. Interestingly, member
states that introduced administrative reforms have a higher level of LRA

involvement. This applies to Belgium, the Czech Republic, Finland, Germany, Spain and Latvia. In the case of Belgium, the Czech Republic, Finland and Spain the LRA involvement scored lower in the previous reports, which hints at the efficiency of the administrative reforms (Committee of the Regions, 2017: 9).

Does LRA Involvement Matter for the Policy Outcome?

We are now aware of the degree of LRA involvement in the various EU member states when preparing, implementing and evaluating the national reform programmes. However, the question is whether their involvement contributes to improved performance, that is, a better policy outcome. Does a higher level of LRA involvement mean that countries perform better? Furthermore, does greater LRA involvement mean a greater potential for political entrepreneurs to push certain policies through?

The monitoring reports indicate the most crucial policy areas where LRA are contributing in the achievement of the Europe 2020 targets. The most frequently mentioned areas are employment, research and development, education, environmental issues, and social inclusion. Of these, employment and research and development are the most crucial areas for entrepreneurship. The area of employment and its headline target – which is to increase the employment rates in the member states – is a major part of the strategy contributing to inclusive growth. The goals also include better conditions for entrepreneurs and vigorous promotion of entrepreneurship (European Commission, 2010: 30). Moreover, the research and development targets include the promotion of an entrepreneurial culture, funding for innovation and for small and medium-sized enterprises (SMEs), and the fostering of an entrepreneurial spirit, particularly among young people in Europe (Committee of the Regions, 2010: 11–22).

With a view to assessing the impact of LRA involvement in the above areas, I constructed correlation models between the LRA involvement scores and the performance of all EU member states in these areas. Figure 5.2 demonstrates that there is only a weak and insignificant correlation (0.18) between LRA involvement and the employment rate. This means that the involvement of LRA has only a slight positive correlation with performance in the area of employment. This outcome is not entirely surprising, as employment is a policy area that is conducted primarily at a national level, where national governments set the labour market policies and targets, and are also responsible for the implementation and enforcement of the policy.

In contrast to employment, Figure 5.3 illustrates a significant correlation (0.37) between LRA involvement and member state performance in

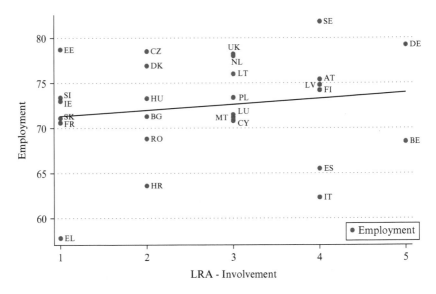

*Figure 5.2   Correlation analysis between LRA involvement and
employment rate*

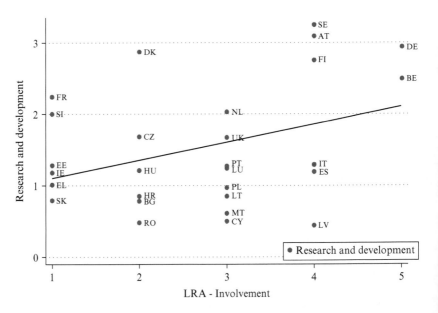

*Figure 5.3   Correlation analysis between LRA involvement and research
and development*

the field of research and development. Research and development belongs to the headline targets in the area of smart growth. Figure 5.3 demonstrates that the higher the level of LRA involvement in the Europe 2020 strategy, the better the country's performance in this area. This implies that the level of LRA policy initiatives and the possibilities for political entrepreneurs to engage in the decision-making process are higher in the area of research and development than in the area of employment. It illustrates further that the potential of political entrepreneurs to act and shape policies and their impacts at local or regional level is dependent on the policy area.

With regard to this outcome, it is interesting to analyse whether LRA involvement has an even stronger impact on the performance of member states in areas where LRA possess more extensive competencies. As environmental issues were mentioned in the monitoring reports as a crucial policy area in which LRA are involved, LRA involvement has been correlated with the recycling rate of municipal waste. The recycling of municipal waste in general is an area where the LRA have more extensive competencies. They are closely involved in initiating policy strategies in this area. This also contributes to the fulfilment of the Europe 2020 strategy in the area of sustainable growth and therefore makes it possible to include all three main areas of growth in the analysis: inclusive growth, smart growth and sustainable growth.

Figure 5.4 demonstrates a strong and significant correlation (0.44)

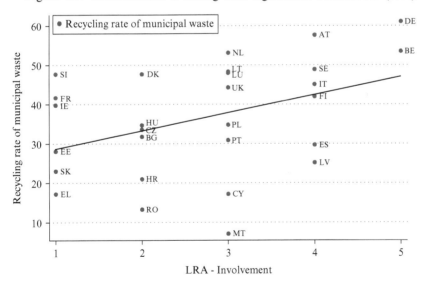

Figure 5.4   Correlation analysis between LRA involvement and recycling rate of municipal waste

between LRA involvement and the recycling rate of municipal waste. This means that greater LRA involvement leads to significantly improved performance of member states in the area of waste management. It further points to the fact that LRA involvement leads especially to a successful policy outcome and the achievement of goals in areas where they possess more extensive competencies.

POLITICAL ENTREPRENEURS AND MULTILEVEL GOVERNANCE

The Europe 2020 strategy is characterised by a comprehensive multilevel governance structure. All levels of governance – including various actors at EU, national and regional levels – contribute to the realisation of the strategy. The various actors are able to have an impact on the policy and to shape the policy outcome. However, they perform very different tasks in achieving the Europe 2020 strategy's headline targets. While institutions at the EU level formulate the goals for the Europe 2020 strategy, the national governments and associated ministries transform the goals into national conditions. The local and regional levels, involving various state and non-state actors, are responsible for implementing the targets at the lowest level, that is, they are responsible for 'making the Europe 2020 strategy real'. The potential for political entrepreneurs to engage in the decision-making process and influence the policy outcomes depends, *inter alia*, on the level of governance. As we have seen in previous chapters, EU institutions or parts thereof may serve as political entrepreneurs when it comes to policy-making. However, these political entrepreneurs are powerful institutions whose potential to have an impact is on a more abstract level, namely in initiating and formulating the strategy and its goals. At the national level, we find national governments and the involved ministries that need to transform the EU goals into national ones. This allows national governments to develop certain country-specific goals, and political entrepreneurs may participate in the process by shaping these goals under national conditions. However, in many areas the practical implementation of EU and national goals is conducted by local and regional authorities. This gives LRA and political entrepreneurs a wide scope and much leeway to actually put a certain policy or goal into practice. As Lipsky (1969; 1980) has argued, at the end of the policy cycle there is the policy implementation, which is in the responsibility of people ('street-level bureaucrats') who put the policies into practice. Actors at this level have the power to shape policies. On the basis of his concept of street-level bureaucracy Lipsky argues that actors at this lowest level of policy-making have a degree of discretion. This means that they have a certain leeway with regard to how to implement, enforce and apply policies or rules, as they have the power to put the policies into practice (Lipsky, 2010: 13–26). Therefore, street-level bureaucrats also have a greater potential to act as powerful political entrepreneurs and influence the policy outcome. In summary, therefore, the lower the level of policy-making, the more potential political entrepreneurs possess to realise certain policies or targets within Europe 2020.

CONCLUDING REMARKS

This chapter asks whether the involvement of LRA contributes to a more successful Europe 2020. As we have seen, the LRA involvement varies significantly between member states. Member states with a long tradition of regional self-government (Austria, Belgium, Germany, the Netherlands and Sweden) involve their LRA to a larger extent than other member states. On the basis of correlation models, the study demonstrates further that there is a positive, but weak, correlation between LRA involvement and member state performance in the area of employment. However, LRA involvement correlates positively and significantly with member state performance in the area of research and development and the area of waste management (strongest correlation). This means that the involvement of LRA in implementing Europe 2020 contributes to improved performance by the country and thus to greater success of the strategy as a whole. This is a clear indication of the need to involve LRA in the Europe 2020 strategy as efficiently as possible with a view to ensuring its success. Even though all areas of growth (smart, inclusive, sustainable) have been included in the study, this analysis is limited to three policy areas. Therefore, assessing LRA involvement in relation to the member states' performance in all policy areas and headline targets will be an interesting topic for further research.

An interesting outcome of this study is that member states with a higher level of LRA involvement also allow for a greater potential for political entrepreneurs. In a multilevel governance system, the potential for political entrepreneurs is encountered at all levels. While the EU level is more abstract and political entrepreneurs have the option to influence and shape the initiation and formulation of the strategy and its goals, the national level transforms the EU goals into national goals, and it is up to the local and regional levels to put the strategy into practice. As in the case of street-level bureaucrats, this gives actors a degree of discretion and the power to make the policy 'real'. Hence, political entrepreneurs are granted much leeway to impact the policy outcome. The potential of political entrepreneurs to shape policies might therefore be strongest at the lowest level of policy-making.

REFERENCES

Agence Europe (2010a). (EU) EU/COMMITTEE OF THE REGIONS: Work of extraordinary meeting of Committee of the Regions' Bureau focuses on a green, competitive and connected economy, Brussels, 15/03/2010, AE 10098, 16.3.2010.

Agence Europe (2010b). (EU) EU/REGIONS: Regions and cities warn that EU 2020 strategy does not have means to deliver promises, Brussels, 01/06/2010, AE 10150, 2.6.2010.

Bache, I. (2010). Partnership as an EU Policy Instrument: a political history. *West European Politics*, **33**(1), 58–74.

Christiansen, T. (2016). Governance in the European Union. In M. Cini and N. Perez-Solorzano Borragan (eds), *European Union Politics*, 5th edn. Oxford: Oxford University Press, pp. 97–109.

Committee of the Regions (2009). The White Paper on multi-level governance, accessed 20 September 2018 at http://cor.europa.eu/de/activities/governance/Pages/white-pape-on-multilevel-governance.aspx.

Committee of the Regions (2010). *First CoR Monitoring Report on Europe 2020, Europe 2020 Monitoring Platform, The EU's Assembly of Regional and Local Representatives, 126th Meeting of the Committee of the Regions Bureau,* December 2010.

Committee of the Regions (2011). *Second CoR Monitoring Report on Europe 2020, Europe 2020 Monitoring Platform, The EU's Assembly of Regional and Local Representatives,* December 2011.

Committee of the Regions (2012). *Third CoR Monitoring Report on Europe 2020, Europe 2020 Monitoring Platform, The EU's Assembly of Regional and Local Representatives,* October 2012.

Committee of the Regions (2013). *Fourth CoR Monitoring Report on Europe 2020, Europe 2020 Monitoring Platform, The EU's Assembly of Regional and Local Representatives,* October 2013.

Committee of the Regions (2014a). *Fifth CoR Monitoring Report on Europe 2020, Europe 2020 Monitoring Platform, The EU's Assembly of Regional and Local Representatives,* October 2014.

Committee of the Regions (2014b). Resolution of the Committee of the Regions on the Charter for Multilevel Governance in Europe, 106th plenary session, 2–3 April 2014, RESOL-V-12.

Committee of the Regions (2015). *Sixth CoR Monitoring Report on Europe 2020 and the European Semester, Europe 2020 Monitoring Platform,* October 2015.

Committee of the Regions (2016). *Seventh CoR Monitoring Report on Europe 2020 and the European Semester, Europe 2020 Monitoring Platform,* October 2016.

Committee of the Regions (2017). *Eighth CoR Monitoring Report on Europe 2020 and the European Semester, Commission for Economic Policy,* October 2017.

Copeland, P. (2012). Conclusion: the Lisbon Strategy – evaluating success and understanding failure. In P. Copeland and D. Papadimitriou (eds), *Evaluating the EU's Lisbon Strategy*. Basingstoke: Palgrave Macmillan, pp. 229–38.

European Commission (2001). Communication from the Commission of 25 July

2001 'European governance – A white paper' [COM(2001) 428 final – Official Journal C 287 of 12.10.2001].

European Commission (2010). EUROPE 2020. A strategy for smart, sustainable and inclusive growth, Brussels, 3.3.2010, COM(2010) 2020 final.

Eurostat (2018). Europe 2020, Indicators, Data Main tables, accessed 13 September 2018 at https://ec.europa.eu/eurostat/web/europe-2020-indicators/eu rope-2020-strategy/main-tables.

Hooghe, L. and G. Marks (2001). *Multi-Level Governance and European Integration*. Lanham: Rowman & Littlefield.

Hooghe, L., G. Marks and A.H. Schakel (2010). *The Rise of Regional Authority: A Comparative Study of 43 Democracies*. London: Routledge.

Kingdon, J.W. (2011). *Agendas, Alternatives, and Public Policies* (updated 2nd edn). Harlow: Pearson.

Knodt, M. (1998). *Tiefenwirkung Europäischer Politik: Eigensinn oder Anpassung Regionalen Regierens?* Baden-Baden: Nomos.

Knodt, M. and M. Große Hültmann (2010). Der multi-level Governance-Ansatz. In H-J. Bieling and M. Lerch (eds), *Theorien der Europäischen Integration* (3rd edn). Wiesbaden: Springer Fachmedien Verlag, pp. 187–205.

Lipsky, M. (1969). Toward a theory of street-level bureaucracy. *IRP Discussion Papers No. 48-69*, accessed 12 October 2018 at http://www.irp.wisc.edu/publica tions/dps/pdfs/dp4869.pdf.

Lipsky, M. (1980). *Street-level Bureaucracy: Dilemmas of the Individual in Public Services*. New York: Russell Sage Foundation.

Lipsky, M. (2010). *Street-Level Bureaucrats as Policy Makers: Dilemmas of the Individual in Public Service* (30th anniversary expanded edn). Russell Sage Foundation, accessed 15 October 2018 at JSTOR, http://www.jstor.org/sta ble/10.7758/9781610446631.

Marks, G. (1993). Structural policy and multilevel governance in the EC. In A.W. Cafruny and G.G. Rosenthal (eds), *The State of the European Community, The Maastricht Debates and Beyond*. Vol. 2. Boulder: Lynne Rienner, pp. 391–410.

Marks, G., L. Hooghe and K. Blank (1996). European integration since the 1980s: statecentric vs. multi-level governance. *Journal of Common Market Studies*, **34**(3), 341–78.

Piattoni, S. (2010). *The Theory of Multi-level Governance: Conceptual, Empirical, and Normative Challenges*. Oxford: Oxford University Press.

APPENDIX

Table 5A.1   Correlation table

	A	B	C	D
A. LRA involvement	1.00			
B. Employment	0.18	1.00		
C. Research and Development	0.37*	0.46***	1.00	
D. Recycling	0.44**	0.46***	0.78***	1.00

Note: * = p < 0.1; ** = p < 0.05; *** = p < 0.01.

6. Europe 2020, EU agencies and political entrepreneurship

Helena Ekelund

The notion of political entrepreneurship within a European Union (EU) context is often associated with the agenda-setting institutions, that is, the European Commission and the European Council, or the decision-making institutions, that is, the Council of the European Union and the European Parliament. For the implementation of strategies, such as the Europe 2020 strategy, the EU is dependent also on EU agencies, however. Although some EU agencies play an important role in the regulation of specific fields, they do not have direct rule-making powers (Busuioc, 2013: 23). For this reason, Wood (2018) argues, the agencies have to become political entrepreneurs in order to gain authority. This chapter sets out to explore political entrepreneurship of EU agencies with regard to the implementation of the Europe 2020 strategy.

Within the context of the Europe 2020 strategy, inclusive growth means 'empowering people through high levels of employment, investing in skills, fighting poverty and modernising labour markets, training and social protection systems so as to help people anticipate and manage change, and build a cohesive society' (European Commission, 2010a: 17). These ideas are not new to the European Union. As early as 1975, two decentralised agencies – the European Centre for the Development of Vocational Training (Cedefop) and the European Foundation for the Improvement of Living and Working Conditions (Eurofound) – were created in order to assist member states and the Community institutions with developing initiatives related to vocational training and living and working conditions, respectively. In 1994, the European Agency for Health and Safety at Work (EU-OSHA), the work of which aims to improve health and safety at work throughout Europe, was set up.[1] These agencies are important partners of the Directorate-General for Employment, Social Affairs and Inclusion,

---

[1]   The European Training Foundation (ETF) was also set up. As this agency assists non-member states it will not be discussed in this chapter.

which deals with many issues of critical importance for the realisation of the Europe 2020 strategy.

As part of the Europe 2020 flagship initiative *Agenda for new skills and jobs*, the Commission states its aim 'to make full use of the problem-solving potential of social dialogue at all levels' (European Commission, 2010a: 18). Social dialogue refers to discussions and consultations with the social partners, that is, trade unions and employers' organisations. The social dialogue is intrinsic to the rationale, governance and functioning of Cedefop, Eurofound and EU-OSHA. These agencies have a tripartite governance structure where national authorities of the member states, employers' organisations and employees' organisations are represented on the governing boards. As a consequence of this, these agencies can be assumed to have well-established ties to the social partners. In order to fulfil their tasks, these agencies also coordinate and participate in various networks of organisations with a stake in achieving exactly what the Europe 2020 strategy means by inclusive growth.

Given their functions and involvement in social dialogue, these agencies ought to be in a good position to engage in political entrepreneurship fostering cooperation between member states, stakeholders and themselves. The aim of this chapter is to investigate if these agencies indeed act as political entrepreneurs in their current work related to the Europe 2020 strategy. The focus is on agencies as institutions, and individual employees within the agencies will not be considered in this chapter.

The chapter will address the following research question: To what extent are the activities and initiatives the agencies engage in with regard to Europe 2020 expressions of political entrepreneurship?

The rest of the chapter is structured as follows. First, a brief background to EU agencies under DG employment is given. This is followed by a discussion of how these agencies can be understood against the background of the definition of political entrepreneurship presented in Chapter 1. The activities and initiatives of each of the three agencies are then examined and discussed to determine to what extent they are expressions of political entrepreneurship. The chapter ends with a summary and some concluding remarks.

BACKGROUND: EU AGENCIES UNDER DG EMPLOYMENT

Currently the European Union lists 32 decentralised agencies on its website (European Union, 2018), and four of these work directly with the Directorate-General for Employment, Social Affairs and Inclusion (European Commission, 2018). One of these, the European Training

Foundation (ETF), has an external focus in that it assists developing and transition countries within the context of the EU's external relations policy. In contrast, Cedefop, Eurofound and EU-OSHA, the three agencies discussed in this chapter, aim to assist the EU institutions and EU member states. The core functions of the agencies are outlined in their governing legislations. Whilst the wording is different for each agency, the prime roles of all of them are to gather and to disseminate information in various ways (Regulation EEC No. 337/75; Council Regulation No. 2062/94; Regulation EEC No. 1365/75). As will be shown later in this chapter, all three agencies have various networks for this purpose. Concrete examples of activities that the agencies may engage in are conducting their own research and facilitating the exchange of best practice through various channels such as publications and conferences.

Cedefop and Eurofound are special in that they were the very first decentralised agencies to be set up in 1975. No more agencies were established until the 1990s when the agencification process really took off in Europe (see for example Ekelund, 2012). EU-OSHA, established in 1994, is one of the agencies set up as part of this wave of agency establishment. European agencies come in different sizes, have a wide variety of functions, different governance structures and levels of financial independence from the EU institutions (see for example Ekelund, 2012). All agencies under DG Employment are advisory agencies, that is, they provide advice but do not have a mandate to make decisions that are binding on individuals (Ekelund, 2012). Financially they are dependent on subsidies from the EU budget. The total revenues for the year 2017 were €17.9 million for Cedefop (Statement of revenue and expenditure of the European Centre for the Development of Vocational Training (Cedefop) for the financial year 2017), €20.5 million for Eurofound (Statement of revenue and expenditure of the European Foundation for the Improvement of Living and Working Conditions for the financial year 2017) and €15.6 million for EU-OSHA (Statement of revenue and expenditure of the European Agency for Safety and Health at Work for the financial year 2017 — amending budget No. 1). According to the EU Agencies Network (2016), Cedefop has 94 employees, Eurofound 94 employees and EU-OSHA 65 employees.

Most decentralised European agencies are governed by a governing board consisting of one representative from each member state and representatives of the European Commission. Cedefop, Eurofound and EU-OSHA stand out from the other agencies by their tripartite governance structures. In addition to representatives of national authorities in each member state, the boards of these agencies also include one representative of an employees' organisation and one representative of an employers' organisation from each member state. The social partners are not only included on the boards of the agencies, but also on their advisory committees (Council of the EU, 2016).

POLITICAL ENTREPRENEURSHIP AND EU AGENCIES

As explained by Pircher (Chapter 3 in this volume), studies of EU-level political entrepreneurship have predominantly focused on the European Commission, although some studies have shown that also the inter-governmental European Council and the Council may act as political entrepreneurs in some circumstances. Hitherto, only one study of the political entrepreneurship of EU agencies has been conducted. In this study, Wood (2018) sets out to map the entrepreneurial strategies of all existing EU agencies. The definition of entrepreneurial strategies used by Wood (2018) differs from the definition used in this study, however. Wood's (2018: 404) baseline definition of entrepreneurial strategies is how agencies 'work informally to spread information and ideas'. Expanding on this, Wood (2018: 407) associates entrepreneurship with leadership, and defines entrepreneurial strategies as '*the potential range of approaches through which EU agencies strategically disseminate information and ideas informally to relevant organisations and actors, in light of their political context*' (emphasis in original). This involves strategically choosing 'particular methods to engage of a broad political sphere on the basis of expectations about how that environment will respond' (Wood, 2018: 408). The methods to choose from are 'media communication; face-to-face networking; and knowledge development and learning' (Wood, 2018: 409). Considering also political salience, by which Wood (2018: 409) means 'the visibility specifically of agencies', he creates a typology of four ideal-type entrepreneurial strategies: technical-functional, network-seeking, insulating and politicised. He classifies Cedefop as a network-seeking agency, meaning that it has 'extensive entrepreneurship methods but low levels of salience' (Wood, 2018: 411). Eurofound and EU-OSHA are both classified as technical-functional, meaning that they score low on entrepreneurial methods as well as salience in Wood's (2018: 415) study.

In so far as it emphasises strategic choices of action, Wood's definition is in line with the definition of political entrepreneurship used in this book. Two crucial differences, however, have to do with the characteristics of the activities and the perceived goal of these activities. Wood (2018: 405) focuses on '"everyday" practices' used to disseminate ideas and information strategically. Furthermore, he links the entrepreneurial strategies with the agencies' own quest for authority, arguing that these strategies are needed if the agencies want to be perceived as credible regulators despite not having direct rule-making powers. This is of course worthwhile to explore as it can tell us more about how agencies influence policies and their implementation. However, being strategic is not necessarily the same as being innovative, and a focus only on strategy does not take the goal of the activities into account. Thus, some of the critiques against previous research on political entrepreneurship described in Chapter 1 of this volume can be levelled against Wood's study of agencies. In particular, by assuming that the goal of the agencies' activities is to establish themselves as credible regulators one assumes that political entrepreneurship is about individual profit, not the common good. Moreover, it is not clear what would distinguish these strategic activities of agencies from their day-to-day activities. It should also be noted that political entrepreneurship in Wood's (2018) definition does not concern specifically the promotion of entrepreneurial activities and economic growth, which the conceptualisation of political entrepreneurship used in this book does.

This book defines political entrepreneurs as '[a]ctors and institutions (politicians/ bureaucrats/ officers/ institutions) within the publicly funded sector that with innovative approaches encourages entrepreneurship/ business and where the goal is growth and employment for the common good' (Silander, Chapter 1 of this volume). In doing so, this book strives to distinguish political entrepreneurship from 'regular, day-to-day political/ public activities in the public sector' (Silander, Chapter 1 of this volume). For an activity to be deemed political entrepreneurial in this study, it has to be innovative somehow, and it needs to encourage entrepreneurship and/or business. Furthermore, this book associates political entrepreneurship with a degree of altruism given the emphasis of the common good. Whilst some general insights about agency activities from the Wood (2018) study will inform the analysis in this chapter, the typology will be largely irrelevant as it concerns everyday activities. Rather, the focus of this chapter will be on determining to what extent the activities of the agencies studied can be regarded as entrepreneurial given the narrower definition of political entrepreneurship used in this study.

As previously mentioned, Cedefop, Eurofound and EU-OSHA are advisory agencies. The agencies' absence of regulatory powers in combination with not being allowed to raise any substantial revenue of their own accord means that the formal mandates of these agencies are rather weak. In contrast to the EU institutions, they have no formal possibility to influence at the agenda-setting or decision-making stages, and they have no right to be consulted. The absence of formal power need not eliminate the possibilities to act as political entrepreneurs, however. Here it is useful to recall the definition of a political entrepreneur as someone who uses 'formal and informal institutions and networks to improve the public sector's activities towards entrepreneurs and entrepreneurship by developing and promoting new norms' (Silander, 2016: 10).

The agencies' potential to be entrepreneurial lies in the tasks and functions they are set up to fulfil, including how they make use of their networks. In a study of Cedefop conducted before the adoption of Europe 2020, Ekelund (2010: 93) has concluded that this agency is well placed to spread norms throughout its networks and to the EU institutions. The study demonstrated that work done by Cedefop is taken up by the Commission, and that labour market enhancing tools, such as the European CV and the European credit system in vocational education and training (VET), devised by Cedefop are now widespread throughout Europe. This clearly shows that Cedefop can plant ideas with the goal of growth and employment for the common good throughout its networks and with the EU institutions. Given their similar nature we can assume that this applies also to Eurofound and EU-OSHA. Theoretically, the agencies can also use innovative approaches to encourage policy-makers at the EU level and at the national level to implement policies that encourage conditions for entrepreneurs. Furthermore, the agencies may draw on their experience of social dialogue, the problem-solving capacity of which is acknowledged by the Commission in the Europe 2020 strategy document (European Commission, 2010a: 18). In the context of agency potential to influence EU institutions, it is also worth noting that the Commission and the Council have recognised the importance of these agencies in meeting new societal and economic needs. The Commission has proposed revised regulations for all three agencies, and in each case added value in line with the Europe 2020 strategy is listed as an objective (European Commission, 2016a; 2016b; 2016c). The Council (2016) has reached agreement on the proposals.

To uncover political entrepreneurship of the agencies within the context of the Europe 2020 strategy, we need to focus on how the agencies are working with the practical implementation of the strategy on an ongoing basis. This will be covered in the next sections.

AGENCY ACTIVITIES AND INITIATIVES RELATED TO THE EUROPE 2020 STRATEGY

Cedefop

A quick glance at Cedefop's website reveals that a lot of what the agency does can be related to the Europe 2020 strategy. To reach the strategy's goals of an employment rate of 75 per cent, people need skills that are sought after by enterprises, Cedefop (2018a) states. Thus, the agency's ambition is to help 'develop the right policies to provide the right skills' (Cedefop, 2018a). In order to do this Cedefop engages in a range of activities related to data-gathering, monitoring and information-sharing. The agency functions like an information hub. It gathers information from a variety of actors, and then disseminates the information throughout its networks. According to Wood (2018), whose definition of political entrepreneurship focuses on strategies for information dissemination without considering the degree of innovation or the goal of the activities, Cedefop has a high level of entrepreneurialism precisely because it is seeking to network. Recalling the narrower definition of political entrepreneurship used in this book, extensive use of networks is not in itself sufficient for activities to be deemed entrepreneurial. This discussion will thus consider to what extent information-sharing and networking are done in innovative ways, and whether or not the goal is regarded as entrepreneurship for the common good.

The agency's work is structured around four overarching themes: analysing policy, developing life-long learning, identifying skills needs and understanding qualifications (Cedefop, 2018b). Within each theme, the agency has a number of projects. At the time of writing, Cedefop has 28 projects, and details about the projects as well as archived projects are available on the agency's website. In terms of their focus, most of the projects can be linked to the aims of the Europe 2020 strategy, and it is not possible to cover everything within the scope of this chapter. Thus, this presentation will focus on the two projects where Cedefop itself makes explicit references to Europe 2020 in the project presentations. These projects are: 'Forecasting skill demand and supply' and 'Early leaving of education and training'.

As part of the 'Forecasting skill demand and supply' project, Cedefop uses quantitative data on skills in Europe to forecast trends 'in employment by sector of economic activity and occupational group' as well as 'level of education of the population and the labour force' (Cedefop, 2018c). The idea is to make data comparable across Europe, not to replace similar activities at the national level. The methodology and results are validated by national experts, and Cedefop (2018d) describes the activities as 'one of the key building blocks of the EU Skills Panorama under the flagship initiative Agenda for New Skills and Jobs of the Europe 2020 strategy'. These activities have not been launched in connection to the strategy, however. The earliest publication related to the project that can be found on Cedefop's website dates to the year 2003. To carry out data-gathering and statistical analysis does not constitute an innovative approach in itself, and Cedefop has not really developed new working methods or activities as part of the project. Moreover, the tasks related to the flagship initiative are carried out in response to a call from above rather than as a new initiative taken by the agency (European Commission, 2010b). Nevertheless, it could be argued that there is a degree of political entrepreneurship here in that the agency uses its established expertise in order to contribute to a new initiative that in turn has the goal of encouraging entrepreneurship/business for the common good.

Within the 'Early leaving of education and training' project, Cedefop (2018e) 'undertakes research and develops tools to empower the role of VET to the fight against early leaving from education and training (ELET)'. As noted in Chapter 1 of this volume, reducing the rate of early school leavers to 10 per cent is one of the goals of the Europe 2020 strategy. Having noted that the problem of early school leaving differs amongst different regions of Europe, Cedefop (2018e) argues that 'high quality, inclusive and flexible VET provision may prevent and remedy leaving education early'. Through its research the agency claims to have found insights into '[p]rotective factors to prevent early leaving from VET', '[m]echanisms for measuring and monitoring ELET at national and EU-level', '[s]uccessful policies and practices in Europe to tackle ELET' and '[g]ood practices for policy impact evaluation'. These insights have then been used to develop a web toolkit for tackling the problem of ELET. The toolkit, which is easily accessible on the agency's website, is 'aimed for policy makers and VET practitioners involved in the design, implementation and evaluation of VET policies and practices to tackle early leaving' (Cedefop, 2018e). Whilst the 'Forecasting skill demand and supply' project only exemplifies a low degree of political entrepreneurship, the 'Early leaving of education and training' project clearly demonstrates that Cedefop can use 'innovative approaches [that] encourages entrepreneurship/business and where the goal is growth and employment for the common good' (Silander, Chapter 1 this volume). Here the agency has developed a new and innovative tool that aims to help tackle a problem identified as an important goal of the Europe 2020 strategy. The tool has the potential to reach a wide audience as it is web-based and free to use (Cedefop, 2018e). As previously mentioned, other tools developed by the agency have become widespread throughout Europe, so relevant policy-makers and practitioners have shown an openness to ideas promoted by the agency.

Results from both projects are communicated and analysed in publications or at various events. Publications often take the form of Cedefop research papers or briefing notes. Events could be anything from brief launching events to more intensive conferences and workshops, and they are often organised by Cedefop itself although the agency also participates in events organised by other actors. Events are often held either at Cedefop or in Brussels, but there are also examples of events organised elsewhere. Some events are open and some of them are by invitation only. It is reasonable to assume that publications issued by the agency are primarily read by actors who are already following the activities of the agency, which means that communicating information through publications does not constitute an innovative approach. When organising or participating in events, the agency may act in an entrepreneurial manner, however. Through these types of events, the agency makes itself visible and reaches new audiences for its ideas. The research conducted by the agency can be regarded as policy research, and in a study of think-tanks Stone (2007) has found that events such as conferences and workshops play an important role in spreading results from policy research. Assuming that this applies also to EU agencies, Cedefop can use these types of events to promote new norms that could improve conditions for entrepreneurs and entrepreneurship.

If we move from the consideration of individual projects, and take a more general view of the agency's work, we see that networks play an important part in the agency's operations. The agency coordinates three networks: ReferNet, Skillsnet and CareersNet (Cedefop, 2018f). Whereas ReferNet is a network of national organisations that play a key role in VET in their countries, Skillsnet is open to researchers and experts working on 'early identification of skill needs and forecasting or in the transfer of research results on future skill requirements into policy and practice' (Cedefop 2018f). This network is linked with the 'Forecasting skill demand and supply' project. ReferNet and Skillsnet were set up several years before the adoption of the Europe 2020 strategy. CareersNet, which involves national experts on lifelong guidance and career development, is a relatively new network that had its first meeting in 2017 (Cedefop, 2018g; Cedefop, 2018h). Whilst networking in itself does not constitute examples of political entrepreneurship as defined in this book, the agency could use the networks in an entrepreneurial way analogous to the use of conferences and events.

Eurofound

Eurofound (2018a) directly links its work to the Europe 2020 strategy, by stating that it 'aims to support the objectives of the Europe 2020 strategy, to ensure that Europe achieves smart, sustainable and inclusive growth'. On the basis of research into living and working conditions in Europe, the agency seeks to identify 'factors for successful change' and to develop ideas for the improvement of these conditions (Eurofound, 2018a). In this way the agency seeks to support the implementation of the strategy

(Eurofound, 2016). The way the agency advertises its work with the Europe 2020 strategy suggests an entrepreneurial ambition: the agency seeks to draw on its expertise to develop new ideas that will contribute to the success of the strategy. Drawing on interview data about activities in general and not specific to the Europe 2020 strategy, Wood (2018: 416) notes a wish from Eurofound to reach out to wider audiences, but that 'resource constraints and demanding workloads' can stand in the way. It is thus not surprising that the agency draws on its core research activities, rather than developing new methods, when seeking to contribute to the strategy.

Currently, the agency's work is organised around six priority areas: working conditions and sustainable work; industrial relations; labour market change; quality of life and public services; the digital age: opportunities and challenges for work and employment; and monitoring convergence in the European Union. Whereas the first four build directly on expertise the agency has built up over the years, the latter two have been selected as '[t]hey capture cross-cutting challenges and paradigmatic changes' (Eurofound, 2016: 7). Within all six areas the agency is carrying out activities predominantly focused on gathering and analysing data. This overview of agency activity will focus on the first four areas, as these are the ones that the agency itself either specifically relates to the Europe 2020 strategy, or, as in the case of 'industrial relations' priority area, includes work that can be mainstreamed into all of the agency's work.

Eurofound (2018b) directly links the priority area 'working conditions and sustainable work' to the Europe 2020 strategy as well as the Commission's 'Agenda for new skills and jobs' from 2010. The key activity within this priority area is to analyse and monitor working conditions through the use of a tool called the European Working Conditions Survey (EWCS). Eurofound (2016: 27) expects that evidence from their analyses will 'inform policies aimed at extending working lives and achieving the employment targets of the Europe 2020 strategy'. The EWCS tool dates back to the 1990s, however, so the survey itself is not connected to the strategy. Results from the analyses are made available through the agency's European Observatory of Working Life (EurWORK), which also transmits results from research related to the priority area 'industrial relations' (Eurofound, 2018c). As noted in the discussion of Cedefop, data analysis itself is not an entrepreneurial activity, but the use of established expertise to achieve new objectives is in a sense entrepreneurial. It is about identifying windows of opportunity to contribute to the strategy. Whilst the agency itself cannot make policy, it could influence policy, and the way to do that is first to identify where policy-makers may be open to taking in the agency's ideas, and second to provide the type of information that is sought after. By targeting its work to priority areas closely linked to the objectives of the Europe 2020 strategy, the agency makes its work relevant to EU institutions and member states implementing the policy. This relevance is essential if the agency wishes to develop and promote ideas that encourage entrepreneurship for the common good. On the basis of the data available for this study, it is not possible to determine to what extent the agency seeks to promote new ideas, and to what extent it is just providing statistical data, however.

Within the priority area 'industrial relations', the focus is on monitoring and analysing trends, and of particular importance here is to understand the dynamics of social dialogue, that is, institutionalised cooperation between employers' and employees' organisations (Eurofound, 2016: 8). The agency's work is not limited to understanding the dynamics, however. Analysing the contribution of social dialogue and 'the role of the social partners in finding and implementing solutions in a wide range of policy fields is mainstreamed in all strategic areas of intervention described in this programme', Eurofound (2016: 8) explains. Throughout its work on industrial relations, the agency relies on its network of contacts throughout the member states. This reliance is typical for agencies that seek to reach out, but that are hampered by a lack of resources (Wood, 2018). The agency may not itself be able to reach all potential policy-makers and implementers throughout Europe, but its national contacts assists the agency in reaching important national decision-makers such as social partners and governmental departments (Eurofound, 2018e). To get its ideas out to wider audiences the agency uses its contacts as multipliers, which can be regarded as a creative strategy to maximise impact despite limited resources.

The focus of the 'labour market change' priority area is on research on changing labour markets with the aim to help policy-makers anticipate and manage structural change (Eurofound, 2016: 10). Similarly to work within the 'working conditions and sustainable work' priority area, whilst the agency specifically links the research conducted to the Europe 2020 strategy, it draws on well-established survey tools that have existed before the strategy's adoption. Results from this work are available through an observatory called European Monitoring Centre on Change (Eurofound, 2018c). Again we can see how the agency is drawing on old tools to research new situations, which is entrepreneurial to an extent.

As observed by Eurofound (2018d), '[q]uality of life is a broad concept', which encompasses 'objective factors such as health, work status and living conditions, as well as the subjective assessments of an individual's life situation and perception of quality of society'. Eurofound (2016: 11) gathers data on these factors using the European Quality of Life Survey

(EQLS), the first round of which was conducted in 2003. The results are made available via the European Observatory on Quality of Life (Eurofound, 2018c). Whilst the area of work is not new to the agency, it makes special note of its relevance for the European platform against poverty and social exclusion, which is one of the flagship initiatives of the Europe 2020 strategy (Eurofound, 2018d). As with the other priority areas, it appears that the agency seeks to make its work relevant to the implementation of the strategy. Whilst its resources do not allow for new and innovative working methods, the agency acts entrepreneurially in that it is very strategic in prioritising areas that are closely linked to the goals of the Europe 2020 strategy.

EU-OSHA

EU-OSHA's field of work is closely linked to the Europe 2020 strategy, and this is depicted in its vision '[*t*]*o be a recognised leader promoting healthy and safe workplaces in Europe based on tripartism, participation and the development of an OSH risk prevention culture, to ensure a smart, sustainable, productive and inclusive economy*' (EU-OSHA, 2017: 7, italics in original). Similarly to Eurofound, the agency thus shows an entrepreneurial ambition in how it is describing its work. It wishes to be seen as a contributor to achieving the goals of the Europe 2020 strategy, and it emphasises its role as a leader within its field of activity. The agency is also similar to Eurofound in that its resources are rather limited (Wood, 2018), and it is dependent on other actors to spread its work. Currently, the agency's work is organised around six priority areas: anticipating change; facts and figures; tools for the management of occupation safety and health (OSH); raising awareness of OSH; networking knowledge; and networking (EU-OSHA, 2017: 14).

Within the anticipating change priority area, the agency works on identifying and anticipating emerging risks in OSH. A lot of this is done through the European Risk Observatory (ERO), which 'gathers and examines data, drawing on research and expert consultations, on trends and underlying factors having an impact on workplaces and workers' safety and health' (EU-OSHA, 2018a). The agency also publishes discussion papers and runs specific projects called foresight projects. As evidenced by the report *Priorities for occupational safety and health research in Europe: 2013–2020* the agency has the Europe 2020 strategy in mind when identifying needs for OSH research (EU-OSHA, 2013). In addition to identifying and anticipating risks, the foresight projects aim to 'provide instruments for policy-makers, researchers and workplace intermediaries to address adequately the future challenges that are identified', and to 'explore how best to transfer the findings from its foresight activities into policy-making' (EU-OSHA, 2017: 15). As of August 2018, there are three ongoing foresight projects: 'Green jobs', 'Nanomaterials' and 'ICT/ digitalisation' (EU-OSHA, 2018a). 'Green jobs' and 'ICT/digitalisation' are both directly linked to the aims of the Europe 2020 strategy. Whilst gathering and analysis of data is not entrepreneurial in itself it can be argued that EU-OSHA acts in an entrepreneurial way. The agency is seeking ways to make its work relevant and to contribute to the goals of the strategy. By devising projects that are closely linked to the aims of the strategy, the agency is making strategic use of its resources, which it has to do in order to have a chance of disseminating norms that encourage entrepreneurship for the common good.

As part of providing decision-makers with facts and figures EU-OSHA (2017: 16–17) conducts overviews of OSH and gathers data through a large-scale survey called European Survey of Enterprises on New and Emerging Risks (ESENER). These activities span several years. The purpose of ESENER is to gather data on how enterprises manage OSH, and then seek to 'identify factors that encourage preventive measures and those that discourage or impede them, as well as helping to define enterprises' needs according to their characteristics – size, sector, location and age' (EU-OSHA, 2017: 16). According to EU-OSHA (2017: 17), the OSH overviews, the scope of which is determined together with stakeholders, 'contribute to the development and sharing of good practice, both at the level of policy and of workplace intervention, which can provide content for campaigning activities'. The way the agency describes its activities bears close resemblance to the definition of political entrepreneurship used in this book. The agency determines what to focus on in collaboration with stakeholders, and there is a focus on developing norms that encourage improved functioning of the labour market for enterprises as well as employees. Improved health and safety at work is obviously beneficial for workers, but the way in which the agency describes its work there is a focus also on the needs of the employers. In other words, it is framed in terms of suggesting a goal to contribute to the common good.

The need for tools for the management of occupational safety and health (OSH) was foreseen already in the agency's founding regulation, and it is provided through the 'Online interactive Risk Assessment (OiRA) tool' (EU-OSHA, 2017: 17). OiRA has been in use since 2010 (EU-OSHA, 2018b), although it is constantly being developed (EU-OSHA, 2017). In its description of the OiRA tool, EU-OSHA (2017) emphasises the involvement of the social partners and national authorities in developing and raising awareness of the existence of the tool. The constant development of OiRA is an example of political entrepreneurial activities on behalf of the agency. As noted also by Wood (2018), EU-OSHA is a rather small agency so it has to be creative in order to get its ideas out there. The OiRA tool is free to use and targeted specifically at small and micro businesses. Its purpose is to help these businesses conduct their own self-assessments of risks related to OSH, which in turn could render them more competitive (EU-OSHA, 2018b). Many business entrepreneurs start off managing their own micro businesses, so by taking innovative approaches, such as developing online tools, that assist this type of business, EU-OSHA is clearly encouraging entrepreneurship. Compliance with OSH legislation must be considered to be for the common good, but, as EU-OSHA (2018b) points out, '[i]t is known that particularly micro and small enterprises face challenges in complying with OSH legislation'. In sum, here we can clearly see how EU-OSHA is using innovative approaches to encourage 'entrepreneurship/ business and where the goal is growth and employment for the common good' (Silander, Chapter 1 in this volume).

Within the raising awareness of OSH priority area, EU-OSHA coordinates the 'Healthy workplaces campaigns'. These campaigns run for two years, and have a number of goals. For example, the campaigns are meant to raise awareness, provide information, share best practice, engage stakeholders and encourage activities with workplace impact (EU-OSHA, 2017: 19). EU-OSHA (2017: 19) describes the campaigns as having a 'network-based approach', and the agency seeks to draw on their contacts with actors such as the EU institutions, social partners, national focal points and the Enterprise Europe Network. The agency coordinates the campaigns, and then its various partner organisations as well as individual workplaces can organise their own activities in accordance with their needs (EU-OSHA, 2017: 19). In addition to these campaigns, the agency communicates and conducts other awareness-raising activities on a variety of topics, often in contact with the national focal points. The agency is also involved in the production of short films, running of seminars and organisation of awards (EU-OSHA, 2017). As a general principle, the agency seeks 'to explore and develop innovative approaches to meeting the challenge of communicating in a multilingual Europe' (EU-OSHA, 2017: 21). An example of this is 'the development of an automated translation management tool' (EU-OSHA, 2017: 20). The awareness-raising activities are not presented as being specifically linked to the Europe 2020 strategy, however. Whilst the agency is focusing on their existing contacts, it is acting entrepreneurially in that it is seeking to communicate in new ways. The agency is also making creative use of its existing contacts by letting them function as multipliers that in turn pass information on to their networks.

For an outside observer it is not obvious what the difference is between the priority areas networking knowledge and networking. Both of them point to the importance for the agency to maintain and develop its contacts with stakeholders including the EU institutions, national governments, the social partners, other EU agencies, international organisations and the Enterprise Europe Network (EU-OSHA, 2017: 22). In its programming document as well as on its website, the agency writes a lot about how it needs to make use of contacts, which suggests that the agency is using innovative approaches to get its ideas out to the public despite having limited resources to do so of its own accord. This focus on networking is necessary as the agency would struggle to fulfil its tasks if it could not create synergies through cooperation. The online encyclopaedia OSHwiki is a concrete expression of this cooperation. OSHwiki, which can be used by anyone, is managed by the agency, and its content is provided by authorised contributors (EU-OSHA, 2017: 21). Just like OiRA discussed above, OSHwiki is an example of an innovative use of electronic tools to get ideas and information out to the wider community, which is a form of political entrepreneurship.

CONCLUDING REMARKS

The three advisory agencies examined in this chapter have very limited ability to take their own initiatives at the policy-formulation stage in comparison with the EU's decision-making institutions. They can play an important role at the implementation stage, however, and this is where they have their greatest potential to act entrepreneurially. Their work could potentially influence policy-makers and provide them with information needed to achieve the goals of the strategy. It is striking that all three agencies make explicit references to the Europe 2020 strategy when presenting what they do and the rationales behind these activities. In particular Eurofound and EU-OSHA show an entrepreneurial ambition in how they advertise their work related to the strategy. How creative the agencies are in 'selling' their work matters, as this could affect their possibilities to get their ideas into the minds of policy-makers. Effective 'selling' increases their chances of having their ideas that encourage entrepreneurship taken up and turned into policy. In order to differentiate the political entrepreneurship of agencies from their day-to-day activities, this chapter has gone beyond studying strategies for information-dissemination. It has considered when activities have been initiated, if any changes to activities have taken place and what the aims and goals of activities are.

The analysis reveals that a common approach of all three agencies is to draw on previous expertise and apply it to a new situation. Over the years each agency has developed a range of working methods for gathering and analysing data related to their respective field of specialisation. Making sure that people have the right skills sought after by enterprises, improving living and working conditions and assisting enterprises in complying with OSH regulations can all be linked to enhancing conditions for entrepreneurship and business for the common good. It can thus be argued that when the agencies use their established expertise to analyse new situations in order to contribute to the Europe 2020 strategy, they are being entrepreneurial to an extent. The methods themselves may not be innovative, but what is innovative is applying them in the new context of seeking to achieve the goals of the strategy. In other words, the agencies have found a window of opportunity to utilise and spread their expertise on what could improve conditions for entrepreneurship in Europe. A clear example of this is the foresight projects devised by EU-OSHA.

Another common approach is the extensive use of networks for the purpose of spreading their research findings. Eurofound and EU-OSHA in particular are very reliant on strategic networking where network partners are used as multipliers that help spread the ideas further. This approach plays a central role in EU-OSHA's work on awareness-raising campaigns. Networking in itself is not necessarily entrepreneurial. It depends how the networks are used. If they are used to spread norms that are beneficial to entrepreneurship where the goal is employment and economic growth for the common good, this could be linked to political entrepreneurship as defined in this book. The same applies to the organisation and participation in events, which is of significant importance to the work of Cedefop. The analysis of this chapter suggests that the agencies have ambitions to use their networks in entrepreneurial ways, and a suggestion for further research is to conduct the expert interviews needed to establish whether the ambition translates into practice.

Whereas Eurofound appears to direct most efforts to its core task of data analysis, Cedefop and EU-OSHA carry out a wider range of activities. One such activity that is closely in line with political entrepreneurship is the development of free to use electronic tools. Cedefop has developed one as part of the 'Early leaving of education and training' project, and EU-OSHA is constantly developing its OiRA tool. These tools allow the agencies to spread norms conducive to entrepreneurship to wide audiences, and the use of new technology is clearly an innovative approach. New technology is also used by EU-OSHA through the OSHwiki tool and in its endeavours to communicate more effectively with multilingual Europe, two other examples of innovative approaches.

To conclude, all three agencies use entrepreneurial approaches when seeking to contribute to the implementation of the Europe 2020 strategy.

REFERENCES

Busuioc, M. (2013). *European Agencies: Law and Practices of Accountability.* Oxford: Oxford University Press.

Cedefop (2018a). 'About Cedefop', accessed 24 August 2018 at http://www.cedefop.europa.eu/en/about-cedefop.

Cedefop (2018b). 'Themes', accessed 24 August 2018 at http://www.cedefop.europa.eu/en/themes.

Cedefop (2018c). 'Forecasting skill demand and supply – future trends', accessed 24 August 2018 at http://www.cedefop.europa.eu/en/events-and-projects/projects/forecasting-skill-demand-and-supply/data-visualisations.

Cedefop (2018d). 'Early leaving from education and training', accessed 24 August 2018 at http://www.cedefop.europa.eu/en/events-and-projects/projects/early-leaving-education-and-training.

Cedefop (2018e). 'Networks', accessed 24 August 2018 at http://www.cedefop.europa.eu/en/events-and-projects/networks.

Cedefop (2018f). 'Forecasting skill demand and supply', accessed 24 August 2018 at http://www.cedefop.europa.eu/en/events-and-projects/projects/forecasting-skill-demand-and-supply.

Cedefop (2018g). 'CareersNet', accessed 24 August 2018 at http://www.cedefop.europa.eu/en/events-and-projects/networks/careersnet.

Cedefop (2018h). '1st CareersNet meeting', accessed 24 August 2018 at http://www.cedefop.europa.eu/en/events-and-projects/events/1st-careersnet-meeting.

Council of the EU (2016). 'European agencies Eurofound, EU-OSHA, Cedefop: Council reached agreement'. Press release 750/16 08/12/2016.

Council Regulation (EC) No. 2062/94 of 18 July 1994 establishing a European Agency for Safety and Health at Work.

Ekelund, H. (2010). 'The agencification of Europe: explaining the establishment of European community agencies'. Unpublished PhD thesis, University of Nottingham.

Ekelund, H. (2012). 'Making sense of the "Agency Programme" in Europe: mapping European agencies'. *Central European Journal of Public Policy*, **6**(1): 26–49.

EU Agencies Network (2016). *The EU Agencies Working for You.* Luxembourg: Publications Office of the European Union.

EU-OSHA (2013). *Priorities for Occupational Safety and Health Research in Europe: 2013–2020.* Luxembourg: Publications Office of the European Union.

EU-OSHA (2017). 'Programming document 2018–2020', accessed 26 August 2018 at https://osha.europa.eu/en/tools-and-publications/publications/programming-document-2018-2020/view.

EU-OSHA (2018a). 'Emerging risks', accessed 26 August 2018 at https://osha.europa.eu/en/emerging-risks.

EU-OSHA (2018b). 'OiRA: free and simple tools for a straightforward risk assessment process', accessed 26 August 2018 at https://osha.europa.eu/en/tools-and-publications/oira.

Eurofound (2016). 'Programming document 2017–2020', accessed 28 August 2018 at https://www.eurofound.europa.eu/publications/work-programme/2016/programming-document-2017-2020.

Eurofound (2018a). 'What we do', accessed 28 August 2018 at https://www.eurofound.europa.eu/about-eurofound/what-we-do.

Eurofound (2018b). 'Working conditions and sustainable work', accessed 29 August 2018 at https://www.eurofound.europa.eu/topic/working-conditions-and-sustainable-work.

Eurofound (2018c). 'Observatories', accessed 29 August 2018 at https://www.eurofound.europa.eu/observatories.

Eurofound (2018d). 'Quality of life and public services', accessed 29 August 2018 at https://www.eurofound.europa.eu/topic/quality-of-life-and-public-services.

Eurofound (2018e). 'Network of Eurofound correspondents', accessed 30 September 2018 at https://www.eurofound.europa.eu/network-of-european-correspondents.

European Commission (2010a). 'Europe 2020 – a strategy for smart, sustainable and inclusive growth'. Brussels, 3.3.2010, COM(2010) 2020 final.

European Commission (2010b). Communication from the Commission to the European Parliament, the Council, the European Economic and Social Committee and the Committee of the Regions: An Agenda for new skills and jobs: A European contribution towards full employment. Strasbourg, 23.11.2010 COM(2010) 682 final.

European Commission (2016a). 'Proposal for a Regulation of the European Parliament and of the Council establishing a European Centre for the Development of Vocational Training (Cedefop) and repealing Regulation (EEC) No. 337/75'.

European Commission (2016b). 'Proposal for a Regulation of the European Parliament and of the Council establishing the European Foundation for the improvement of living and working conditions (Eurofound), and repealing Council Regulation (EEC) No. 1365/75'.

European Commission (2016c). 'Proposal for a Regulation of the European Parliament and of the Council establishing the European Agency for Safety and Health at Work (EU-OSHA), and repealing Council Regulation (EC) 2062/94'.

European Commission (2018). 'Agencies and partners', accessed 20 August 2018 at http://ec.europa.eu/social/main.jsp?langId=en&catId=85.

European Union (2018). Decentralised agencies, accessed 20 August 2018 at https://europa.eu/european-union/about-eu/agencies/decentralised-agencies_en.

Regulation (EEC) No. 337/75 of the Council of 10 February 1975 establishing a European Centre for the Development of Vocational Training.

Regulation (EEC) No. 1365/75 of the Council of 26 May 1975 on the creation of a European Foundation for the improvement of living and working conditions.

Silander, D. (2016). 'The political entrepreneur', in C. Karlsson, C. Silander and D. Silander (eds), *Political Entrepreneurship: Regional Growth and Entrepreneurial Diversity in Sweden*. Cheltenham, UK and Northampton, MA, USA: Edward Elgar Publishing, pp. 7–20.

Statement of revenue and expenditure of the European Centre for the Development of Vocational Training (Cedefop) for the financial year 2017 (2017/C 84/01).

Statement of revenue and expenditure of the European Foundation for the Improvement of Living and Working Conditions for the financial year 2017 (2017/C 84/04).

Statement of revenue and expenditure of the European Agency for Safety and Health at Work for the financial year 2017 – amending budget No. 1 (2017/C 248/01).

Stone, D. (2007). 'Recycling bins, garbage cans or think tanks? Three myths regarding policy analysis institutes'. *Public Administration*, **85**(2): 259–78.

Wood, M. (2018). 'Mapping EU agencies as political entrepreneurs'. *European Journal of Political Research*, **57**(2): 404–26.

PART III

Policies on smart, sustainable and inclusive growth

7. Policy evaluation in competitiveness: towards more results-oriented industrial policies

Charlie Karlsson and Sam Tavassoli

Today there is a large amount of interest in industrial policy among policy-makers particularly within the European Union, which is the result of several challenges that governments are facing. First, it is due to globalisation and increasing competition from emerging economies, which has created a new geography of growth, production and trade. The situation that has emerged is particularly due to the rise of China and its growing integration into world trade and foreign direct investments, challenging the competitiveness of many old industrial countries (Karlsson et al., 2015). Second, it is due to a new geography of innovation with an increased diffusion of information technologies and a growing priority given to science and technology particularly in developing countries (Karlsson et al., 2012). Third, it is the effect of climate change and the need to develop new 'green' infrastructures, goods and services that can handle negative environmental externalities and increase the production of renewable energy (Wallace and Silander, 2018). Fourth, it is the result of concerns in some countries that the manufacturing sector has declined so much and that critical knowledge and capabilities have been irreversibly lost (Warwick, 2013). The manufacturing sector can be seen as a strategic sector due to its contribution to R&D, productivity, employment, exports and GDP as well as its importance to other sectors via backward and forward demand and supply linkages. This implies that it is a sustainable strategy in the long term for rich countries to concentrate on the high value-added downstream and upstream intangible activities in the value chain and abandon the low value-added activities related to production. Fifth, it is the result of the financial and economic crisis that started in 2008, which stimulated a search for new growth mechanisms in many countries. This led many politicians and economists to question the capacity of free markets to secure a large enough flow of finance and an allocation of that flow to investments in the 'right' sectors that could restore economies to their trend paths. Sixth, it is a result of the fact that many countries face increasing demographic pressures due to ageing and declining labour forces, which leads them to search for new sources of growth, such as innovation-induced productivity growth including investments in intangible assets.

The new interest in policy models that consider the higher integration of global economies has led the European Union to formulate the Europe 2020 Strategy (approved in June 2010). The purpose of this strategy is to provide a new framework for economic and particularly industrial policy in Europe based upon three priorities: (1) smart growth, that is, an economy based on knowledge and innovation; (2) sustainable growth, that is, a resource-efficient, greener and more competitive economy; and (3) inclusive growth, that is, a high-employment economy with social and territorial cohesion. Industrial policy, indeed, became the flagship of the Europe 2020 Strategy, which indicates the overall aim of EU industrial policy to promote European industrial competitiveness, thus placing more emphasis on factors such as the growth of SMEs, the supply and management of raw materials, and well-paid jobs.

There are only a few policy areas in recent decades that have attracted more interest among economists than industrial policy[1] (Allen et al., 2006; Chimoli et al., 2009; Naudé, 2010; Lin, 2012; OECD, 2012; 2013). Moreover, there is probably no other policy area where economists disagree more than in the field of industrial policy. They all agree on the importance of macroeconomic stability, high rates of physical, R&D and human capital investments and well-functioning institutions as critical components of economic growth. However, there is considerable disagreement on the very role of industrial policy in developed as well as developing economies.

Given the prevailing uncertainty concerning the very role and design of industrial policies, there are strong motives to continue to study industrial policies and to evaluate their effects and costs. To provide clarity about the intentions of the political entrepreneurs and to facilitate better policy design and implementation, the trend is today increasingly to recommend policies that are amenable for monitoring and evaluation exercises. One of the key ingredients of such policies is that they permit the use of outcome or results indicators, that is, that they are results-oriented (Rodrik, 2004). Nowadays, leading-edge policy-related research regards the use of monitoring and evaluation exercises based on outcome/results indicators

---

[1] Sometimes in the literature terms such as 'enterprise policy', 'innovation policy', 'entrepreneurship policy' and 'SME policy' are used. We here see them all included in the concept of 'industrial policy'.

tied to the goals, objectives and intentions of any industrial policy as being essential for assessing the impacts of industrial policies. This is the only means to guarantee that policies are designed and implemented as closely as possible to the agreed societal objectives that the policy is intended to influence. However, this use of monitoring and evaluation exercises is still rare both in practice and in literature.

Against the above background, the purpose of this chapter is: (1) to carry out a survey of the problems involved in policy evaluation in general and specifically in the evaluation of industrial policies with reference to the Europe 2020 strategy; and (2) to sketch the role of policy monitoring and evaluation in an industrial policy life-cycle model. This contributes to better understanding of challenges facing policy-makers and researchers to design a holistic policy evaluation framework that is result-oriented. The chapter is organised as follows: the next section discusses policy evaluation from the perspective of the European Union. The third section introduces the concept of policy evaluation, followed by a discussion of the purpose of policy evaluations and the general problems that evaluators meet. The fifth section discusses special challenges related to the evaluation of industrial policy. The sixth section highlights special problems related to industrial policy evaluation in the presence of spillovers. The seventh section presents a logic cause-and-effect evaluation model, which provides the foundation for a discussion in the eighth section of an ideal industrial policy circle. The ninth section illustrates the role of policy monitoring and evaluation in an industrial policy life-cycle model. Concluding remarks are presented in the final section.

POLICY EVALUATION – A EUROPEAN PERSPECTIVE

Policy-makers today have access to a somewhat richer flow of evidence on the nature and performance of past industrial policies, which might give a feeling that they can avoid some of the earlier mistakes in industrial policy. Nevertheless, there is a strong need for *all* governments to go through their industrial policies at regular intervals and evaluate and compare them with what other governments do, since industrial policies often relate to (1) vested interests; (2) difficult problems; and (3) substantial costs and risks including rent-seeking among economic agents (Krueger, 1990; Ades and Di Tella, 1997; Pack and Saggi, 2006; Acemoglu and Robinson, 2013). Much of the analysis has focused on understanding the behaviour of elites and political entrepreneurs and how institutional 'insiders' are driven by their wish to capture policy-related rents. It is among other things the increasing awareness of the role played by these complex governance issues that has led to an increase in the interest of evaluations of industrial policy. It is particularly within the EU with its many different policy levels that these complex governance issues are important given the differences between the member states in terms of institutions, culture and history.

A fundamental problem with industrial policy, particularly within the EU, is that it implies multi-level governance involving multiple partners operating at different spatial scales and different hierarchical jurisdictions. Finding ways to build complementarities between different policy arenas involving both political and business entrepreneurs is essential and there are arguments suggesting that such complementarities can best be developed at the regional or local level. However, mobilising different political entrepreneurs and business entrepreneurs and other stakeholders to build such complementarities is a very complex challenge, and requires a consideration of the various incentive mechanisms involved. Here is a strong need for policy learning, which can't take place without proper evaluation.

In order to overcome institutional opposition and rent-seeking, it is necessary to develop a vision that can directly engage a range of different elites, political entrepreneurs and constituencies and persuade them to cooperate and align themselves with the industrial policy initiatives (Rodrik, 2014). Only by developing a broad-based consensus is it possible to develop an overarching framework on which policy prioritisation decisions can be based in a variety of different settings. However, without evaluations of the decided policies and their effects, there is a clear risk that the consensus will break down over time.

It is important in this context to understand that all industrial policies and specifically those within the European Union arise from a complex bargaining process between different political entrepreneurs, different other stakeholders, different parties, different interest and lobbying groups and different constituencies. This implies that every industrial policy to a varying extent necessarily represents a compromise between diverging interests and views. An agreement between differing groups is essential in order for an industrial policy to be decided upon and for such a policy to operate (Stiglitz et al., 2010) and this implies that the motivation underlying each industrial policy must reflect a dialogue spanning a complex patchwork of perceptions, incentives and interests. However, each industrial policy that is implemented needs to have an overall encompassing vision in order for there to be any functional agreement between the different parties involved and this vision must also reflect the fundamental underlying intentions of the actual policy. Moreover, there should also be a clear set of sufficiently narrowly defined objectives which the policy is focused on achieving, in order to make it possible to observe and to evaluate the effects of the policy action.

Despite calls for industrial policy evaluation in Europe, it was not until the mid-1990s that evaluations of industrial policy interventions at the firm level really began to take off. The increased impetus for evaluation during the 1990s was largely driven by the EU who emphasised the need to provide accountability and to assess the impact of significant EU transfers to guarantee an efficient use of public resources. The implementation within the Europe 2020 Strategy led to a further emphasis on policy evaluation *ex ante* as well as *ex post*. A critical aspect of the new EU industrial policy within the Europe 2020 Strategy, which should promote an industrial renaissance, was that it had to be firmly set within the European Union and also within the institutions of the Eurozone. This was necessary to coordinate industrial policy with macroeconomic, monetary, fiscal, trade, competition, regulatory and other EU-wide policies to achieve full legitimation to the actions by the policy-makers at the European level for influencing what is produced and how it is produced. This has required major changes in EU regulations, specifically those that prevent public action from distorting the operation of markets.

POLICY EVALUATION – AN INTRODUCTION

An increasing emphasis has been placed on systematising and improving evaluations of industrial policy by developing and testing new methodological approaches to policy evaluation, which has led to widespread changes in evaluation practices. Changes in the orientation, focus and measures of industrial policy have also raised new sets of methodological challenges for policy evaluators. Despite the changes that have taken place, one can in this connection observe that evaluations of industrial policies are still less common than evaluations in other policy sectors, such as labour market policies, education policies and health care policies. Furthermore, most of the existing evaluations of industrial policy concern industrial policy initiatives in newly industrialised countries or developing countries. The number of evaluations of industrial policy initiatives in the rich Western countries is quite small and many of them are limited in scope or have distinct methodological problems. Several authors have complained about this lack of evaluations of industrial policy.[2]

---

[2] For example: 'The recent discussion of *new* industrial policy including the desirability of fostering learning and obtaining benefits from agglomeration economies offered by industrial clusters has received little systematic evaluation.' Pack and Saggi (2006: 285).

A policy evaluation can be defined as a systematic and objective assessment of the merit, worth and value of ongoing governmental projects, programmes or policies in terms of its design, inputs, management, processes, outputs, outcomes and impacts in relation to its goals to guide future policy decisions (cf. Vedung, 1997; DAC, 2002: 22), which in principle asks the key question: 'What works and in what circumstances?' (Hart, 2007: 297). It should be performed as an analytically rigorous process aimed at isolating and determining the impact of specific public policy initiatives (Storey, 2000) by contrasting the policy outcome with a 'counter-factual' scenario.[3] An evaluation 'seeks to determine . . . the relevance, efficiency and effectiveness of an activity in terms of its objectives' including implementation and administration (Papaconstantinou and Polt, 1997: 10), that is, the results of the policy.

For policy-makers it is critical to know if the policies they have decided to implement have the intended effects and, if that is the case, which are the underlying mechanisms of the policy measures, as a support for future policy-making (Guy, 2003). Policy evaluations are necessary for policy-makers in the sense that they provide an instrument for them to determine the true nature of their policies as well as the efficiency of these policies and hence they make it possible for the policy-makers to improve them or terminate them and instead implement other policies (Batterbury, 2006). This is true for industrial policy as well as for all other policy areas.

Policy evaluations are an instrument to revise policy objectives for ongoing policies and to get ideas about how policy objectives for new policies should be formulated (Batterbury, 2006). They give information about 'best practice' policies in different contexts and information about how public funds should be allocated to optimise the societal benefits given the high opportunity costs of public funds and the limited public budgets.

Moreover, policy evaluations are important not only for future decisions by policy-makers. They are also a means for policy-makers to fulfil the requirements for accountability to the general public, the business community and different kinds of stakeholders and particularly to show the taxpayers that they are getting value for their taxes. Accountability

---

'Unfortunately while enterprise policy is widespread across developed economies there is very little evaluation of impact.' Greene and Storey (2007: 213).

[3]   It is important to observe that the results of evaluations may depend on who performs them. There are indications that evaluations sponsored by government funding departments and/or agencies delivering the policy and conducted by private sector for-profit organisations are more likely to be favourable to the policy than evaluations by independent (usually academic) researchers working on a not-for-profit basis and sponsored by parties other than those funding or delivering the policy (Curran et al., 1999).

of policy-makers, that is, politicians and public agencies, is one of the prerequisites for a democracy. This implies that they generally need to ensure that the policies that they decide on and implement are evaluated to be able to show the voters and the taxpayers that they are getting value for money and that the taxpayers' money is spent in those areas that give them the highest return on their money.

It might be important to stress here that professional policy-making not only involves *ex post* evaluations but also:

- *ex ante* evaluations, which give information about the likely impacts of different policies; and
- *process monitoring and evaluations*, which offer opportunities to make policy adaptations during policy implementation and operation.

POLICY EVALUATION – PURPOSE AND SOME GENERAL PROBLEMS

In this section, we discuss the purpose of policy evaluations together with some of the general problems that policy evaluators must handle. Policy evaluations are a critical and fundamental component of all attempts to improve public policies in any field, since there are numerous questions for which policy-makers want clear answers (Hansen, 2005): To what extent have the goals been achieved? Which impacts can be documented? Has the level of activity been satisfactory? Have there been any implementation problems? What has the performance been as a whole? Has the productivity been satisfactory? Has the effectiveness been satisfactory? Has the socio-economic profitability been satisfactory? Are the economic agents satisfied? Are the stakeholders involved satisfied? Is the quality satisfactory? What works in different contexts for different economic agents? Does the underlying policy theory hold?

Turning next to the question of which evaluation models and techniques to choose, we find that a large variety of tools are available, which differ in terms of their rationale, purpose, complexity, data requirements and underlying assumptions (Georghiou and Roessner, 2000). The existence of several evaluation models and methods raises some difficult questions for policy evaluators (Hansen, 2005). Which criteria should be used to select a proper evaluation method? How to secure the reliability and empirical validity of different evaluation methods? In the following, we will provide some hints concerning what factors must be considered to be able to answer these questions.

Unfortunately, it is no understatement to claim that the field of policy evaluation is underdeveloped. Robust evaluation methodologies need strong theoretical underpinnings. For example, Lenihan (2011, 330) makes the remark that 'Evaluation as a "science" is lacking when it comes to "theory"' and this hampers the development of new evaluation methods particularly when it concerns the evaluation of industrial policy.

The first step in any policy evaluation is to specify the objectives, that is, the goals, of the policy, since no evaluation is possible without clear and in principle measurable objectives (Storey, 2000). A problem here is that objectives are not always specified in the policy documents or that the specification is non-transparent. Thus, it is often required that the evaluator must assume or interpret what the policy objectives might be. A closely related issue is when the policy objectives will be achieved, which determines the time horizon for the policy evaluations.

It is a waste of money, time and people to carry out evaluations and report impacts if the evaluation methodology is not sophisticated enough. There are substantial risks involved here, since it seems that less sophisticated evaluation methodologies are more likely to report evidence of positive policy impacts than more sophisticated methodologies (Storey and Potter, 2007). Thus, it is important that it is professional evaluators that choose the evaluation methodology and not the policy-makers, since the choice of methodology can influence the outcome of the evaluation. Since the 1960s there has been a rich body of literature on methods and models for policy evaluation (Rossi and Freeman, 1993; Patton, 1975 and 2008). An evaluation methodology is of course critical for a proper evaluation of industrial policy. It is important here to stress that the use of sophisticated evaluation methods is dependent upon access to appropriate data.[4]

When evaluations are used to assess a public policy, the natural goal is to generate the best knowledge possible about the actual impact of the policy, which implies that it should be (1) based on relevant empirical evidence; (2) corroborated by facts; and (3) reliable, that is, using reliable methods. There are four types of empirical evidence that are required to evaluate public policies (Laurent et al., 2009):

- Factual evidence of the existence of policy effects based upon a description and verification of the actual situation before and after the policy.

---

[4] A remark one can make here is that all proper evaluations of industrial policy are dependent upon access to appropriate longitudinal data sets that are maintained over time. Snapshot evaluations are unlikely to provide insights into important policy impacts (Lenihan, 2011).

- Evidence of causality, which confirms a relationship of cause and effect between a policy input and a policy output *ceteris paribus*.
- Evidence of effectiveness, that is, evidence that the value of the policy input including administration costs is justified given the value of the output.
- Evidence of 'harmlessness', that is, evidence of an absence of serious adverse effects for economic agents outside the target population, for example small displacement effects.

It must in this connection be observed that not all types of evidence are equally reliable, and the reliability of evidence can be classified in the following order, from the greatest to the least:

1. Evidence obtained through randomised controlled trials.
2. Evidence obtained from data from representative situations for hypothesis testing and statistical validation of the robustness of the results.
3. Evidence obtained from cohort studies or controlled case studies.
4. Evidence obtained from historical or geographical comparisons.
5. The opinions of respected authorities.

However, in many evaluations several types of evidence are involved and need to be combined, which raises many questions for evaluators (Laurent and Trouvé, 2011). Extra problems emerge when information from 'treated' and 'non-treated' economic agents is collected through a survey either of a sample of the population or of the full population. In the case when a sample is used, the question always emerges as to whether the sample is representative or not. The next problem is whether there are response biases or not. When a survey concerns business firms, we may observe that there are two types of response biases: (1) larger firms are more likely to respond than smaller firms (Goffee and Scase, 1995); and (2) firms in some industries are more likely to respond than others (Curran and Blackburn, 1994).

CHALLENGES RELATED TO THE EVALUATION OF INDUSTRIAL POLICY

As with all policy evaluations there is a fundamental problem involved in identifying, measuring and evaluating the direct and indirect policy effects. This problem is worsened due to the existence of interdependencies and inter-firm and intra- and inter-industry spillovers (Tavassoli et al.,

2017). Furthermore, there certainly are positive and negative interaction effects between industrial policies and policies in other areas, such as soft and hard infrastructure policies. On top of this one must consider the influences of positive and negative external events and shocks.

The evaluation studies that exist are often characterised by various factual and methodological problems[5] as well as problems with approaches and assumptions (Chang et al., 2013). Some studies define targeted industries in terms of general characteristics without checking that these industries in practice were favoured by government policies (Chang, 1995). Other studies use the actual degree of government support to define targeted sectors but run into the problem that many important industrial policy measures, such as coordination and regulation measures, cannot by definition be captured by quantifiable indicators.

Many selective and targeted industrial policies are about externalities, linkages, coordination and structural shifts across industries (and localities) with the aim of upgrading the structure and functioning of the entire economy. Under such circumstances, it is not sufficient to evaluate industrial policies only in terms of the direct outcomes in the targeted industries and localities. The evaluation must also consider the indirect effects of industrial policies on the rest of the economy, that is, their impacts, using system-level evaluation methodologies. A genuine problem with any attempt to evaluate the effects of an individual industrial policy on economy-wide goals is that the theoretical links between the interventions in an individual project and the wider impacts on the economy and on society are difficult to establish and they tend to be rather vague. Furthermore, many types of industrial policies involve, in relative terms small, individual interventions and this makes the evaluation of the wider impacts of such policies difficult and complicated when we consider the total size of the economy. Furthermore, the individual interventions may influence each other both positively and negatively.

Another problem is that the resources spent on the different interventions might come from several governmental organisations and agencies at different spatial levels as well as from non-government organisations. These types of policy initiatives are unlikely to be 'coherent' without clear coordination and without adequate dialogue between the different policy-makers involved. In cases like this, the recommendation is to adopt a more 'realist' type of evaluation methodology (Davies et al., 2000; Pawson, 2006; Storey, 2008; Gault, 2013), which uses various indicators

---

[5] 'The conceptual difficulties involved in statistical inference in this area are so great that it is hard to see how statistical evidence could ever yield a convincing verdict' (Rodrik, 2008: v).

and tracking devices and approaches to get insights into the policy impacts. Realist approaches to policy evaluation use a combination of quantitative and qualitative evaluation techniques to generate a portfolio of evidence including outcome and impact indicators (Abreu, 2012), which in ideal cases point in the same direction. Such indicators must always be associated with a baseline value of each indicator before the policy intervention and with a target value, which is the intended value after the policy intervention at a certain point in time or at several points in time.

The evaluation questions here concern whether it is possible to identify indirect effects of industrial policy, that is, impacts, in terms of a higher capacity to generate innovative technologies, new and improved products, new and more competitive firms, structural shifts in the economy and a higher capability to compete in the world market. These impacts to the extent they are realised are over time reflected in the rate of productivity and economic growth. However, there might be a need to complement such general indicators, such as the share of knowledge-intensive as well as high-tech industries and products, and world market shares overall and for dynamic 'leading' industries and products.

In the case of industrial policy evaluations, there is a strong need to complement the traditional methodologies that concern themselves with narrowly defined economic impact metrics and measure impact solely at the level of the 'treated' firms. Evaluation methods in other policy areas might give some inspiration here. It is necessary to evaluate the effects in the short, medium and long term as well as the effects for diverse types of economic agents as well as for the economy and the society at large. Specifically, this is necessary for evaluating 'new' public policies with their focus on cooperation, collaboration and networking, involving not only several types of firms but also universities, research institutes and public agencies at national, regional and local levels.

The results-oriented public policies are generally considered as being a sensible and meaningful way to think about policy design and implementation in the field of public policy analysis. However, surprisingly few policies are results-oriented in terms of both design and implementation. Many public policy interventions have little explicitly measurable objectives integrated in their design and very few are therefore possible to monitor and evaluate properly. Many policies have multiple, sometimes competing goals as well as too many goals. Others have stated goals, such as increasing GDP, which are too far away from what the policy can achieve to be meaningful. What is needed to make monitoring and evaluation meaningful is a small number of clearly stated objectives and intended outcomes, which are close enough to the policy actions to be theoretically connected to those same actions, and which are also possible to track via the use of a number of indicators. Otherwise, it will be impossible to determine whether the observed outcomes after the policy has been implemented are actually due to the policy actions. Fortunately, there is today a growing body of literature on the requisite properties of good output and results indicators (see for example Abreu, 2012).

Storey and Potter (2007) show in a review of evaluations of SME and entrepreneur policies that most studies didn't use matching or take account of selection biases. One could add here that it is very difficult, particularly for small firms, to construct matched samples, since there is a great heterogeneity of small firms and their external conditions (Storey, 2000). They operate in all industries, markets and regions of the economy, while at the same time firms in the same industry and same locality may serve different markets (Curran and Blackburn, 1994). They are run by people of different ages and genders, with different social, educational and ethnic backgrounds, have very different aims and operate with different technologies and different labour and skill mixes (Curran, 2012). Further problems are created by the extensive churning in the small business population.

We may observe that quantitatively-based aggregated evaluations of industrial policies offer little information on how individual firms respond to the policy and thus on the internal mechanism of firms. Firms, and specifically small firms, are heterogeneous and thus the policy impact may be quite asymmetrical. The results of aggregate evaluations hide how owners/managers/entrepreneurs might change their goals and/or behaviour, the operational procedures of the firm and relations with external stakeholders due to the policy. Thus, there is a need to complement aggregate evaluations with micro-economic evaluations including qualitative components that open the black box of the firm.

INDUSTRIAL POLICY EVALUATION IN THE PRESENCE OF SPILLOVERS

In the discussion above, we assumed away any possibilities of interaction and spillover effects between economic agents in the target population and other economic agents, that is, we apply the 'Stable Unit Treatment Value Assumption' (SUTVA) (Rubin, 1986). As noted earlier, it is not uncommon for evaluations of industrial policy to focus on the policy impact among the firms in the target population without considering the potential spillovers (positive as well as negative) to non-targeted firms. This is of course not optimal, since the positive and negative externalities that may result from every industrial policy, in the form of knowledge spillovers, cross-sectional substitution and crowding-out effects, can and often will affect non-targeted incumbent firms and potential entrepreneurs both inside and outside the eligible policy areas (Neumark and Simpson, 2015).[6]

Knowledge spillovers are often seen as a positive externality but if the new knowledge leaks out too fast from the firm that generated it so that the knowledge-investment costs cannot be recouped together with certain profit for the investing firm it is a negative externality, which will induce firms not to invest in new knowledge. Cross-sectional substitution is a potentially negative externality, which occurs when targeted firms take some of the business opportunities that non-targeted firms would have exploited in the absence of the industrial policy (De Castris and Pellegrini, 2012; Tavassoli and Carbonara, 2014; Tavassoli and Jienwatcharamongkhol, 2016). Crowding-out effects are another potentially negative externality, which occurs when the activities of targeted firms crowd out non-targeted firms from the market.

Furthermore, many industrial policies, such as place-based policies, are implemented precisely with the objective of generating positive spillover effects by trying to take advantage of potential positive spatial externalities (De Castris and Pellegrini, 2012). This indicates that there is a strong need to develop and apply evaluation methods that can deal with spillover effects. Interestingly, there are rather few such evaluation methods and as a result, rather few empirical evaluation exercises (Cerqua and Pellegrini, 2017). The reason for this situation is that it is difficult empirically to disentangle the spillover effects from other confounding factors. This is troublesome since the founding rationale for several industrial policies consists in generating positive externalities.

Generally, spillover effects are difficult to detect at meso or macro levels (local, regional and national level, respectively), which implies that it is necessary to use evaluation methodologies that use firms and other economic agents as the unit of observation, which includes incumbent non-targeted firms and new start-ups. An example of an international-level spillover is the 'manufacturing renaissance' when certain manufacturing sectors are starting to return to Western countries (Tavassoli et al., 2015). Obviously, the tracing of positive and negative spillover effects involves intricate identification problems, given that the spillovers can go through

---

[6] Several scholars have noted that if a substantial amount of public money has been put in the market, a special type of spillover effects called general equilibrium effects might be engendered, which may change the relative price structure in the economy (see for example Goolsbee, 1998). However, when the monetary value of the industrial policy measures is small compared with the total public budget, the general equilibrium effects might be considered negligible (Criscuolo et al., 2012).

several different links and they can happen in a substantial period after the policy-makers started to implement a given industrial policy. Of course, evaluations should be made by an attempt to inform the policy-makers and other stakeholders about the extent of each externality, respectively the extent to which positive externalities have been taken advantage of and negative externalities have been abated. However, it is possible to single out each individual spillover/externality effect only when resorting to extremely strong assumptions (Cerqua and Pellegrini, 2017).

It is essential that evaluators recognise that industrial policy has the potential or the purpose to cause interaction and spillover effects of varying spatial extension. Today, they can base their evaluations on a rich body of literature on the importance and character of social interactions, networking, peer effects, spillovers and other externalities that has emerged in recent decades (Manski, 1993; Karlsson et al., 2005; Tavassoli and Carbonara, 2014). In a situation where target economic agents may interact directly or indirectly with non-target economic agents or where the policy measures are designed to facilitate interaction between targeted and non-targeted economic agents, it is no longer possible to measure the policy effect by comparing the outcome for the targeted group with a control group, that is, the SUTVA principle doesn't apply (Baum-Snow and Ferreira, 2015). If industrial policy incentives are effective in generating spatial externalities and spatial spillovers, they should be possible to measure empirically by the presence of a positive spatial correlation in some outcome variables, such as productivity, growth or employment (De Castris and Pellegrini, 2012).

A LOGIC CAUSE-AND-EFFECT EVALUATION MODEL

Policy evaluations are basically focused on the additionality, that is, net positive outcomes (desired outcomes or even unanticipated outcomes), of one specific policy measure (Bellandi and Caloffi, 2010). In other words, the additionality is a measure of how much of the observed output can be attributed to the policy intervention beyond any doubt. One could think that it should be relatively easy to measure the additionality using before-and-after evaluation designs. However, in practice it is quite difficult as the *ceteris paribus* condition is not fulfilled (Curran, 2012). Normally, industrial policy measures operate over at least several months and often much longer. This implies that there is a very high probability that the external context may change both marginally and structurally over the life of the policy measure. These changes will, with a high probability, influence the behaviour and performance of both 'treated' and 'non-treated' economic agents, which will tend to bias the measurement of the additionality of the actual policy.

We can think of an industrial policy as a planned and organised action to reduce or eliminate economy-wide, regional or local economic and/or societal problems. For simple and single industrial policy interventions it is easy to imagine a logic cause-and-effect evaluation model that runs from goals via inputs, activities, results/outputs and outcome to impact (cf. Wren, 2007).

- The *goals* for an industrial policy specify (1) the intended changes in the results/output indicators among the target group for the policy and represent a situation or conditions for the economic agents in the target population that policy-makers and preferably all stakeholders involved consider desirable to achieve at different points in time; and (2) the desired economy-wide impacts of the policy.
- The *inputs* stand for the resources – public as well as private – mobilised through the policy intervention and include budgets, staff, equipment, technologies, partners and so on. The value of these resources can be measured either in terms of financial costs or in terms of opportunity costs.
- The resources allocated to the specific policy are used to initiate *activities*, which might include various actions, processes, networking, cooperation, collaboration, facilitation, funding, events, provision, delivery, re-organisations, initiatives to new organisations and so on.
- The purpose of these activities that generate *results/outputs*, that is, services, information, knowledge, training, education, skills, capabilities, changes in incentives and so on – an additionality – through a process that can be viewed as a production process. Such production processes might be quite complex and the activities, sub-processes and mechanisms might vary between different recipients of the policy intervention and are often treated as a black box.
- These results/outputs are what induce the policy *outcomes*, which represent the direct short- and medium-term effects on the target population in the form of changes in attitudes and/or behaviour, increases of investments in personnel, R&D, innovation, production processes, marketing, exports and/or organisation, increased firm growth, increased new firm formation/entrepreneurship and so on.
- *Impacts* represents the medium- and long-term economy-wide and societal effects of the policy outcomes in terms of increased productivity, employment, economic growth, increased welfare and so on, as well as on sustainability and equity.

The results/output and impact indicators reflect the policy goals, which indicates what the policy-makers intend to achieve, change, influence and/ or facilitate. These indicators are normally metrics with a clear measurement unit, but they can and possibly should be supported by qualitative indicators. Unfortunately, it is often the case that goals and outcome or results indicators are not clearly stated and defined in measurable terms. Often too many goals are specified and it is not unusual for the goals to conflict with each other. Sometimes the goals are specified at such an aggregated level – take GDP growth as an example – that the effects of individual industrial policies or policy mixes are not discernible. Another problem concerns which time perspective to choose for evaluations, since the effects of industrial policies might come with considerable lags – lags that vary for different industrial policies.

The most robust and sophisticated monitoring and evaluation systems which provide most insights are those which incorporate and integrate quantitative and qualitative evaluation methodologies which are intended to complement each other and to respond to different issues and needs. Quantitative indicators are what permit *ex post* and counter-factual type evaluation approaches (Scarpa, 2012), while qualitative and case study techniques allow for a detailed understanding of how the expected links between policy measures and indicators function (Vanclay, 2012).

Quantitative evaluation methodologies have advantages and disadvantages depending upon the specific evaluation situation. They can under the right circumstances provide rather clear answers concerning actual policy results/outcomes and indications about potential policy impacts and they can be independently verified. On the other hand, (1) they are associated with high costs related to data collection; (2) they are demanding econometrically; (3) they don't provide information about context and the mechanisms behind the policy impact; (4) they might give a false impression about precision; (5) they have a narrow focus on effectiveness and efficiency; (6) they are difficult to use for industrial policies that use indirect interventions to influence the business environment and cooperation among economic agents; and (7) they struggle with the 'control group problem'.

In an analogous manner, qualitative evaluation methodologies have their advantages and disadvantages. Their advantages are that (1) they allow for engaging participants and stakeholders in the policy learning process; (2) they can assess a wide range of evaluation criteria; (3) they offer a deeper understanding of the processes and mechanisms leading to results/outcomes and impacts; and (4) they allow the pick-up of unintended consequences. However, qualitative evaluation methods also have clear disadvantages in the sense that (1) they may use respondents and interviewers who are biased or poorly informed; (2) they rarely provide clear answers; (3) they tend to 'describe' rather than 'evaluate'; (4) they carry the risk of including 'unrepresentative' groups; and (5) they have difficulties in judging effectiveness and efficiency and in establishing a cause-and-effect relationship.

A critical evaluation problem is that it is difficult to be sure that the whole output can be attributed to the policy intervention. Thus, a key question involves the extent to which the observed positive outcomes can be attributed reliably to the policy evaluated (Lenihan, 2004). Of course, we must acknowledge that observed positive outcomes might have materialised fully or partly without any policy initiative. To imagine what output might have resulted in the absence of policy intervention, a counterfactual production process is designed that produces a counterfactual output. This counterfactual output is known as the deadweight of a policy intervention. The size of the deadweight is estimated by comparing the actual policy outcome with the outcome in a counterfactual scenario with no policy intervention to try to solve the identified problem. However, the deadweight is difficult to measure as it is extremely difficult to establish a counterfactual scenario. What is often done as an alternative is to ask owners/managers/entrepreneurs what they would have done in the absence of the actual policy measure, which is always problematic.

The difference between the actual output and the counterfactual output is the outcome of the policy intervention. The outcome is the short-run direct market effect of the policy intervention that over time might generate an impact, that is, a long-run effect on the wider economy, through external effects, which include:

1. Displacement effects, that is, displacement of other activities in output and input markets in the economy due to the policy intervention.
2. Linkage effects, that is, effects in other markets via backward and forward linkages generated by the price mechanism.
3. Feedback effects, that is, long-run effects in the actual market due to linkage effects and possibly broader macroeconomic feedback effects.
4. Multiplier effects, that is, effects in future periods due to the extra income generated by the policy initiative.

Evaluations must also consider to what extent displacements are taking place. An example of a displacement effect is when 'treated' firms take market share from 'non-treated' firms, that is, crowd-out 'non-treated' firms. Thus, displacement is the degree to which increased output or value-added from or employment in 'treated' firms displaces output, value-added or employment in 'non-treated' firms in the market place (Lenihan et al.,

2005) and can hence be looked upon as a negative external policy effect. In a similar manner, we can talk about displacement from a spatial point of view when output or employment in 'treated' localities or regions displace output or employment in 'non-treated' localities or regions (Tervo, 1990). In fact, displacement is very difficult to estimate mainly because it can take so many forms (Curran, 2012). A proper evaluation demands a careful analysis of all firms (regions) of being affected directly or indirectly by the industrial policy that is evaluated, which in practice is extremely difficult. Many evaluations do estimate displacement, but most estimates are unfortunately guesses or are expressed as minimum/maximum values.[7]

The difficulties of evaluating industrial policies do not stop with the problems connected with getting to grips with systemic policy effects, such as displacement and linkage effects. Another type of evaluation problem is that the evaluation methodology must account for the long-run effects due to the cumulative dynamics in the economy. Accordingly, it is not enough to account for the existence of time lags, qualitative transformations, discontinuities, truncations and reversals. It is also necessary to explicitly consider the question of the relevant time scale, that is, the time required to reach the intended impacts on the overall economy (Andreoni, 2011).

Having stated the reasons for using a substantial number of evaluation metrics, we now come to the question of whether it is possible to develop a logic model in this case that depicts the 'assumptions about the resources to support program activities and produce outputs, and the activities and outputs needed to realize the intended outcomes of a program' (Cooksy et al., 2001: 119). Logic models provide a multi-dimensional guide as to what should be assessed and measured (Storey and Potter, 2007). They aid policy planning *ex ante*, implementation, process evaluation and impact evaluation *ex post*. They can incorporate effects on multi-level layers based upon a potential chain of cause and effect and can potentially also evaluate the effects on the wider economy and even society at large. However, they have problems handling positive and negative externalities induced by the policy interventions (Lenihan, 2011). Nevertheless, the framework of a logic model has the potential to help policy-makers understand the linkages between problems/conditions, activities, outcomes and impacts of a policy (Lynch et al., 2009).

Well-designed logic models identify external effects occurring elsewhere in input and output markets, linkage effects, long-run feedback effects

---

[7] To the extent that the effects for the wider economy are marginal, the impacts for the wider economy can be evaluated by means of cost–benefit analysis. If, however, the effects are not marginal the effects for the wider economy must be evaluated by means of a general equilibrium approach.

and multiplier effects, that is, the interactions between economic agents and the external economic environment (Wren, 2007). They can also be used to compare the actual operation of policies with an ideal situation. Logic models offer some key advantages (Goldman and Schmaltz, 2006) since they (1) have the power of visual communication; (2) put policy elements into context; (3) allow observations of critical policy processes and outcomes within a dynamic framework; (4) offer a framework for interpreting information; (5) facilitate comparisons between the 'real' and an 'ideal' policy; and (6) help making stakeholders and actors responsible for processes and outcomes by aiding the classification of options for setting priorities and supporting the effective allocation of resources.

However, establishing a causal relationship between the policy measures and the outcomes for the policy variables is not enough to claim that a certain industrial policy is successful. A complete evaluation of an industrial policy must also consider:

1. Appropriateness that concerns the importance of the policy problem in focus and its relative priority, that is, whether the actual industrial policy has focused on an essential problem for society.
2. Adequacy that concerns how much of the actual problem the industrial policy in question is supposed to handle, that is, how much of the total problem has been dealt with.
3. Effectiveness that concerns to what extent the stated goals are achieved because of the policy activities.
4. Efficiency that concerns the resource costs to achieve the policy outcome.
5. Productivity that concerns the relationship between the policy outcomes and the resources used.

And finally, there is a need for an *ex post* cost–benefit analysis to determine whether society is better off after a certain industrial policy has been implemented.

AN IDEAL INDUSTRIAL POLICY CIRCLE

Here and in the next section, we will sketch an ideal industrial policy circle with integrated policy evaluation to get a general framework for discussing the evaluation and monitoring of industrial policies. In such an ideal world, all industrial policies have a sunset clause after which they are wound down, unless they show clear positive results based on rigorous evaluation exercises. That would be a significant step from the existing system whereby resources are assigned once and, in effect, retained indefinitely with little regard for results or alternative priorities.

Results-oriented industrial policies require monitoring and evaluations to be an integrated part of the policy process. Evaluation should here be understood as a process and should never only be undertaken as an *ex post* accounting exercise to determine whether the public resources have been spent wisely or not. Results-oriented indicators are required both for the *ex ante* and *ex post* evaluations of the intended and the realised policy impacts, respectively. At the same time monitoring and process evaluations are required for the implementation process and the ongoing steering of the policy to allow for feedbacks and learning during the implementation process. Monitoring tracks the implementation and progress of a policy intervention with the goal of supporting the programme administration. Evaluation and monitoring assesses the theoretical policy foundations, the policy design and planning process, the policy implementation, and the results of the intervention to support decisions about program continuation, program change or program termination (Hempel and Fiala, 2011).

Thus, monitoring and evaluation exercises are critical parts of results-/outcome-oriented industrial policies and the reason they are so essential is that such policies demand an explicit theory of expected effects that links the policy goals with the policy interventions that in each case are specified *ex ante*. The articulation of such a theory *ex ante* makes a difference compared to a pure political logic to policy design and instead establishes outcome-/results-based criteria for policy design and implementation. With such an approach, industrial policies will be designed to a great extent according to what effects they have on the behaviour of economic agents rather than on any political logic governed by the distribution of political rents. For this to function, there must exist *ex ante* a logical and well-motivated set of expected links between each policy action and the behavioural responses among the economic actors directly or indirectly affected by the policy action. A theory of expected policy effects is fundamental because the development of results-/outcome-oriented policies and the pertinent use of results-/outcome-indicators and the associated monitoring and evaluation activities cannot be applied without a well-defined and clearly articulated theory of expected effects, which makes up the underlying motivation not only for the specific policy as such but also for each of its policy interventions. Furthermore, unless there is a well-articulated theory of expected effects it will not be possible to reach an agreement between the stakeholders involved regarding the preferred policy and its pertinent priorities (Stiglitz et al., 2010).

It is important to stress here that no theory of expected effects supporting an industrial policy can be 100 per cent flawless because our theoretical and empirical knowledge about what works under what circumstances is limited. Furthermore, all industrial policies are implemented in a context characterised by risk and uncertainty and this applies particularly for new industrial policies, which have never been applied in any context and thus never tried, tested, adjusted and evaluated. This concerns industrial policies focusing innovation and entrepreneurship – phenomena related to newness and novelty (Gordon and McCann, 2005). However, this certainly doesn't imply that industrial policy operates in a knowledge vacuum, since the theory of expected effects underlying the policy logic is derived both from a higher-level aggregate theoretical and empirical framework[8] and from experience of recent micro-economic analytical evidence and empirical examples of similar or the same industrial policies elsewhere. There are examples of specific industrial policy initiatives that have their basis in some previous pilot projects which have generated evidence that justifies the current policy approach. However, most new industrial policy initiatives take place in a context characterised by a certain degree of *ex ante* risk and uncertainty, which requires experimentation and 'self-discovery' (Hausmann and Rodrik, 2003) to understand what works in each specific context. This implies that part of the theory of expected effects supporting the logic behind the industrial policy is something that must be experienced as a learning-by-doing phenomenon rather than something that is entirely constructed *ex ante*.

We must here observe that the approach to new industrial policy initiatives discussed here in many respects works in a methodological direction that is the opposite of traditional formal economic models. Formal economic models are typically deducing hypotheses in a top-down manner using an analytical framework – hypotheses that are tested econometrically *ex post* using the appropriate datasets. This approach is not useable for designing new industrial policies, since it requires that a well-specified model can be constructed *ex ante* and the data already exist on which the model can be tested. However, in the case of new industrial policy initiatives, the data on which to perform an *ex ante* analysis typically don't exist in advance and can only be collected at some point in the future. The reality is that new industrial policy initiatives tend to be based on partial, indirectly related or incomplete data. The reason is that such

---

[8] In the economics literature, we find general theoretical models, which demonstrate the critical role of innovation and entrepreneurship for aggregate economic growth (Aghion and Howitt, 1998), as well as econometric models, which demonstrate how innovation proceeds via a series of linkages between stages (Crépon et al., 1998). However, these models and econometric results are at a level of aggregation and generality, which prevents them from providing specific guidance concerning what to do in any particular context or case (Hughes, 2012).

industrial policies tend to be focused on new policy arenas or apply new policy concepts to established policy arenas. This implies that no suitable dataset exists in advance on which all aspects of the new policy design and implementation can be tested.

The result of the state of the art is that the process of designing new industrial policy initiatives tends to move in a much more inductive manner that relies on applying monitoring and evaluation on available data with their limitations together with bottom-up observations and collection of experiences. This represents a realist type of perspective (Davies et al., 2000; Pawson, 2006) rather than a pure logical positivist perspective including a well-specified analytical model *ex ante*. Thus, this approach advances in a more iterative manner collecting knowledge, experiences and evidence as they arise. However, this also implies that new data must be collected during the life of the industrial policy to make *ex post* evaluations possible and that the data collected must be relevant for testing if the expected effects assumed by the theory of expected effects are realised. This type of data generation process reflects more of a bottom-up inductive approach rather than a top-down deductive approach. Key issues to be evaluated include relevance, effectiveness and efficiency of the industrial policy and the potential to improve it. Thus, we understand that to decide on priorities for industrial policy initiatives, it is necessary to perform a detailed analysis of the current economic and industrial structure and trends based on the best available current evidence for the actual policy level (national, regional and/or local), which can provide the necessary baseline indicators for policy evaluation.

AN INDUSTRIAL POLICY LIFE-CYCLE MODEL

Based upon the discussion above, we can now sketch a policy life-cycle model (cf. Hogwood, 1987) for an optimal industrial policy process as follows. It is also summarised in Figure 7.1.

1. A clear description of the *policy problem*, that is, the gap between the actual and a desired situation, and its character and causes based upon a detailed analysis and a presentation of baseline indicators.
2. The formulation of one (or a few) clear, specific and measurable *goal(s)* concerning the effects of the industrial policy at (1) the micro-level, that is, among the economic agents in the target population (and for policies focusing on externalities and spillovers also among other economic agents); (2) the meso-level in terms of the

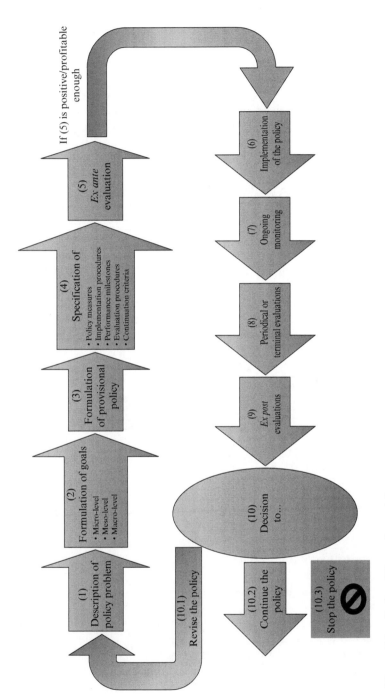

Figure 7.1   Policy life-cycle model

functioning of clusters, regional innovation systems and so on; and (3) at the macro-level, that is, impacts in terms of productivity, employment and GDP. Preferably, it (they) is (are) expressed as the intended changes of results/outcome indicators with theoretical links to intended economy-wide impacts. Goals must be specific, measurable, achievable/attainable, relevant and time-bound. This is necessary to make *ex ante* and *ex post* evaluations possible. Evaluation can only be performed in policy frameworks where the intended results/outcomes and impacts are specified. The results/outcome and impact indicators, which normally will contain both 'level' and 'change' indicators, must be chosen by the policy-making authorities in such a way that they best capture the behavioural changes, which are intended to be engendered by the policy interventions.

3. The formulation of a logic *provisional policy model* that clarifies/ presents (1) the hypotheses, that is, policy assumptions, concerning the relationship and mechanisms between possible policy measures, that is, the activities, and the goal(s) concerning the results/outcome indicators and the economy-wide impacts; (2) the risks that the goals will not be attained; and (3) the design of theory-based monitoring and evaluation activities that are planned. Considerations of how the policy shall be evaluated must be incorporated into the formulation of the policy model. This implies that different types of indicators including baseline indicators that can link the logic of the intervention to the monitoring and evaluation activities must be identified. The indicators needed include input/resource indicators, process/ activity indicators and performance indicators in the form of output indicators, results/outcome indicators and impact indicators (cf. Arthurs et al., 2009).

4. A specification of (1) the *policy measures* in terms of resources, activities and costs to be used to achieve the policy goals; (2) the pertinent *implementation procedures*; (3) the performance targets and milestones for inputs/resources, activities, outputs, results/outcomes and impacts; (4) the subsequent monitoring and evaluation procedures that will be applied over the lifetime of the policy intervention; and (5) the criteria for the continuation of the policy at prespecified dates in the future if the policy initiatives do not have a termination date. At this stage, it must also be specified what share of the costs should be used for monitoring and evaluations. To guarantee that enough resources are allocated for this purpose, it is preferable that a minimum percentage is mandatory and that a higher percentage is allocated for industrial policies where monitoring and evaluation is more complicated.

5. An *ex ante evaluation* preferably combined with an *ex ante* cost–benefit analysis. *Ex ante* evaluation is fundamental to assess whether the proposed interventions and the related implementation processes are relevant and coherent and whether the expected results/outcomes and impacts are realistic. It is also important as a test of the indicators and procedures designed for subsequent monitoring and evaluation. *Ex ante* evaluations give policy-makers an opportunity to get insights about and reflect on the expected range of results/outcomes at various stages in the policy implementation but also on how the results/outcomes might change if some of the policy parameters are changed.[9] They help policy-makers to ensure that they invest in policies where the expected return on the investment is greatest. *Ex ante* evaluations can also support the design of policies that achieve the specified goals at the lowest cost, or that maximise the impacts at a given cost (Todd and Wolpin, 2008).

6. *Policy decision and implementation* given that the *ex ante* evaluation is positive/profitable enough from a societal point of view.

7. Ongoing *monitoring and process evaluation* is used to observe the ongoing behaviour of the public agencies responsible for implementing the policy and the economic agents in the target population as well as the results/output indicators to provide valuable inputs for the management of the ongoing policy intervention to assess how the policy is progressing over time. The purpose of monitoring and process evaluation is to help the public agencies responsible to manage the intervention and to ensure that there is an early warning system if targets, milestones and goals are not going to be met.

8. *Periodical and terminal evaluations*, respectively, occur at certain predetermined times in the life of a policy or immediately after the closure of a policy and ensure there is an institutional memory and that all relevant data and qualitative information from those directly involved in the implementation are preserved. Periodical evaluations give policy-makers an understanding of immediate next steps, particularly when quick decisions are needed on the continuation or closure of policies.

9. *Ex post evaluation* is the activity by which the results/outcomes and impacts are assessed and is preferably combined with an *ex post* cost–benefit analysis. It takes place after implementation is complete or after an appropriate operational period and when end results/outcomes and impacts are known or can be estimated. *Ex*

---

[9] Roper et al. (2004).

post evaluation gives information on the effects of specific measures and whether the activities delivered the expected results effectively and efficiently. It typically uses a combination of a realist perspective alongside an *ex post* counterfactual analysis based on logical positivist principles. It is used to deliver accountability to stakeholders and the general public and is used to design future interventions based on concrete empirical knowledge of what has worked and what has not.

10. *Decision by policy-makers whether to revise the policy (10.1), continue the policy (10.2), or stop the policy (10.3),* where the evaluation results are used as an input in the policy revision.

Of course, what is critical here is that the industrial policies are results-oriented, which among other things implies that the policy goals, the logic of intervention, the theory of expected effects, the design of the policy, results/outcome and impact indicators and the databases constructed for monitoring and evaluation are employed during the whole policy circle and are all treated as closely interrelated issues which cannot be divorced from each other. However, there is no 'one-size-fits-all' blueprint or template for the design and evaluation of results-oriented industrial policies. On the contrary, the results orientation and the policy monitoring and evaluation aspects must be built into every policy design right from the beginning. Hence, adopting a results-oriented approach to industrial policy-making imposes analytical discipline on all aspects of the policy process as well as a need for engagements among and preferably agreements with economic agents in the target population and/or organisations representing them and other stakeholders involved with intentions, analysis and expectations as a foundation. This implies that applying a purely political logic to the industrial policy process doesn't work. A clarity in terms of intentions, analysis and expectations in the industrial policy process facilitates policy transparency and accountability with an associated openness to measurement, monitoring and evaluation. Such an approach makes it possible to develop a culture of policy learning and improvements of institutions (Sedlacko and Martinuzzi, 2012).

CONCLUDING REMARKS

The purpose of this chapter was to carry out a survey of the problems involved in policy evaluation in general and specifically in the evaluation of industrial policies and to sketch the role of policy monitoring and evaluation in an industrial policy life-cycle model. We claim that the application of such a model would help improve the industrial policy process and make industrial policy more results-oriented, guarantee an evaluation culture and increase the potential for policy learning.

REFERENCES

Abreu, M. (2012), Good Practices in the Selection and Use of Outcome Indicators, accessed 16 October 2018 at http://citeseerx.ist.psu.edu/viewdoc/download?doi=10.1.1.593.65&rep=rep1&type=pdf.

Acemoglu, D. and J.A. Robinson (2013), *Why Nations Fail: The Origins of Power, Prosperity, and Poverty*, New York: Crown Business.

Ades, A. and R. di Tella (1997), National Champions and Corruption: Some Unpleasant Interventionist Arithmetic, *Economic Journal* **107**, 1023–42.

Aghion, P. and P. Howitt (1998), *Endogenous Growth Theory*, Cambridge, MA: MIT Press.

Allen, C., D. Herbert and G. Koopman (2006), The European Commission's New Industrial Policy, *EIB Papers No. 12/2006*, European Investment Bank, Luxembourg.

Andreoni, A. (2011), Productive Capabilities Indicators for Industrial Policy Design, *UNIDO Working Paper 17*, United Nations Industrial Development Organisation, Vienna.

Arthurs, D., E. Cassidy, C.H. Davis and D. Wolfe (2009), Indicators to Support Innovation Cluster Policy, *International Journal of Technology Management* **45**, 263–79.

Batterbury, S.C.E. (2006), Principles and Purposes of European Union Cohesion Policy Evaluation, *Regional Studies* **40**, 225–36.

Baum-Snow, N. and F. Ferreira (2015), Causal Inference in Urban and Regional Economics, in G. Durnaton, V. Henderson and W. Strange (eds), *Handbook of Urban and Regional Economics 5*, Amsterdam: Elsevier, pp. 3–68.

Bellandi, M. and A. Caloffi (2010), An Analysis of Regional Policies Promoting Networks of Innovation, *European Planning Studies* **18**, 67–82.

Cerqua, A. and G. Pellegrini (2017), Industrial Policy Evaluation in the Presence of Spillovers, *Small Business Economics* **49**, 671–86.

Chang, H-J. (1995), Explaining 'Flexible Rigidities' in East Asia, in T. Killick (ed.), *The Flexible Economy: Causes and Consequences of the Adaptability of National Economies*, London: Routledge, pp. 199–224.

Chang, H.J., A. Andreoni and M.L. Kuan (2013), *International Industrial Policy Experiences and the Lessons for the UK*, Future of Manufacturing Project: Evidence Paper 4, Foresight, Government Office for Science, London.

Chimoli, M., G. Dosi and J.E. Stiglitz (2009), *Industrial Policy and Development*, Oxford: Oxford University Press.

Cooksy, L.J., P. Gill and P.A. Kelly (2001), The Program Logic Model as an Integrative Framework for Multimethod Evaluation, *Evaluation and Program Planning* **24**, 119–28.

Crépon, B., E. Duguet and J. Mairesse (1998), Research Innovation and Productivity, An Econometric Analysis at the Firm Level, *Economics of Innovation and New Technology* **7**, 115–56.

Criscuolo, C., R. Martin, H. Overman and J. van Reenan (2012), The Causal Effects of an Industrial Policy, *NBER Working Paper 17842*, National Bureau of Economic Research, Cambridge, MA.

Curran, J. (2012), What is Small Business Policy in the UK for? Evaluating and Assessing Small Business Policies, *International Small Business Journal* **18**, 36–50.

Curran, J. and R.A. Blackburn (1994), *Small Firms and Local Economic Networks. The Death of the Local Economy?* London: Paul Chapman.

Curran, J., R. Berney and J. Kuusisto (1999), *A Critical Evaluation of Industry SME Support Policies in the United Kingdom and the Republic of Ireland – An Introduction to SME Support Policies and Their Evaluation*, Ministry of Trade and Industry, Helsinki.

DAC (2002), *Glossary of Key Terms in Evaluation and Results-Based Management*, Working Party on Aid Evaluation, Development Assistance Committee, OECD, Paris.

Davies, H.T.O., S.M. Nutley and P.C. Smith (2000), *What Works? Evidence-Based Policy in Public Services*, Bristol: Polity Press.

De Castris, M. and G. Pellegrini (2012), Evaluation of Spatial Effects of Capital Subsidies in the South of Italy, *Regional Studies* **46**, 525–38.

Gault, F. (ed.) (2013), *Handbook of Innovation Indicators and Measurement*, Cheltenham, UK and Northampton, MA, USA: Edward Elgar Publishing.

Georghiou, L. and D. Roessner (2000), Evaluating Technology Programs: Tools and Methods, *Research Policy* **29**, 657–78.

Goffee, R. and R. Scase (1995), *Corporate Realities. The Dynamics of Large and Small Organizations*, London: Routledge.

Goldman, K.D. and K.J. Schmaltz (2006), Logic Models: The Picture Worth Ten Thousand Words, *Health Promotion Practice Published* **7**, 8–12.

Goolsbee, A. (1998), Investment Tax Incentives, Prices, and the Supply of Capital Goods, *Quarterly Journal of Economics* **113**, 121–48.

Gordon, I.R. and P. McCann (2005), Innovation, Agglomeration and Regional Development, *Journal of Economic Geography* **5**, 523–43.

Greene, F.J. and D.J. Storey (2007), Issues in Evaluation: The Case of Shell Livewire, in D.B Audretsch, I. Grilo and A.R. Thurik (eds), *The Handbook of Research on Entrepreneurship Policy*, Cheltenham, UK and Northampton, MA, USA: Edward Elgar Publishing, pp. 213–33.

Guy, K. (2003), Assessing RTD Program Portfolios in the European Union, in P. Shapira and S. Kuhlmann (eds), *Learning from Science and Technology Policy Evaluation: Experiences from the United States and Europe*, Cheltenham, UK and Northampton, MA, USA: Edward Elgar Publishing, pp. 174–203.

Hansen, H.F. (2005), Choosing Evaluation Models. A Discussion of Evaluation Design, *Evaluation* **11**, 447–62.

Hart, M. (2007), Evaluating EU Regional Policy: How Might We Understand the Causal Connections between Interventions and Outcomes More Effectively?, *Policy Studies* **28**, 295–308.

Hausmann, R. and D. Rodrik (2003), Economic Development as Self-Discovery, *Journal of Development Economics* **72**, 603–33.

Hempel, K. and N. Fiala (2011), *Measuring Success of Youth Likelihood Interventions: A Practical Guide to Monitoring and Evaluation*, Global Partnership for Youth Employment, Washington, DC.

Hogwood, B. (1987), *From Crisis to Complacency: Shaping Public Policy in Britain*, Oxford: Oxford University Press.

Hughes, A. (2012), Choosing Races and Placing Bets: UK National Innovation Policy and the Globalisation of Innovation Systems, in D. Greenaway (ed.), *The UK in a Global World. How Can the UK Focus on Steps in Global Value Chains that Really Add Value?*, Centre for Economic Policy Research, London, pp. 37–70.

Karlsson, C., U. Gråsjö and S. Wixe (eds) (2015), *Innovation and Entrepreneurship in the Global Economy: Knowledge, Technology and Internationalization*, Cheltenham, UK and Northampton, MA, USA: Edward Elgar Publishing.

Karlsson, C., B. Johansson and R.R. Stough (2005), Industrial Clusters and Inter-Firm Networks, in C. Karlsson, B. Johansson and R.R. Stough (eds), *Industrial Clusters and Inter-Firm Networks*, Cheltenham, UK and Northampton, MA, USA: Edward Elgar Publishing, pp. 1–25.

Karlsson, C., B. Johansson and R.R. Stough (2012), *The Regional Economics of Knowledge and Talent: Local Advantage in a Global Context*, Cheltenham, UK and Northampton, MA, USA: Edward Elgar Publishing.

Krueger, A.O. (1990), Government Failures in Development, *Journal of Economic Perspectives* **4**, 9–23.

Laurent, C. and A. Trouvé (2011), Competition of Evidences and the Emergence of the 'Evidence-Based' or 'Evidence-Aware' Policies in Agriculture, Paper presented at the 122nd EAAE Seminar 'Evidence-Based Agricultural and Rural Policy Making: Methodological and Empirical Challenges of Policy Evaluation', Ancona, 17–18 February.

Laurent, C., J. Baudry, M. Berriet-Solliec, M. Kirsch, D. Perraud, B. Tinel, A. Trouvé et al. (2009), Pourquoi s'intéresser à la notion d'Evidence-based Policy?, *Revue Tiers-monde* **200**, 853–73.

Lenihan, H. (1999), An Evaluation of a Regional Development Agency's Grants in Terms of Deadweight and Displacement, *Environment and Planning C* **17**, 303–18.

Lenihan, H. (2004), Evaluating Irish Industrial Policy in terms of Deadweight and Displacement: A Quantitative Methodological Approach, *Applied Economics* **36**, 229–52.

Lenihan, H. (2011), Enterprise Policy Evaluation: Is There a 'New' Way of Doing It?, *Evaluation and Program Planning* **34**, 323–32.

Lenihan, H., M. Hart and S. Roper (2005), Developing an Evaluative Framework for Industrial Policy in Ireland: Fulfilling the Audit Trail or an Aid to Policy Development?, *ESRI Quarterly Commentary*, Summer, pp. 69–86.

Lin, J. (2012), *New Structural Economics: A Framework for Rethinking Development and Policy*, Washington, DC: World Bank.

Lynch, N., H. Lenihan and M. Hart (2009), Developing a Framework to Evaluate Business Networks: The Case of Ireland's Industry-Led Network Initiative, *Policy Studies* **30**, 163–80.

Manski, C. (1993), Identification of Endogenous Social Effects: The Reflection Problem, *The Review of Economic Studies* **60**, 531–2.

Naudé, W.A. (2010), Industrial Policy: Old and New, *UNU-WIDER Working Paper 106*, Helsinki.

Neumark, D. and H. Simpson (2015), Place-Based Policies, in G. Duranton, V. Henderson and W. Strange (eds), *Handbook of Urban and Regional Economics 5*, Amsterdam: Elsevier, pp. 1197–287.

OECD (2012), Beyond Industrial Policy – Emerging Issues and Trends, *Draft STI Working Paper on Industrial Policy DSTI/IND (2012)19*, OECD, Paris.

OECD (2013), *Perspectives on Global Development 2013 – Shifting Up the Gear: Industrial Policies in a Changing Economic Landscape*, Paris: OECD.

Pack, H. and K. Saggi (2006), Is There a Case for Industrial Policy? A Critical Survey, *World Bank Research Observer* **21**, 267–97.

Papaconstantinou, G. and W. Polt (1997), Policy Evaluation in Innovation and Technology: An Overview, in OECD (ed.), *Policy Evaluation in Innovation and Technology: Towards Best Practices*, Paris: OECD, pp. 9–14.

Patton, M.Q. (ed.) (1975), *Alternative Evaluation Research Paradigms*, Grand Forks, ND: University of North Dakota Press.

Patton, M.Q. (2008), *Utilization-Focused Evaluation*, 4th edn, London: Sage Publications.

Pawson, R. (2006), *Evidence-Based Policy: A Realist Perspective*, London: Sage Publications.

Rodrik, D. (2004), Industrial Policy for the Twenty-First Century, *CEPR Discussion Paper No. 4767*, Centre for Economic Policy Research, London.

Rodrik, D. (2008), Normalizing Industrial Policy, *Working Paper No. 3*, Commission on Growth and Development, The International Bank for Reconstruction and Development/The World Bank.

Rodrik, D. (2014), When Ideas Trump Interests: Preferences, Worldviews, and Policy Innovations, *Journal of Economic Perspectives* **28**, 189–208.

Roper, S., N. Hewitt-Dundas and J.H. Love (2004), An Ex Ante Evaluation Framework for the Regional Benefits of Publicly Supported R&D Projects, *Research Policy* **33**, 487–509.

Rossi, P.H. and H.E. Freeman (eds) (1993), *H.E. Evaluation: A Systematic Approach*, 5th edn, Newbury Park, CA: Sage Publications.

Rubin, D.B. (1986), Comment: Which Ifs Have Causal Answers, *Journal of the American Statistical Association* **81**, 961–62.

Scarpa, D. (2012), *Guidance for the Design of Quantitative Survey-Based Evaluation*, accessed 16 October 2018 at https://pdfs.semanticscholar.org/b3e9/8c5319e9c51dcd5db5d23266a6c2337b4de6.pdf.

Sedlacko, M. and A. Martinuzzi (2012), *Governance by Evaluation for Sustainable Development: Institutional Capacities and Learning*, Cheltenham, UK and Northampton, MA, USA: Edward Elgar Publishing.

Stiglitz, J.E., A. Sen and J-P. Fitoussi (2010), *Report by the Commission on the Measurement of Economic and Social Progress*, accessed 16 October 2018 at http://www.voced.edu.au/content/ngv:44133.

Storey, D.J. (2000), Six Steps to Heaven: Evaluating the Impact of Public Policies to Support Small Businesses in Developed Countries, in D.L. Sexton and H. Landström (eds), *The Blackwell Handbook of Entrepreneurship*, Oxford: Blackwell, pp. 176–93.

Storey, D.J. (2008), Entrepreneurship and SME Policy, *World Entrepreneurship Forum*, 2008 edn.

Storey, D.J. and J. Potter (2007), *OECD Framework for the Evaluation of SME and Entrepreneurship Policies and Programmes*, Paris: OECD.

Tavassoli, S. and N. Carbonara (2014), The Role of Knowledge Variety and Intensity for Regional Innovation. *Small Business Economics* **43**(2), 493–509.

Tavassoli, S. and V. Jienwatcharamongkhol (2016). Survival of Entrepreneurial Firms: The Role of Agglomeration Externalities. *Entrepreneurship & Regional Development* **28**(9–10), 746–67.

Tavassoli, S., L. Bengtsson and C. Karlsson (2017), Strategic Entrepreneurship and Knowledge Spillovers: Spatial and Aspatial Perspectives. *International Entrepreneurship and Management Journal* **13**(1), 233–49.

Tavassoli, S., B. Kianian and T.C. Larsson (2015), Manufacturing Renaissance: Return of Manufacturing to Western Countries, in C. Karlsson, U. Gråsjö and S. Wixe (eds), *Innovation and Entrepreneurship in the Global Economy: Knowledge, Technology and Internationalization*, Cheltenham, UK and Northampton, MA, USA: Edward Elgar Publishing, pp. 261–80.

Tervo, H. (1990), Factors Underlying Displacement: An Analysis of Finnish Regional Incentive Policy Using Survey Data on Assisted Firms, *Applied Economics* **22**, 617–28.

Todd, P.E. and K.I. Wolpin (2008), Ex Ante Evaluation of Social Programs, *Annales d'Économie et de Statistique* **91/92**, 263–91.

Vanclay, F. (2012), *Guidance for the Design of Qualitative Case Study Evaluation*, accessed 16 October 2018 at http://ec.europa.eu/regional_policy/sources/doc gener/evaluation/doc/performance/Vanclay.pdf.

Vedung, E. (1997), *Public Policy and Program Evaluation*, New Brunswick, NJ: Transaction Publishers.

Wallace, D. and D. Silander (eds) (2018), *Climate Change, Policy and Security – State and Human Impacts*, London: Routledge.

Warwick, K. (2013), Beyond Industrial Policy: Emerging Issues and New Trends, *OECD Science and Technology and Industry Papers*, No. 2, Paris: OECD Publishing.

Wren, C. (2007), Reconciling Practice with Theory in the Micro-Evaluation of Regional Policy, *International Review of Applied Economics* **21**, 321–37.

8. Research and innovation
Anne Haglund-Morrissey[1]

The European Commission has over the years, in particular since the eruption of the 2008 global financial crisis, repeatedly argued for the importance of research and innovation (R&I) investment as a smart, lasting way out of the crisis and, in the current period of economic recovery, as a source of renewed growth, to strengthen the European Union's (EU) global competitiveness, and to address global societal challenges (cf. Ulnicane, 2016: 328; EC, 2018h). R&I plays an important role both in addressing global challenges such as climate change, clean energy and active and healthy ageing, and in triggering smart, sustainable and inclusive growth, as well as job creation. By producing new knowledge, R&I is fundamental in the development of new innovative products, processes and services, which in turn enable higher productivity, industrial competitiveness, employment and ultimately prosperity. This explains why R&I is the core pillar of the Europe 2020 strategy, where the specific target is 'improving the conditions for innovation, research and development', in particular with the aim of 'increasing combined public and private investment in R&D [research and development] to 3 per cent of GDP' by 2020 (EC, 2010b).

A number of actions and instruments have been put in place to reach the Europe 2020 target of 3 per cent of EU Gross Domestic Product (GDP) invested in R&D. The 'Innovation Union' was introduced as one of seven Europe 2020 flagship initiatives, which 'Horizon 2020' – the EU's largest ever R&I programme (2014–20) – was designed to implement. The European Research Area (ERA) was put at the centre of the Europe 2020 Innovation Union flagship, with the ambition to create attractive conditions for carrying out research and investing in R&D-intensive sectors, where Horizon 2020 would finance its further development. Commission activities to reach the Europe 2020 R&I-related objectives are now

---

[1] The content of this chapter does not reflect the official opinion of the European Commission. Responsibility for the information and views expressed therein lies entirely with the author.

embraced by the 'Open Innovation, Open Science and Open to the World' policy objectives of the current EU R&I policy.

This chapter addresses how the Commission and its Directorate-General for Research and Innovation (DG RTD), as a part of the EU R&I policy, uses various policy initiatives, instruments and actions to encourage Europe to become a better global science performer, to remove obstacles to innovation, and to transfigure the way public and private sectors work together in line with the R&D objective of the Europe 2020 strategy. It focuses on the role of the Commission and its DG RTD as a political entrepreneur at a supranational level, and on how it works with and develops stimulating actions and monitoring instruments to assist the EU Member States in reforming their systems to improve the levels and quality of public R&I investment, to promote the exchange of best practices, and to monitor progress such as through the European Semester coordination, the Horizon 2020 Policy Support Facility, and the further development of the ERA, where the financial instrument of Horizon 2020 is key. Reforms and transformations at both European and national level are encouraged in order to contribute to smart, sustainable and inclusive growth, as well as job creation.

As noted in Chapter 1, political entrepreneurs in this book are in general 'politicians, public servants, bureaucrats and institutions that seek to create new, innovative favourable formal and informal institutional conditions . . . for growth and employment'. When it comes to political entrepreneurs such as the Commission, as also noted by Edler and James (2015: 1256), those are often based on 'individuals who are able to mobilise both internal and external expertise as well as the support of the internal hierarchies and thus the capacity of the Commission in the broader, inter-institutional space'. Commission Directorates-General (DGs), with their informational and expertise advantage, can play an important role as bottom-up political entrepreneurs to shape the political agenda along their favoured frames (cf. Schön-Quinlivan and Scipioni, 2017: 1173).

The Commission has in previous research been seen as the principal source of ideas behind Europe 2020 and the motor driving the agreement, where the DG for Economic and Financial Affairs has played an important role as political entrepreneur for its general shaping and development (cf. Copeland and James, 2014: 10–14). This chapter, however, focuses on how the DG RTD contributes to the Europe 2020 objectives by taking initiatives that boost European R&I and that optimise its impact. It is argued that priority is given to R&I investment, the promotion of reforms in national R&I systems, and an increase in funding levels of the EU framework programme to enable recovery and growth in times of crisis.

In the area of R&I, there are various ways in which the Commission can have an impact on and effect change and reforms that contribute to growth as a supranational political entrepreneur. The Commission can do so through: (1) the legitimacy it possesses by building on pre-existing norms of policy-making; (2) being an expertise and knowledge-based authority, where the institutional memory of DG RTD plays a fundamental part; (3) undertaking continuous encouragement; (4) establishing alliances and interaction with Member States and other key stakeholders in the R&I community; (5) selling the solution during the policy window opened by the financial crisis; and (6) contributing towards the social construction of a narrative regarding a problem, and an intersubjective understanding of a (supranational) solution (cf. Maltby, 2012: 437. See also Kaunert and Della Giovanna, 2010; Kingdon, 1995). DG RTD plays a key role in the EU machinery through outlining, developing and implementing the EU R&I policy with a view to reinforcing the science and technology base, encouraging innovation, addressing framework conditions and turning societal challenges into innovation opportunities that will help deliver on the Commission's priorities and provide solutions to European citizens (see EC, 2018g). It is therefore key when exploring the R&I component of the Europe 2020 strategy.

EU RESEARCH AND INNOVATION POLICY AND THE ROLE OF DG RTD

The EU's research and innovation (R&I) policy can be understood as a gradual development and expansion based on a functional need for and long tradition of integration specific to this field (research collaboration and researchers' mobility has a long international tradition), and the existing large diversity of national R&I systems across the Member States. It has further become characterised by the main instruments used: the Open Method of Coordination (OMC) and funding instruments through Framework Programmes (FPs) for research.

Science and technology (S&T) cooperation at Community level was initially conducted on a sector-by-sector basis, notably research on coal and steel production, and nuclear research included in the Treaties establishing the European Coal and Steel Community (1951) and the European Atomic Energy Community – Euratom (1958). The latter also established the Joint Research Centre (JRC) as an internal Community research centre managed by the Commission (Reillon, 2017: 3–4; EC, 2015a: 3).[2] The major EU policy instrument in this area was launched in 1984 through the first EU Framework Programme for research (FP1) to

---

[2] The JRC, which initially focused on nuclear energy research, is today, as one of the Directorates-General of the European Commission, a science and knowledge service with

allocate funds on a competitive basis for collaborative European research and technological development projects involving universities, research centres, companies and other organisations. The Single European Act (1986) introduced cooperation and coordination of national research policies as the objectives of the common research policy as a Community competence, and provided a firm legal basis for the adoption of the following FPs.[3] Emphasis was put on applied research to support the competitiveness of European industry. There was only a small programme in the 1980s to support basic/fundamental research, which however has become more significant in the last decade (EC, 2015a: 3–4).

The launch of the ERA through the ERA Communication, adopted under Philippe Busquin, Commissioner for Research, in January 2000, became an important foundation for the EU research policy, and the FP would be the main tool to implement it (cf. Reillon, 2017: 17; EC, 2015a: 4).[4] The ERA was to be part of the Lisbon strategy (March 2000), aiming to make the EU the most competitive and dynamic knowledge-based economy in the world, in a context where the average research effort in the EU was lagging behind major global competitors (Hervás Soriano and Mulatero, 2010: 289; Edler, 2012: 170–71; EC, 2000: 4).[5] With the Treaty of Lisbon in 2007, the completion of ERA became a Treaty requirement, and the same year two important policy innovations were launched: the European Research Council (ERC) that supports fundamental research carried out by individual teams (currently accounting for 17 per cent of Horizon 2020) and the European Institute for Innovation and Technology (EIT) for managing collaborative initiatives between research, education and business (EC, 2015a: 4; Reillon, 2016: 6).

The current EU R&I policy has its legal basis in Title XIX of TFEU and Title II, Chapter 1 of the Euratom Treaty. Art. 179 (TFEU) specifies that the EU:

> shall have the objective of strengthening its scientific and technological bases by achieving a European research area in which researchers, scientific knowledge and technology circulate freely, and encouraging it to become more competi-

scientists who carry out research to provide independent scientific advice and support to EU policy.
[3] FP2 was the first framework programme adopted with this legal basis.
[4] The idea of an ERA had already been put forward by Antonio Ruberti, European Commissioner for Research 1993–95, based on the ideas of Ralf Dahrendorf, European Commissioner for Research 1973–74. However, Commissioner Busquin transformed the ERA idea into a real political project (EC, 2015a: 22).
[5] The inception of the ERA in 2000 triggered the use of articles introduced already in 1986 for the establishment of public–public and public–private partnerships (Articles 185 and 187 of the Treaty on the Functioning of the European Union, TFEU).

tive, including in its industry, while promoting all the research activities deemed necessary by virtue of other Chapters of the Treaties.

To pursue these objectives, the EU should carry out activities *complementary* to those of the Member States (Art. 180 TFEU), such as:

- implementing research, technological development (RTD) and demonstration programmes, by promoting cooperation with and between undertakings, research centres and universities;
- promoting cooperation in the field of Union RTD and demonstration with third countries and international organisations;
- disseminating and optimising the results of activities in Union RTD and demonstration;
- stimulating the training and mobility of researchers in the EU.

The competences of the EU in the area of RTD are shared with the Member States (TFEU, Art. 4:3). The EU and the Member States should coordinate their research and technological policies (Art. 181:1 TFEU), and the Commission may use 'initiatives aiming at the establishment of guidelines and indicators, the organisation of exchange of best practice, and the preparation of the necessary elements for periodic monitoring and evaluation' to promote such coordination (TFEU, Art. 181:2). Articles 182–6 TFEU specify the details of the Framework Programme (FP) for R&I, which sets out all the Union activities. In implementing the FP, the EU can also participate in research programmes undertaken by several Member States (Art. 185 TFEU) and set up joint undertakings or any other structure necessary for the implementation of EU research programmes (TFEU, Art. 187). Regarding obligations stemming from the Euratom Treaty, 'the Commission shall be responsible for promoting and facilitating nuclear research in the Member States and for complementing it by carrying out a Community research and training programme' (Euratom Treaty, Art. 4:1).

DG Research (and Education) was first established in 1973, which gave the European research policy an institutional memory and policy-making capacity. Other DGs continued to have responsibilities in R&D for their sectors, but DG Research became the lead administrative body for EU research policy (cf. Gornitzka, 2015: 88). The obligations and activities of today's DG RTD are based on the provisions in Chapter XIX of TFEU and Title II, Chapter 1 of the Euratom Treaty as described above. The types of interventions can be summarised in the following (cf. EC, 2016b: 4–5):

- definition and implementation of EU R&I policy;

- analysis of national R&I policies and efforts to increase the effectiveness and efficiency of R&I systems in Europe through more R&I investment with higher impact, and formulating country-specific recommendations (contributing to the European Semester), as well as coordination with Member States in order to achieve the ERA;
- establishing framework conditions that foster and support R&I, based on an analysis of potential barriers to effective R&I in Europe;
- contribution to resolving specific global societal challenges;
- launching of international agreements and initiatives, promotion of international cooperation with strategic third countries and international organisations, and contributing to EU external action priorities;
- management of funding programmes; i.e. Horizon 2020 (including policy-related activities such as definition of Work Programmes), Euratom, Research Fund for Coal and Steel (RFCS), preparation of future programmes, and coordination of the Research family of DGs.[6]

The administrative rules of the FPs were from the beginning based on the principle of direct management by the Commission. Member State authorities with competence in R&D policy could through FP programme committees oversee the Commission's implementation of them. In the first decades, FPs were entirely managed by DG RTD (Gornitzka, 2015: 88). However, in 2008, the Research Executive Agency (REA) was set up in order to separate policy-making (DG RTD) and implementation (Agency).[7] Besides executive agencies implementing R&I actions, Joint Undertakings have been set up together with partners in the private sector to develop and implement specific Joint Technology Initiatives. The Commission also participates in the so-called Article 185 initiatives, which are public–public partnerships established between the Commission on one side and various national R&D programmes managed by participating Member States on the other (EC, 2016b: 4–5).

---

[6] The following DGs are part of the European Commission Research Family, besides DG RTD: DG AGRI, DG CNECT, DG EAC, DG ENER, DG GROW, DG HOME, DG MOVE, DG JRC.

[7] Today, four Executive Agencies are part of the European Commission Research family: the Executive Agency for Small and Medium-sized Enterprises (EASME), the European Research Council Executive Agency (ERCEA), the Innovation and Networks Executive Agency (INEA) and the Research Executive Agency (REA). DG RTD is the leading partner DG, and is chairing the Steering Committee of ERCEA and REA.

R&I AS A KEY COMPONENT OF EUROPE 2020 TO PROMOTE GROWTH

Although the 2008 global financial crisis constituted a challenge for Member States' investments in R&I, for the Commission it also came to offer new arguments for and opportunities to promote R&I as the main driving force for economic recovery. In general, the Commission's response in the area of R&I to the crisis can be characterised by a priority given to R&I investment during times of austerity, the promotion of reforms in national R&I systems, and an increase in funding levels of the EU Framework Programme.

When the European Economic Recovery Plan (EERP) was presented by the Commission in November 2008, support for R&I was one of the priorities put forward for tackling the financial crisis (EC, 2008: 15). This followed the focus of the Lisbon Strategy, launched in 2000 with the objective of the EU becoming a knowledge-based economy based on an ambitious R&I agenda, and with the introduction of a 3 per cent EU GDP spending target for R&D (EC, 2010a: 12; Edler, 2012: 168). Thus, when challenged by the financial crisis, the Commission reinforced the key messages from the Lisbon strategy, namely that investment in knowledge policies, structural reforms of national R&I systems and support for innovative businesses constitute important preconditions for future growth (cf. EC, 2008: 15–16). Similar messages about innovation as a way out of a crisis, and EU cooperation as a way to pool R&I resources in times of austerity have become a dominant discourse in EU R&I policy, repeated in the main policy documents and endorsed by the Commissioners and other key actors (cf. Ulnicane, 2016: 331–2).

The role of R&I in addressing the crisis was again on the EU agenda in 2010 when the Lisbon strategy was replaced by the Europe 2020 strategy for smart, sustainable and inclusive growth (EC, 2010b) under the newly appointed Barroso II Commission, with Máire Geoghegan-Quinn as Commissioner for Research, Innovation and Science. The 'smart' aspect of the strategy was based on developing a knowledge-based and innovative economy. Whereas the decision to relaunch the Lisbon strategy happened irrespective of the 2008 financial crisis (it was launched in 2000 to last until 2010), the crisis was an important factor when the Europe 2020 strategy was launched in 2010. The strategy stated that the crisis had exposed Europe's structural weaknesses including lower levels of investment in R&D and innovation than those of the EU's main global competitors, insufficient use of ICT, and reluctance in some parts of the societies to embrace innovation (EC, 2010b: 3–5).

The Europe 2020 strategy suggested a number of headline targets to be achieved by 2020. The '3 per cent target' for R&D investment of the Lisbon Strategy became a key objective of Europe 2020, where an indicator to reflect R&D and innovation intensity also would be developed (Hervás Soriano and Mulatero, 2010: 298). Despite the fact that its introduction in the Lisbon Strategy displayed the importance and visibility of R&I policy at the EU level, and although many Member States until 2010 had increased public R&D investments, weak performance of some of the Member States meant that the EU's overall performance had improved only marginally since 2000.[8] The Lisbon Strategy had thus not reached its R&I objectives (EC, 2010a: 12; 2010b: 9; Edler, 2012: 170, 183–4).

The headline indicator 'gross domestic expenditure on R&D' was introduced to show the proportion of GDP dedicated to R&D. It reflects the extent of R&I undertaken in a country in terms of resources input, where one-third of the funding should come from the government sector (of which the EU's FP only would constitute a minority) and two-thirds from business (Eurostat, 2016; EC, 2016b: 4). When assessing the development after the introduction of the '3 per cent target', one can notice that after a period of somewhat continuous growth between 2007 and 2014, R&D expenditure in the EU reached 2.04 per cent of GDP in 2014, up from 1.77 per cent in 2007. However, progress has been slow and the most recent figures point to a stagnation, with the 2015 R&D expenditure decreasing slightly to 2.03 per cent of GDP, which has moved the EU further away from its 3 per cent target. Member States have set their own targets ranging from 4 per cent to below 0.5 per cent. R&D expenditure is the highest in northern and western European countries (in particular Finland and Sweden), and the lowest in eastern and southern Member States, where the recession was felt more strongly, with severe effects on their R&I systems. In general, investment in R&D is forecast to increase to 2.2 per cent by 2020 (Eurostat, 2018: 2–3, 18. See also Izsak and Radosevic, 2016: 281). Thus, despite efforts on the Commission's side, it seems unlikely that the 3 per cent Europe 2020 target will be met by 2020.

The Innovation Union Flagship Initiative

Besides the 3 per cent target, the Commission put forward seven flagship initiatives to catalyse progress under the priority themes of smart, sustainable and inclusive growth of the Europe 2020 strategy. Among these, the 'Innovation Union' flagship in particular addresses R&I with the aim of re-focusing R&D and innovation policy on societal challenges, such as

---

[8]   From 1.85 per cent to 1.9 per cent of GDP.

climate change, energy and resource efficiency, health and demographic change. The Innovation Union Communication marked a clear shift by considering innovation to be 'the overarching policy objective' and that the EU and the Member States had to 'adopt a much more strategic approach to innovation' (EC, 2011a: 4).

The Innovation Union initiative was designed to address six priority areas: strengthening the knowledge base and reducing fragmentation; getting good ideas to the market; maximising social and territorial cohesion; creating European Innovation Partnerships; leveraging EU policies externally; and making it happen (EC 2010b: 10–11). It further identified concrete actions to be undertaken at EU and Member State level.

At national level, Member States would reform national (and regional) R&D and innovation systems to foster excellence and smart specialisation, reinforce university–business cooperation, implement joint programming and enhance cross-border cooperation. They should further ensure a sufficient supply of science, maths and engineering graduates, and prioritise knowledge expenditure, including using tax incentives and other financial instruments to promote greater private R&D investments (EC, 2011a).

At EU level, the Commission would work to:

- complete the ERA, develop a strategic research agenda focused on societal challenges, and enhance joint programming with Member States and regions;
- improve framework conditions for business to innovate;
- launch 'European Innovation Partnerships' (EIPs) between the EU and national level to speed up the development and deployment of the technologies needed to meet identified challenges;
- strengthen EU instruments to support innovation (for example structural funds, rural development funds, R&I FP); and
- promote knowledge partnerships and links between education, business, R&I, including through the EIT.

The Commission identified 34 specific commitments for action to be delivered under the six priority areas, and its achievements in delivering those were presented in the last State of the Innovation Union report by DG RTD from 2015 (see EC, 2015b).

In order to compare Member States' R&I policies and performance, assessing relative strengths and weaknesses of national R&I systems, and to help countries identify areas they needed to address, the 'European Innovation Scoreboard' was launched in 2001. The report forms a comprehensive benchmarking and monitoring system of R&I trends in Europe, compared with international competitors. The report is published on a yearly basis by the DG for Internal Market, Industry, Entrepreneurship, and SMEs, together with DG RTD. The 2018 edition shows that Sweden remains the EU innovation leader, followed by Denmark, Finland, the Netherlands, the UK and Luxembourg (EC, 2018a: 7).[9]

Current Priorities to Encourage Progress Towards the Europe 2020 Priorities

Challenges still persist in the European R&I system that impede progress towards the Europe 2020 priorities, including low quality of the public R&I system in some Member States, mainly as a result of their lower public R&D investment; weak knowledge flows and science–business linkages; and insufficiently attractive framework conditions for R&D investment and entrepreneurial activity (see further below). The Commission has therefore in recent years put in place a number of policy actions and instruments to address these challenges.

In 2015, Carlos Moedas, Commissioner for Research, Science and Innovation 2014–19, defined the strategic policy goals of the EU's R&I policy as 'Open Innovation, Open Science, and Open to the World', which succeeds the earlier R&I policy, Innovation Union. Emphasis is placed on making science and innovation more open, collaborative and global to further address the Europe 2020 R&I objectives. In order to improve European R&I, the following actions are seen as needed (EC, 2016a):

- *Open innovation* – helping Europe to capitalise on the results of R&I and create shared economic and social value by bringing more actors into the innovation process, boosting investment, maximising the impact of innovation and creating the right innovation ecosystems.
- *Open science* – supporting new ways of doing research and diffusing knowledge by using digital technologies and new collaborative tools, to ensure excellent science and open access to data.
- *Open to the world* – fostering international cooperation to jointly tackle global societal challenges more effectively, access the latest knowledge and the best talent worldwide, create business opportunities in new and emerging markets, and use science diplomacy as an influential instrument of external policy.

This '3 Os' policy brings together some of the most recent actions and instruments to address persistent challenges. The Commission has

---

[9] From 2010 to 2015, it was called the 'Innovation Union Scoreboard', in line with the Innovation Union initiative.

established three pillars of action for its Open Innovation Policy, namely reforming the regulatory environment, boosting private investment and maximising impacts. Some specific actions under the first pillar include: the establishment of the Scientific Advice Mechanism for providing the Commission policy-making activities with independent scientific advice; the 'Innovation Deals', which make it possible for innovators to question EU rules posing obstacles to innovation; a pilot on the Innovation Principle so that future new EU legislation should be assessed on its potential consequences on innovation; and the Horizon 2020 Policy Support Facility, which provides Member States and Horizon 2020 Associated Countries with practical support in the design, implementation and evaluation of R&I policy reforms. Under the second pillar the Commission has set up a European Venture Capital Fund of Funds (VentureEU) to support businesses as they start up and grow and maximising the use of the European Fund for Strategic Investments (EFSI) for mobilising private funding for strategic investments and for risk finance for small businesses; and innovation procurement schemes to address societal challenges and to support European industrial leadership. Under the third pillar, the Commission focuses on the implementation of the 'Seal of Excellence', which identifies promising Horizon 2020 project proposals and recommends them for further funding from alternative sources; and the establishment of a European Innovation Council to help convert knowledge and science into market-creating products and services (EC, 2016a: 26–8; 2016b: 23–4; Eurostat, 2018: 18).

Activities in the area of *Open Science* includes the establishment of the Open Science Policy Platform, the creation of the European Open Science Cloud, the advancement of open access and data policies, the removal of legal barriers to the use of text and data mining techniques for R&I and the fostering of research integrity, and making science more inclusive.

With regard to the priority of *Open to the World*, since 2012 the Commission has used a strategy for international cooperation in R&I, and cooperation takes place in R&I projects, networking between projects, joint or coordinated calls, and specific joint initiatives. The Commission is collaborating with the Member States and Associated Countries through the Strategic Forum for International S&T Cooperation (SFIC), and there are S&T policy dialogues with key international partner countries, regions and organisations with a focus on improving the framework conditions for engaging in international cooperation (EC, 2016a: 60–64; Eurostat, 2018: 19–20; EC, 2018g: 18–20).

COMMISSION ACTIVITIES TO ADDRESS THE EUROPE 2020 STRATEGY R&I PRIORITIES

As a political entrepreneur, DG RTD is working on several fronts to achieve the Europe 2020 3 per cent target: it carries out activities to strengthen Europe's R&I systems and to achieve the ERA through working with Member States; it establishes framework conditions to capitalise on the results of European R&I by involving all actors in the innovation process; and it works on an effective implementation of Horizon 2020 and other RTD programmes, and to maximise synergies with other EU programmes (EC, 2018g: 14–25). When analysing the Commission as a political entrepreneur and addressing its efforts in reaching the Europe 2020 R&D objectives, the examples of DG RTD's activities below can for analytical reasons be grouped into: (1) encouraging and monitoring reforms of national R&I policies; and (2) supporting and using an increasing volume of funding instruments.

Encouraging and Monitoring Reforms of (EU and) National R&I Policies

Through the Open Method of Coordination (OMC), DG RTD plays an important role as a political entrepreneur and works with the Member States to improve the levels and quality of public R&I investment (see also Prange and Kaiser, 2005: 292). It does so in particular through the European Semester of economic policy coordination under the Europe 2020 strategy (a regular reporting and review process which started during the Lisbon Strategy); the Horizon 2020 Policy Support Facility (PSF) to support the design, implementation and evaluation of national R&I reforms; and through the development of the European Research Area (ERA). The OMC process gives the Commission substantial influence over European R&I through its monitoring and agenda-setting role (cf. Chapter 1).

European Semester mechanism
The implementation of the Europe 2020 strategy has been monitored since 2011 within the framework of the European Semester, a yearly cycle aimed to facilitate the governance of economic policy. The two key milestones of the process are (1) the publication by the Commission of a single analytical economic assessment per Member State – the *Country Report* – analysing the country's economic situation and reform agendas; and (2) the proposals by the Commission of *Country-Specific Recommendations* for every Member State, providing tailor-made policy advice in areas deemed as priorities for the next 12–18 months and adapting priorities identified at

EU level (in the Commission's Annual Growth Survey) to the national level.

At the launch, it was decided that the reporting of Europe 2020 and the Stability and Growth Pact reporting would be done simultaneously, 'while keeping the instruments separate and maintaining the integrity of the Pact' (EC, 2010b: 4. See also Copeland and James, 2014: 12). In November preceding the actual year's cycle, the Annual Growth Survey (AGS) identifies the economic and social priorities of the Union and its Member States for the year ahead. The Country-Specific Recommendations (CSRs) build on the analysis presented in the latest Country Reports, highlighting persistent challenges in the European R&I system that impede progress towards the Europe 2020 priorities such as long-term growth. A network of European Semester officers based in the Member States has been established, and consultative meetings with national authorities, social partners and other relevant stakeholders are held across Europe to discuss how the key challenges identified in the reports could translate into CSRs. The Commission also consults Member States on the analytical parts of the Country Reports prior to their publication (EC, 2018k: 2). It is, however, up to the Member States to implement (or not) the recommendations.

In order to ensure an adequate integration of R&I aspects in the Country Reports and in the CSRs, DG RTD develops a comprehensive evidence-based approach targeting (1) the identification for each Member State of its main R&I policy challenges, that is, the key bottlenecks hampering the full contribution of R&I to smart, sustainable and inclusive growth; and (2) the assessment of the adequacy of the Member State policy response to the identified challenges (EC, 2016b: 17; EC, 2018g: 5).

According to the Commission (EC, 2017h), current persistent challenges in the European R&I system could be grouped into three main categories:

1. *Low quality of the public R&I system in some Member States, mainly as a result of their lower public R&D investment.* Here, relevant performance indicators used are 'bibliometrics' (impact of scientific publications); the number of European Research Council grantees in a country (to show scientific excellence); and the number of top-performing universities in a country according to international rankings.
2. *Weak knowledge flows and science–business linkages.* Here, one of the key elements assessed is the level of public–private collaboration through direct investment by firms in projects carried out by public research organisations.
3. *Bottlenecks in innovation investment.* Here, companies need to operate in an environment that allows them to transform knowledge effectively

into economic returns. This depends not only on the quality and quantity of S&T outputs, but also on the framework conditions in which they operate.

For the most recent exercise, the AGS of November 2017 highlighted that the 'virtuous triangle' of boosting investment, pursuing structural reforms and ensuring responsible fiscal policies is delivering results. In February 2018, the Commission released the Country Reports with substantial R&I content. DG RTD contributed to nine Country-Specific Recommendations, adopted by the Council in May 2018 (on Belgium, the Czech Republic, Germany, Estonia, Spain, France, Ireland, Luxembourg and the Netherlands), which reflect the key policy priorities of the AGS, while taking into account the current more favourable economic and social situation. They call upon the Member States concerned to strengthen their national science and innovation systems, with the clear message that besides introducing the necessary reforms, the EU and its Member States need to step up investment in R&I, and respect the objective of investing 3 per cent of GDP in R&D (EC, 2018g: 5). In this process, DG RTD engaged throughout 2017 in an in-depth dialogue with Member States' national administrations on the identified European Semester challenges and policy responses, and encouraged Member States to take maximum ownership and actions (EC, 2018g: 15).

Overall, one can note that R&D is increasingly supported by governments' efforts to finance public R&D activities, increased profitability in the private sector and improving financing conditions (EC, 2018k: 4). Further, innovation and investment in R&D and digitisation policies in general seem to have a positive and durable impact on productivity. However, priorities and digitalisation levels vary significantly across and within Member States in terms of infrastructure or the availability of digital skills. Therefore, the Commission recommends a strengthening of public or private R&D in terms of investment or effectiveness through better targeting for some countries; and for other countries, a closer collaboration between business and research institutions (see further EC, 2018k: 11).

Although the monitoring and reporting activities linked to the European Semester in general are seen as a way to facilitate national R&I reforms, they have also received some criticism from representatives of national governments and experts, such as that they are increasing the reporting burden on national governments (cf. Ulnicane, 2016: 334).

Horizon 2020 policy support facility
The Annual Growth Survey identifies R&I as one of the seven priorities for Member State structural reforms to boost investment and growth.

It highlights reforms to increase the impact of public funding through improved R&I strategies, programmes and institutions, as well as reforms to ensure an investment-friendly environment to stimulate business innovation. In this context, the Commission launched in March 2015 the Horizon 2020 Policy Support Facility (PSF) as a new instrument that gives Member States and Horizon 2020 Associated Countries practical support to design, implement and evaluate reforms that enhance the quality of their R&I investments, policies and systems. Such reforms concern, for example, the stimulation of stronger and closer links between science and business or the introduction of performance-based funding of public research institutes (EC, 2016a: 22–3; 2016b: 17–18). In order to promote such reforms, the PSF provides Member States and Associated Countries access to independent high-level expertise and analyses through services such as Peer Reviews of the national R&I systems, recommendations and support to specific reforms or project-based mutual learning exercises (MLEs). It is a demand-driven service that responds to requests from national authorities on a voluntary basis. In addition, the PSF provides a Knowledge Centre via a dedicated website with information and analysis on R&I performance and policy responses in each Member State.

In 2015, three pilot PSF activities were launched: a peer review of the Bulgarian R&I system, a pre-peer review of the Hungarian R&I system, and a MLE on policies to foster business R&I investments. In 2016, DG RTD's activities to support national reforms and mutual learning included the implementation of: (1) PSF reports (including specific recommendations) for Moldova, Hungary and Ukraine; (2) specific support to Slovakia and Malta, and three MLEs (that is, on administration of tax incentives; evaluation of business R&D grants; and evaluation of complex public–private partnerships); and (3) additional PSF activities, such as MLEs on performance-based funding of public research, and interoperability of national research programmes and specific support to Slovenia and Romania (EC, 2016b).

Even though a rhythm of 10 PSF actions per year was foreseen (EC, 2016b), due to the high interest from Member States and countries associated with Horizon 2020, 14 actions were carried out or launched by DG RTD in 2017. In 2018, it is expected that an additional 14 PSF actions will be carried out (EC, 2018g: 15).

Developing the European Research Area (ERA)
As set out in TFEU Article 179, the Union has the objective of achieving a European Research Area (ERA) in which researchers, scientific knowledge and technology circulate freely. When launched, its objectives were to address the fragmentation, isolation and compartmentalisation

of national research systems and 'the lack of coordination in the manner in which national and European research policies are implemented' (EC, 2000: 9; 2015a: 24). DG RTD supports the efforts of Member States and research organisations to implement the policies and reforms needed to achieve this objective. Following the conclusions of the European Council of 4 February 2011, the Commission intended to create by 2014 all the conditions necessary for the Member States and other stakeholders to complete the ERA. According to the 'Communication on the European Research Area – Progress Report 2014' the conditions for the completion of ERA are now in place. However, the completion of ERA, as with the Internal Market, is a gradual process and further implementation efforts are therefore needed. The ERA concept also evolves over time as new challenges and policy priorities arise; for example in relation to Commissioner Carlos Moedas' priorities of Open Science, Open Innovation and Open to the World, where a successful ERA is seen as a prerequisite for these priorities. This requires the Commission and the Member States to review ERA-related initiatives to take advantage of the new opportunities and remove any new barrier (EC, 2016b: 18).

A specific OMC approach is inherent in ERA, aiming to promote a tighter coordination and cooperation among national research policies and programmes, through the establishment of indicators, benchmarking exercises, MLEs of policy-makers and coordination schemes of programme managers (cf. Edler, 2012: 173–4). Every year the Commission issues the ERA Monitoring Mechanism, which assesses progress in the implementation by Member States, research stakeholder organisations and the Commission of the set of ERA actions identified in the ERA Communication of July 2012. The most recent ERA progress report, adopted in January 2017, confirms that ERA has made strong progress over recent years. All headline indicators show progress over time according to the EU28 averages, although large disparities exist, both in performance levels and in growth rates between countries. However, there is still room for further progress on all priorities (see EC, 2017e).

DG RTD is foremost of several initiatives contributing towards achieving the ERA. In 2017, these included:

- the publication of the Staff Working Document on the Long-Term Sustainability of Europe's Research Infrastructures, which identifies actions to be taken in support of the sustainability of Research Infrastructures with a medium to long-term vision;
- the preparation of the 2018 Roadmap for the European Strategy Forum on Research Infrastructures (ESFRI) to strengthen the European Research Infrastructures ecosystem;

- the establishment of four[10] new European Research Infrastructure Consortia (ERICs), bringing the total number of established ERICs to 17;
- the continued management of Euraxess, which provides an on-line platform for job market search for researchers; and of the gateway to Science4Refugees, which is a Commission initiative to help refugee researchers find suitable jobs; and
- making the RESAVER Pension Fund (Pan-European Pension Fund for Research Professionals) fully operational. RESAVER was established in 2016 to enabling mobile employees to move between different countries and change jobs without losing their supplementary pension. (EC, 2018g: 16–17)

Supporting and Using an Increasing Volume of Funding Instruments

In addition to the Commission's attempts to facilitate structural reforms and to encourage an increased level of R&I funding at the national level through the Europe 2020 strategy, the Commission has gradually augmented its funding for R&I within the EU's long-term budget – the Multiannual Financial Framework (MFF) – as seen through the current MFF 2014–20, but even further in the proposed MFF for 2021–27. The gradual evolution of the EU R&I policy in recent decades can be seen as rather path-dependent. For each new MFF, a new FP is prepared that amends and revises priorities and rules of the previous FPs and includes some innovations (see also Ulnicane, 2016: 329–30, 337).

The first framework programme for research (FP1) back in 1984 was designed to help address the then economic crisis and support European industry to become more competitive (EC 2015a: 10). It also aimed at modernising public research organisation structures, limiting duplication of research activities in the Community and limiting intra-Community competition. Since then, in total eight framework programmes have been launched, with the Commission's FP9 proposal – Horizon Europe – currently being negotiated among the EU Member States. Similar research areas have been funded throughout the history of the FPs (whose individual budgets in general have increased by each FP), such as energy, health and biotechnology, ICT (with the highest overall budget), environment and climate, materials and processes, transport and space and agriculture and fisheries, whereas new areas were added in FP6 and FP7 (social sciences and humanities, and security research). New instruments

---

[10] LifeWatch hosted by Spain, CESSDA and ECCSEL both hosted by Norway, and INSTRUCT21 hosted by the United Kingdom.

and structures have also been gradually introduced, in particular from FP6 onwards (Reillon, 2017: 13, 26–8).

Although this is a rather path-dependent development, each new FP has also been influenced by new political priorities and policy developments. The development of the ERA concept in 2000 marked a clear shift in the evolution of the FP. FP6 and FP7, adopted in 2002 and 2006 respectively, were designed to implement this EU research policy. FP7 was designed to help reach the 3 per cent R&D target with an increased budget, and it was expected to be the catalyst to increase public and private spending for innovation-related activities. The adoption of the Europe 2020 strategy and the Innovation Union flagship initiative in 2010 influenced the structure of Horizon 2020 (FP8) from 2014, which became the Union's main contribution to reach the '3 per cent target' (Reillon, 2017: 19, 30; EC, 2015a: 21). In general, the early focus in the FPs on strengthening the competitiveness of European industry has in the last FPs been complemented by a focus on social challenges and basic research (EC, 2015a: 5, 19).

While the budget for the FPs has grown steadily since the 1980s and has considerably increased for FP7 (see Table 8.1), in the case of Horizon 2020, the increased funds (by 30 per cent) were presented as a direct response to the financial crisis (EC, 2015a: 8). Horizon 2020's priorities and three-pillar structure of Excellent science, Industrial leadership and Societal challenges include a stronger focus on the societal and economic impact of R&I and commercialisation and links with the Europe 2020 strategy goals of smart, sustainable and inclusive growth. Due to the crisis,

Table 8.1   Evolution of the budget of the EU framework programme (FP) for research (in billion EUR)

Framework Programme	Years	Billion EUR
FP1	1984–1987	3.3
FP2	1987–1991	5.4
FP3	1990–1994	6.6
FP4	1994–1998	13.2
FP5	1998–2002	14.9
FP6	2002–2006	19.3
FP7	2007–2013	55.9
Horizon 2020	2014–2020	80
Horizon Europe	*2021–2027*	*97.6 (+ Euratom 2.4)*[a]

Note: a   As in the proposal from the European Commission (2018h).

Source: Composed from data from European Commission (2015a) and (2018j).

an important focus of Horizon 2020 was put on applied research, which has already been significant for EU policy in strongly linking research and economic growth, but funds for basic/fundamental research (that is, ERC) have also been considerably increased. To address the needs of 'catching up' countries (countries with weaker performance in Horizon 2020), a specific objective of 'spreading excellence and widening participation' was also included (EC, 2011b).[11]

While the allocation of nearly 80 billion EUR to Horizon 2020 has been presented as an important Commission response to the crisis, it is important to keep in mind, as underlined in the TFEU, that the role of R&I needs to be seen holistically, and is not limited to a framework programme. Although being Europe's largest R&I programme, Horizon 2020 accounts for only a small proportion of the public R&I effort in Europe.

The proposed *Horizon Europe* programme (FP9), which builds on previous FPs, will become even bigger than Horizon 2020, with a proposed budget of 97.6 billion EUR (3.5 billion EUR of which will be allocated under the InvestEU Fund; see below). This amount is complemented by 2.4 billion EUR for the Euratom Research and Training Programme. Horizon Europe is designed to strengthen the EU's scientific and technological bases, to further boost Europe's innovation capacity, competitiveness and jobs, and to deliver on citizens' priorities and sustain the European socio-economic model and values (EC, 2018j). The ERA will be reinforced, and the three-pillar structure of Horizon Europe is aligned with the three political priorities of Commissioner Moedas: Open Innovation, Open Science and Open to the World (EC, 2018h):

- *Open Science* will continue to focus on excellent science and high-quality knowledge to strengthen the EU's science base through the ERC, Marie-Skłodowska Curie Actions and Research Infrastructures. As a 'bottom-up', investigator-driven pillar, it will continue to give the scientific community a strong role.
- *Global challenges and Industrial competitiveness* will support research on societal challenges, setting EU-wide missions with ambitious goals around challenges such as the fight against cancer, clean

---

[11] The FP7 interim evaluation (November 2010) identified that some Member States, mainly those that joined the EU after 2004, had low participation rates in FP7 projects. Widening actions under the Spreading Excellence and Widening Participation part of Horizon 2020 address the causes of low participation by fully exploiting the potential of Europe's talent pool. It ensures that the benefits of an innovation-led economy are both maximised and widely distributed across the EU, where synergies with European Structural and Investment Funds are an important component.

mobility and plastic-free oceans. Industrial leadership will be prominent, and the activities of the JRC are included.

- *Open Innovation* aims at making Europe a front-runner in market-creating innovation, where a European Innovation Council (EIC) will offer a one-stop shop for high potential and breakthrough technologies and innovative companies with potential for scaling up, and where the EIT is further strengthened.

In relation to the Commission's Horizon Europe proposal, it is argued that about two-thirds of Europe's economic growth over the last decades has been driven by innovation. This shows again the argument that increasing the budget for the FP will contribute to growth and employment (EC, 2018f): 'Each euro invested by the programme can potentially generate a return of up to 11 euro of GDP over 25 years. Union investments in R&I are expected to directly generate an estimated gain of up to 100 000 jobs in R&I activities in the "investment phase" (2021–2027).'

Besides funds provided to R&I through the FPs, the Commission has moved some funds (2.2 billion EUR) from Horizon 2020 to the new European Fund for Strategic Investments (EFSI) aiming to overcome the investment gap in the EU by mobilising private funding both for strategic investments in infrastructure and innovation, and also for risk finance for small businesses. EFSI has two parts: an Infrastructure/Innovation Window aiming for 240 billion EUR of investments, implemented by the European Investment Bank (EIB); and an SME Window aiming for 75 billion EUR of investments, implemented by the European Investment Fund (EIF). Research, development and innovation is one of the priority sectors targeted by EFSI (EC, 2016a: 25; 2018g: 18–20). In the MFF 2021–27, the fund is renamed InvestEU, and it is proposed that the EU budget contribution will be 15.2 billion EUR to mobilise more than 650 billion EUR of additional investment across Europe. InvestEU will feature a dedicated 'R&I thematic window' that is closely linked to the objectives of Horizon Europe, and it is expected to boost financing for R&I in the EU by an estimated 200 billion EUR from 2021 to 2027, thanks to the crowding of other public and private investment (EC, 2018h).

The Commission also aims at establishing synergies with other EU programmes. In the years to come, Horizon Europe and Euratom will promote synergies with other future EU programmes and policies to promote faster dissemination at national and regional level and uptake of R&I results. Such programmes include the EU Cohesion Policy, the new European Defence Fund, ITER, the Digital Europe Programme and the Connecting Europe Facility Digital (EC, 2018h).

CONCLUDING REMARKS

This chapter has focused on the initiatives and activities of the European Commission and its DG RTD as a supranational political entrepreneur in the field of R&I to promote European competitiveness, growth and employment in line with the Europe 2020 objectives. Many Commission activities are based on the previous approach to economic crises, where the first framework programme (FP1) was designed to overcome the then economic crisis and support the competitive capacity of the Member States to promote growth and employment. We have seen that the 2008 crisis reinforced some of the key elements from the earlier Lisbon Strategy about R&I as a crucial area for creating a knowledge-based economy and sustaining Europe's global competitiveness. These ideas guided both the European Economic Recovery Plan and the Europe 2020 strategy, and were taken up in the European Semester process, the MFF for 2014–20 and by Horizon 2020, whose design was directly linked to the crisis and to be the Union's main contribution to reach the '3 per cent target'.

The OMC, introduced with the Lisbon Strategy, dominates as a method for the EU to influence policy areas such as R&I where there are significant differences among the Member States and/or where the EU's means to influence are more limited due to the shared competence, compared to policy areas of exclusive competence. The OMC in this context has primarily been about the Commission initiating and encouraging benchmarking, MLEs and exchanges of best practice between Member States, based on the voluntary and more intergovernmental mode of cooperation among Member States. The OMC also gives the Commission substantial influence as a political entrepreneur through its monitoring and agenda-setting role, which is visible in the EU's R&I policy and among the activities carried out in the context of Europe 2020.

As we have seen, the EU has by each FP increased its funding for R&I, in particular since FP7, and the Horizon Europe proposal constitutes the largest budget ever devoted to R&I in the EU's MFF. The Commission as a supranational political entrepreneur has thus succeeded in increasing the volume of the budget allocated to EU-level R&I over time. This has been possible with the support of the scientific community for the utility of an EU-level programme, and by convincing Member States why EU programmes are useful for them. Each new FP is based on the previous one in terms of its scope where similar areas have been funded throughout the history of the FP, although new areas have been added, in particular since FP6. The current focus on societal challenges and supporting activities in the innovation process has been in place since the 1990s, which will continue in Horizon Europe. The evolution of the framework programmes can thus be seen as rather path-dependent; each new FP is based on the previous one, where the overall orientation and activities are adjusted and expanded in scope with new political priorities. In line with this, the Commission's Horizon Europe proposal can be seen as an evolution of Horizon 2020 with its three-pillar structure, focus on excellence and global societal challenges, and continued focus on the needs of 'catching-up' countries, and pilot activities introduced in Horizon 2020 will become important priority areas in Horizon Europe (such as the European Innovation Council). Also the monitoring instruments involved in the European Semester follow this logic and build on earlier coordination instruments developed during the Lisbon Strategy.

As a supranational political entrepreneur, the Commission works closely with Member States and encourages exchanges of best practice between them, and develops stimulating actions and monitoring instruments to assist them in carrying out reforms to improve the levels and quality of public R&I investment that together contribute to smart, sustainable and inclusive growth and employment. However, one can also note that the role of the Commission as a political entrepreneur is highly dependent on many external factors. The success of Commission activities is to a large extent reliant on the willingness and capacity of Member States to undertake reforms and to strengthen their public investments in R&D. The R&I policy area is a field of shared competence, and as we have seen, the EU's FP only counts for a small percentage of public funds available for R&D in Europe. In order to have a substantial impact on the overall European R&D spending in line with the Europe 2020 objectives, Member States will need to contribute with the lion's share of this. Even though investment in R&I at Union level can have a positive effect on growth, the difficulties in public finances across the Member States since the 2008 crisis erupted have often led to reductions in national research budgets. This is an important external factor having a direct impact on the achievement of the Europe 2020 objectives, and also explains the variety of activities DG RTD is carrying out in order to encourage Member States to invest more in R&I (through the European Semester and ERA monitoring activities, the support actions through the Horizon 2020 Policy Support Facility and so on). Also, the focus on 'spreading excellence and widening participation' introduced in Horizon 2020 to address the needs of 'catching-up'/'widening' countries can be seen in this context.

Also private sector investments, which are important for growth and development, are linked to various external factors, such as the development of the general global and European economy, and conditions that either encourage or hinder innovation. Legislation and administrative barriers can hamper or even prevent innovation. In some areas, the possibilities for the Commission are often limited (for example in areas of taxation), but in others the Commission can launch EU-level action, or facilitate and encourage developments at Member State level in order to reduce such barriers to innovation. In this vein, we have seen that DG RTD is focusing on the establishment of framework conditions to encourage innovation. In addition, the financial crisis has also meant difficulties for the flow of finance to riskier investments, which is another obstacle to innovation. This explains recent Commission initiatives related to access to finance for innovators and SMEs. Moreover, other developments and challenges in the world, which require swift action or a change in priorities, also have an impact on DG RTD's activities. The outbreak of Mad Cow Disease, Ebola and the Zika virus, the recent migration crisis, extreme weather conditions and natural disasters are all events that have prompted a new focus.

Although its efforts to reach the Europe 2020 '3 per cent target' in R&D spending by 2020 are constrained due to the above-mentioned external factors, the Commission has as a supranational political entrepreneur substantial means to influence the development of R&I policy at European level, and has a large impact on activities carried out at national level. The Commission activities build on previous ways and approaches in dealing with past crises, and its authority in the field of R&I is based on its substantial knowledge (the informational and expertise advantage of its DG RTD), and by building alliances with Member States and other key stakeholders in the R&I area. The Commission's influence as a political entrepreneur is also based on arguments used, underlining the importance of R&I investment at both EU (an increase in volume of the FPs) and national level (to reach the '3 per cent target'), to sell a solution (way out of the crisis and to create growth and employment) where the crisis in this context can be seen as a policy window. This use of repeated arguments contributes towards the social construction of a narrative related to a challenge, which convinces others of the importance and value of a solution and approach at supranational level.

REFERENCES

Commission of the European Communities (1975), *The Scientific and Technical Research Committee (CREST). Its Origin, Role and Function*, EUR 5393 e, Luxembourg: Commission of the European Communities Directorate-General 'Scientific and technical information and information management'.

Copeland, P. and S. James (2014), Policy windows, ambiguity and Commission entrepreneurship: explaining the relaunch of the European Union's economic reform agenda, *Journal of European Public Policy*, **21**(1), 1–19.

EC (2000), *Communication from the Commission to the European Council, the European Parliament, the Economic and Social Committee and the Committee of the Regions. Towards a European research area*, Brussels, 18.1.2000, COM(2000) 6 final.

EC (2008), *Communication from the Commission to the European Council. A European Economic Recovery Plan*, Brussels, 26.11.2008, COM(2008) 800 final.

EC (2010a), *Commission Staff Working Document. Lisbon Strategy evaluation document*, Brussels, 2.2.2010, SEC(2010) 114 final.

EC (2010b), *Communication from the Commission. EUROPE 2020: A strategy for smart, sustainable and inclusive growth*, Brussels, 3.3.2010, COM(2010) 2020.

EC (2011a), *Europe 2020 Flagship Initiative Innovation Union*, SEC(2010) 1161, Communication from the Commission to the European Parliament, the Council, the European Economic and Social Committee and the Committee of the Regions, Directorate-General for Research and Innovation.

EC (2011b), *Communication from the Commission to the European Parliament, the Council, the European Economic and Social Committee and the Committee of the Regions, Horizon 2020 – The framework programme for research and innovation*, Brussels, 30.11.2011, COM(2011) 808 final.

EC (2012), *Communication from the Commission to the European Parliament, the Council, the European Economic and Social Committee and the Committee of the Regions, A Reinforced European Research Area Partnership for Excellence and Growth*, Brussels, 17.7.2012, COM(2012) 392 final.

EC (2013), *Communication from the Commission to the European Parliament, the Council, the European Economic and Social Committee and the Committee of the Regions, Measuring innovation output in Europe: towards a new indicator*, Brussels, 13.9.2013, COM(2013) 624 final.

EC (2014a), *Communication from the Commission to the European Parliament, the Council, the European Economic and Social Committee and the Committee of the Regions, Taking stock of the Europe 2020 strategy for smart, sustainable and inclusive growth*, Brussels, 19.3.2014, COM(2014) 130 final/2.

EC (2014b), *State of the Innovation Union, Taking stock 2010–2014*, COM(2014) 339, Directorate-General for Research and Innovation.

EC (2015a), EU Research funding programmes 1984–2014. *Horizon Magazine*, Special Issue. Directorate-General for Research and Innovation.

EC (2015b), *State of the Innovation Union 2015*, Directorate-General for Research and Innovation.

EC (2016a), *Open Innovation, Open Science, Open to the World – a vision for Europe*, Directorate-General for Research and Innovation, Luxembourg: Publications Office of the European Union.

EC (2016b), *Strategic Plan 2016–2020 Directorate-General for Research and Innovation*, Ref. Ares(2016)1051529 – 01/03/2016.

EC (2017a) *Annual Activity Report: Directorate General Research and Innovation*, DG RTD AAR 2016, Ref. Ares(2017)1880009 – 07/04/2017.

EC (2017b), *ERA Progress Report 2016, ERA Monitoring Handbook*, Accompanying Science-Metrix Study, *'Data gathering and information for the 2016 ERA monitoring' – Technical Report*, EUR 28430 EN, Directorate-General for Research and Innovation.

EC (2017c), *ERA Progress Report 2016, Report from the Commission to the Council and the European Parliament, The European Research Area: Time for implementation and monitoring progress,* COM(2017) 35, Directorate-General for Research and Innovation.

EC (2017d), *European Innovation Scoreboard 2017: Annex B Performance per indicator,* Directorate-General for Internal Market, Industry, Entrepreneurship and SMEs, Unit F1 – Innovation Policy and Investment for Growth.

EC (2017e), *European Research Area Progress Report 2016, Staff Working Document,* EUR 28430 EN, Directorate-General for Research and Innovation.

EC (2017f), *European Research Area Progress Report 2016, Technical Report,* EUR 28430 EN, Directorate-General for Research and Innovation.

EC (2017g), *Management Plan 2018,* DG RTD, Ref. Ares(2017)6345021 – 22/12/2017.

EC (2017h), *European Semester Thematic Factsheet. Research and Innovation. European Commission,* 16.11.2017.

EC (2018a), *European Innovation Scoreboard 2018,* Directorate-General for Internal Market, Industry, Entrepreneurship and SMEs; and Directorate-General for Research and Innovation.

EC (2018b), *Communication from the Commission to the European Parliament, the Council, the European Economic and Social Committee and the Committee of the Regions, Horizon 2020 interim evaluation: maximising the impact of EU research and innovation,* Brussels, 11.1.2018, COM(2018) 2 final.

EC (2018c), MISSIONS, Mission-Oriented Research & Innovation in the European Union: A problem-solving approach to fuel innovation-led growth, by Mariana Mazzucato, Directorate-General for Research and Innovation.

EC (2018d), *Science, Research and Innovation Performance of the EU 2018, Strengthening the foundations for Europe's future,* Directorate-General for Research and Innovation.

EC (2018e), *Communication from the Commission to the European Parliament, the European Council, the Council, the European Economic and Social Committee and the Committee of the Regions. A renewed European Agenda for Research and Innovation – Europe's chance to shape its future. The European Commission's contribution to the Informal EU Leaders' meeting on innovation in Sofia on 16 May 2018.* Brussels, 15.5.2018 COM(2018) 306 final.

EC (2018f), EU budget: Commission proposes most ambitious Research and Innovation programme yet, Press Release, Brussels, 7 June.

EC (2018g), *2017 Annual Activity Report, Directorate-General for Research and Innovation,* Ref. Ares(2018)1735281 – 29/03/2018.

EC (2018h), *Proposal for a Regulation of the European Parliament and of the Council establishing Horizon Europe – the Framework Programme for Research and Innovation, laying down its rules for participation and dissemination.* COM(2018) 435 final. 7 June.

EC (2018i), EU Budget for the Future. *Horizon Europe.* 2 May.

EC (2018j), EU Budget for the Future. *Horizon Europe. EU funding for research and innovation 2021–27.* 7 June.

EC (2018k), Communication from the Commission to the European Parliament, the European Council, the Council, the European Central Bank, the European Economic and Social Committee, the Committee of the Regions and the European Investment Bank – 2018 European Semester – Country-specific recommendations, 23.5.2018 COM(2018) 400 final.

Edler, J. (2012), *Research and Innovation and the Lisbon Strategy,* in P. Copeland and D. Papadimitriou (eds), *The EU's Lisbon Strategy,* Basingstoke: Palgrave Macmillan.

Edler, J. and A.D. James (2015), Understanding the emergence of new science and technology policies: Policy entrepreneurship, agenda setting and the development of the European Framework Programme, *Research Policy* **44** (2015), 1252–65.

Eurostat (2016), *Smarter, Greener, More Inclusive? Indicators to Support the Europe 2020 Strategy*, 2016 edn, Luxembourg: Publications Office of the European Union.

Eurostat (2018), Europe 2020 indicators – R&D and innovation, Statistics Explained, accessed 12 February 2018 at http://ec.europa.eu/eurostat/statisticsexplained/.

Gornitzka, A. (2015), Executive governance of European science – technocratic, segmented and path dependent?, in L. Wedlin and M. Nedeva (eds), *Towards European Science: Dynamics and Policy of an Evolving European Research Space*, Cheltenham, UK and Northampton, MA, USA: Edward Elgar Publishing.

Hervás Soriano, F. and F. Mulatero (2010), Knowledge policy in the EU: from the Lisbon Strategy to Europe 2020, *Journal of the Knowledge Economy*, **(2010)**1, 289–302.

Izsak, K. and S. Radosevic (2016), EU research and innovation policies as factors of convergence or divergence after the crisis, *Science and Public Policy*, **44**(2), 274–83.

James, A.D. (2018), Policy entrepreneurship and agenda setting: comparing and contrasting the origins of the European research programmes for security and defense, in N. Karampekios, I. Oikonomou and E.G. Carayannis (eds), *The Emergence of EU Defense Research Policy*, Cham: Springer.

Kaunert, C. (2007), 'Without the power of purse or sword': the European arrest warrant and the role of the Commission, *Journal of European Integration*, **29**(4), 387–404.

Kaunert, C. and M. Della Giovanna (2010), Post-9/11 EU counter-terrorist financing cooperation: differentiating supranational policy entrepreneurship by the Commission and the Council Secretariat, *European Security*, **19**(2), 275–95.

Kingdon, J.W. (1995), *Agendas, Alternatives and Public Policies*, London: Longman.

Maltby, T. (2012), European Union energy policy integration: a case of European Commission policy entrepreneurship and increasing supranationalism, *Energy Policy*, **55**(2013) 435–44.

Prange, H. and R. Kaiser (2005), Coordination in the European Research Area, *Comparative European Politics*, **2005**(3), 289–306.

Reillon, V. (2016), Research in the European Treaties, Briefing March 2016, EPRS – European Parliamentary Research Service, European Parliament.

Reillon, V. (2017), *EU framework programmes for research and innovation. Evolution and key data from FP1 to Horizon 2020 in view of FP9*. European Parliament, European Parliamentary Research Service (EPRS), September.

Schön-Quinlivan, E. and M. Scipioni (2017), The Commission as policy entrepreneur in European economic governance: a comparative multiple stream analysis of the 2005 and 2011 reform of the Stability and Growth Pact, *Journal of European Public Policy*, **24**(8), 1172–90.

Ulnicane, I. (2015), Broadening aims and building support in science, technology and innovation policy: the case of the European Research Area, *Journal of Contemporary European Research*, **11**(1), 31–49.

Ulnicane, I. (2016), Research and innovation as sources of renewed growth? EU policy responses to the crisis, *Journal of European Integration*, **38**(3), 327–41.

9. Gender equality policy

Charlotte Silander

Gender equality policy is often considered to be the most developed dimension of the European Union's (EU's) social dimension (Hyman, 2008; Hix, 2005). The EU has put pressure on individual member states through directives in the area of working life to act in a way they would otherwise have never done (Walby, 1999; Rees, 2006). On the other hand, gender equality policy has been an area of contradictions. Many improvements have come as part of trade-offs in the form of large packages serving to integrate the European market with the risk to weaken social protection on national levels (Rossilli, 2000) and is a policy in line with the neo-liberal model of capitalism (Young, 2000).

Gender equality has traditionally been described as an *intrinsic value*, meaning that gender equality is valued for itself rather than as an instrument for achieving other goals. This is also in line with the gender equality goal of the 2030 Agenda for Sustainable Development, adopted by all United Nations (UN), aiming to achieve gender equality and empower all women and girls. However, gender equality can also be viewed as an *instrumental* value. The literature shows evidence from a wide range of countries that gender equality in education and in employment impact positively on economic growth (Klasen and Lamanna, 2009; Kabeer and Natali, 2013; Klasen, 2006). Gender inequality reduces the average amount of human capital in a society, harming economic performance by excluding talented women and restricting the overall pool of talent (Klasen, 2006; Dollar and Gatti, 1999).

Gender equality in the EU can be described in terms of a move from the strategy of *equal treatment*, with a strong focus on equal rights for workers resulting in a number of directives and legislation that have influenced the member states, followed by the use of *positive action* and to the current situation and the use of *mainstreaming* (Rees, 2006). Equal treatment for workers has a strong legal base in the EU. However, most areas related to gender equality (for example, social policy, educational policy and research and development) have a weak legal basis in EU legislation wherein their roles are limited to promote cooperation between member states and, when necessary, support and supplement their efforts. In these areas, policy-shaping takes place through the framework of the open coordination method. This chapter explores what kind of strategies the EU use to achieve targets set out in the Europe 2020 document and how these can be understood from a gender perspective and in the view of political entrepreneurship. The concept of political entrepreneurship originated from Dahl (1961: 6) as an overarching concept for all actors in the political arena (the public sector) who work to create the conditions for other entrepreneurs and for the common good (that is, the good of society) (Bergmann-Winberg and Wihlborg, 2011; Minstrom, 2004; Schneider et al., 1995). This includes politicians and civil servants in government departments, public authorities, departments of public work and engines of economic growth. Here, the focus will be on political entrepreneurship from a structure-oriented perspective, discussing how formal institutional arrangements may be changed to stimulate growth.

For such an analysis, *Europe 2020 – A strategy for smart, sustainable and inclusive growth* is highly relevant. It was launched by the European Commission in 2010, succeeding the European Single Market programme (1986–92) and the Lisbon Strategy (2000–10). The document referred to *smart growth* as promoting an economy based on knowledge and innovation, *sustainable growth* based on resource efficiency and a greener economy and *inclusive growth* providing for social integration. This is done by proposing five measurable EU targets for 2020 that will steer the process and be translated into national targets: employment; research and innovation; climate change and energy; education; and combating poverty. The aim of the chapter is to analyse Europe 2020 and related documents from a gender perspective. The overall question to be explored is: How do Europe 2020 and related documents relate to gender equality and women? This overall question is followed up by:

- Is gender equality viewed as an objective in itself or as a measure for reaching other objectives?
- Which strategies does the EU have for strengthening gender equality?
- What actions have taken place in order to achieve gender equality and with what results?
- What signs of political entrepreneurship exist?

This chapter is based on an analysis of documents originating from the European Commission and its directorates-general (DGs) and documents from the Council of Ministers or related working groups. A strategic selection has been used in which documents related to Europe 2020 were included as well as assessment reports, evaluations and monitoring reports. In total, 15 EU documents were analysed, covering the period from 2000 to 2018.

This chapter is divided into three sections. After the introduction follows a section dealing with the history of gender equality in the EU, addressing different theoretical views on gender equality. This section also discusses the use of 'new modes of governance' in the EU and their relation to mainstreaming. After that follows a section that deals with how gender is related to four areas of Europe 2020: employment, research & development, education and the fight against poverty. The related targets of Europe 2020 are summed up in a table and the results are discussed in the last section.

THE IDEOLOGICAL BASE FOR GENDER EQUALITY

The history of EU gender equality has proceeded through three phases of *equal treatment*, *positive action* and *mainstreaming* (see also Rees, 2006). The first two phases are closely connected to women's participation in the workforce, where the legal basis for action in the area of gender equality is anchored. The third phase, mainstreaming, is argued to widen the scope of gender equality by also addressing representation, decision-making and private spheres of life.

Equal Treatment

The strategy of *equal treatment* is based on the idea of equality as sameness and indicates that rules and actions must apply to both women and men. According to the equal treatment perspective, the lack of gender equality exists because women historically have been excluded from the labour market, politics and other social contexts (Verloo and Lombardo, 2007). The strategy aims to remove any direct form of gender discrimination which leads to the unequal treatment of men and women. Each individual should have the same access to rights and opportunities and be treated according to the same principles and standards.

The origin of the principle of equal treatment in the EU goes back to Article 119 in the EEC Treaty of 1957 (later 141, now 157) on women's and men's rights to equal pay. The Article was originally introduced into the Treaty in reference to distortion of market competition. France was worried that lower salaries and limited social benefits for women in other member states would distort competition in the European market. In this context gender equality was not a goal, but a means to reach fair competition in relation to principles of a free, competitive market and economic growth.

Article 119 clearly referred to women as paid workers; however, it still provides an important basis for the development of legislation for equal opportunities in the EU. Article 119 was nevertheless a principle without clear legal definition, and it did not come with any organisational capacity for action. In the 1970s, the Defrenne vs Sabena case (case no. 43/75) gave substance to the Article as the European Court of Justice (ECJ) ruled that the Belgian flight attendant Gabriell Defrenne could not be forced to retire at 40 when this was not the case for her male counterparts. Defrenne had complained that the lower pension rights and lost future earnings violated her right to equal treatment on grounds of gender (Hoskyns, 1996). The ECJ ruled in favour of Defrenne and held that the Article was enforceable not merely between individuals and the government, but also between private parties. By doing so, the principle of *direct effect* was enforced, meaning that the provisions would have direct force without the need to be transposed into national law. In this way, Article 119 served as a basis for the Commission to establish a framework for supporting national harmonisation of women in paid work. Although the Commission did try to bring about proposals relating to non-work-related issues of gender equality, the main focus continued to be on women as workers and the principle of equal treatment continued to be characterised as an economic issue.

The legislation on gender equality in relation to work is comprehensive and includes the *Directive of equal pay for equal work* (Directive 75/117/EEC), the *Directive on equal treatment regarding the access to employment, vocational training and promotion* (Directive 76/207/EEC) and the *Directive on equal treatment in connection with social security* (Directive 79/7/EEC). The strong focus on working life is further emphasised by the narrow interpretation of the ECJ in, for example, the Hofmann case (Case 184/83) that ruled that 'The Equal treatment directive was not designed to settle questions concerned with the organization of the family, or to alter the divisions of responsibilities between parents'. Although equal treatment legislation was limited to the labour market, the early legislation on equal treatment forms an important base for equal treatment policy in the EU. Feminist scholars like Rees (2006) have nonetheless argued that the policy is flawed in focusing exclusively on the formal rights of women as workers. Feminists have also criticised this approach to gender equality as it seeks to change society without really challenging the male norms or the existing patriarchal structures (Squires, 1999). The equal treatment approach stems from the basic principle of men and women as similar and the belief that if hindrances and distortions in society are removed and men and women are treated equally, then inequality will disappear accordingly.

Positive Action

If the strategy of equal treatment focuses on men and women as similar, the approach of *difference* problematises the existence of an unquestioned norm that women need to imitate or be compensated for. The *positive actions approach* recognises that the differences between men and women are due to a complex range of social, historical and economic reasons that have led to unequal choices among, and access to, careers (Rees, 2006). Because men and women are different, it is necessary with specific actions to overcome their unequal starting positions in society (Pollack and Hafner-Burton, 2000). The solution is therefore to address these differences by targeting women specifically. In addition, positive action can include positive discrimination in which the share of women is increased by the use of affirmative actions or quotas (Rees, 2006). Instead of equality of possibilities, the focus is on equality of outcomes.

During the 1980s and 1990s, EU politics gradually moved from equal treatment approaches towards positive action approaches (Rees, 2006). A directive dealing with part-time work (Directive 97/81/EC) targeted structural discrimination against part-time workers (of which a majority were women) in terms of benefits and working conditions. Another directive dealt with the protection of health and safety for pregnant women and women breastfeeding (Directive 92/85/EEC). Both directives aimed to facilitate the process for women to combine work with family life. The directives were to a large extent motivated by economic goals and the need to enlarge the workforce in order to combat demographic changes of an ageing population and decreasing birth rates (Calvo et al., 2009: 317). Other examples of positive action were the adoption of action programmes by the Commission aiming at projects related to childcare and women's rights networks.

Both decisions made by the ECJ reaffirmed the rights of the member states to adopt positive actions. The inclusion of Justice and Home Affairs into the Maastricht Treaty also served to open up the possibility for the EU to act on violence against women. The agreement on social policy in the Maastricht Treaty confirmed the EU's orientation towards workers by including the wording of Article 119. By introducing a paragraph, it was stressed that member states should not be prevented from maintaining or adopting measures providing for specific advantages in order to make it easier for women to pursue vocational activity or compensate for disadvantages in their professional careers (TEU Article 6§3). This statement made it clear that member states were free to take positive actions to combat discrimination. Together, all these initiatives made it possible for the EU to act beyond the narrow equal treatment approach.

Mainstreaming

Although positive actions may have some impact on certain areas, they do not address systematic culture change. The idea of gender equality as *transformation* problematises the gendered world itself, as *gender mainstreaming* is put forward as a means for change (Squires, 2005). Underpinning the 'transforming' or gender mainstreaming approach is the idea that existing structures and institutions are not gender-neutral, but favour one gender over another, usually men, in a variety of subtle and often invisible ways. This approach also recognises that differences exist between the sexes yet embraces these differences as bringing added value to the working environment. In the EU, gender mainstreaming is defined as: 'the (re)organisation, improvement, development, and evaluation of policy processes so that a gender equality perspective is incorporated in all policies and at all stages by the actors normally involved in policy-making' (Council of Europe, 1996).

Many scholars argue that mainstreaming of gender equality has given the EU the possibility to take action in a number of areas where they have no provisions in the treaties. Domestic violence is one such area, and the inclusion of women in science is another (Calvo et al., 2009). In this way, mainstreaming changed the limitation of the EU to move outside areas covered in the treaty, although the mandate to act is still more diffuse (due to this very lack of provisions in the treaty). The idea of mainstreaming had existed in the EU since the beginning of the 1990s, but it was the 1995 Platform for Action decided in Beijing that was the real starting point. The European Commission and its member states had actively pushed for mainstreaming at the Beijing meeting and the EU delegation played a leading role in promoting the policy (Calvo et al., 2009: 319). The Beijing Platform defined mainstreaming, and all participating nations agreed to work to incorporate the gender perspective into all policy-making areas (Pollack and Hafner-Burton, 2000; Calvo et al., 2009). In 1996, mainstreaming was officially adopted by the European Commission, defined as the organisation of policy processes according to the definition above. In 1996, the Commission adopted the Fourth Action Program on Equal Opportunities for Women and Men (1996–2000), wherein mainstreaming was presented as the single most important component (Pollack and Hafner-Burton, 2000). Three themes were introduced in order to reach gender equality: the first was that mainstreaming should be the organising principle. The mainstreaming approach was further strengthened by the Treaty of Amsterdam in 1997, which included several new provisions in the area of equal opportunities, such as a reinforcement of the old Article 119 and the introduction of the co-decision procedure for equal opportunity legislation strengthening the role of the European Parliament, traditionally a strong gender equality supporter.

New Modes of Governance

Traditional policy-making patterns in the EU are increasingly being complemented by the use of 'soft' governance tools such as benchmarking, recommendations on best practices and guidelines, which allow for member states to coordinate policy as well as act as executives, because the member states are responsible for their compliance to the measures they have agreed to on the EU level. Gender mainstreaming can be considered a typical illustration of the soft tools and 'new modes of governance', as it is a non-binding and flexible instrument in clear contrast with the traditional regulatory and economic instruments that have historically been central to EU gender equality policy (Hantrais, 2008). Gender is explicitly highlighted as an area for which the use of soft tools is needed in order to push for the development of gender equality and work against discrimination (European Commission, 2010b: 15). The reason for this is the lack of provisions in the treaties in most of the areas that relate to gender equality. An exception is equal treatment related to working life.

The use of soft tools takes place through the Open Method of Coordination process (OMC). In the process, the Commission plays a monitoring and agenda-setting role. The Council of Ministers then sets the policy goals and guidelines by unanimity. Member states submit annual reports on their progress and these reports are commented on and evaluated by the Commission. The OMC is applied in areas where the national situation differs substantially or where only limited competences exist on the EU level, which is the case in the area of gender equality (but also in areas such as employment policy, social policy, education policy and R&D). OMC has developed as a compromise, as it retains member-state responsibility for an area while giving the EU a coordinating and policy-shaping role (Warleigh-Lack and Drachenberg, 2011: 207). The process was launched as part of the package from the Lisbon meeting of 2000 together with the European Employment Strategy (European Council, 2000).

The OMC represents a voluntary and intergovernmental mode of cooperation. It is not a uniform process; instead, it works differently depending on area. However, a few common steps exist. The first step is to set fixed guidelines for the Union combined with a timetable. This step is driven by the Commission targets set by the member states (in close cooperation with the Commission). An example is the targets set in Europe 2020 and the related flagship documents. Step 2 is to establish quantitative and qualitative indicators and benchmarks to strive for, and which in step 3 will be translated into national and regional policies by setting specific targets and adopting measures for reaching them. The Commission draws up a report on progress made towards the objectives that are set both at the EU level and within the member states. The progress and fulfilment of the targets set up are evaluated in national reports. These reports also form bases for mutual learning processes, during which officials and stakeholder representatives meet during conferences and workshops in order to represent and discuss important issues and progress. The OMC process is considered to have important consequences for policy-making at both European and national levels both in the areas of employment and education (Warleigh-Lack and Drachenberg, 2011).

GENDER EQUALITY IN EUROPE 2020

Employment

In Europe 2020, gender equality is mentioned as a strong European value, together with the importance of democratic institutions, consideration for economic, social and territorial cohesion and solidarity, respect for the environment, and cultural diversity (European Commission, 2010a: 9). However, although related to other European values, Europe 2020 primarily addresses women as a supply to the labour market. Gender equality is first and foremost a tool for economic growth and welfare. On first impression, gender equality does not seem to play an important role (the term only appears three times), but a closer look reveals that women are viewed as central for a European economic recovery as they constitute an important pool of recruitment in order to meet the main target of 75 per cent of the population in the workforce: 'Policies to promote gender equality will be needed to increase labour force participation thus adding to growth and social cohesion' (European Commission, 2010a:17). Women's employment rate is lower than men's: in 2010, it was 63 per cent, compared to men's at 76 per cent (European Commission, 2010a: 7). In order to reach the target of 75 per cent of the population in the workforce, the pool of women needs to be used: 'The employment rate of the population aged 20–64 should increase from the current 69% to at least 75%, including through the greater involvement of women, older workers and the better integration of migrants in the work force' (European Commission, 2010a:10). Hence, from the perspective of gender equality, Europe 2020 almost exclusively deals with ways to increase women's participation in the workforce. This situation is further emphasized as the demographic situation in Europe is viewed as highly problematic and Europe 2020 calls for a need to make full use of the populations. Gender equality is therefore put forward as an important way to reach the employment target (European Commission, 2010a). Employment rates need to be raised all over, but women are emphasised as an important potential group (European Commission, 2010a:3).

Three ways are suggested to increase the chances for women to contribute to the following target: 'support measures to reconcile work and private life, gender mainstreaming, and actions for tackling gender-based segregation in the labour market' (European Commission, 2010b: 21). The first way calls for policies on work–life balance. Here, the Commission urges the member states to facilitate the reconciliation of work and family life at home to promote 'new forms of work–life balance and active ageing policies and to increase gender equality' (European Commission, 2010a: 19). A review of the document indicates that an important measure to reconcile work and private life and to promote new forms of work–life balance as mentioned is to increase the participation in early childhood education: 'In order to increase labour participation access to childcare facilities and care for other dependents are important' (European Commission, 2010a: 18). Second, the need for gender mainstreaming is mentioned; however, no specific actions are expressed. A third and more substantial action is to evaluate the impact of employment-relevant non-discrimination directives (European Commission, 2010b: 16). The development of gender equality work and work on discrimination should further take place through the use of soft tools (European Commission, 2010b: 15). In addition to these strategies, female participation in the workforce should further be supported by the increasing introduction of flexicurity policies (European Commission, 2010b: 3). Female participation calls for an increase of flexibility in the work organization or of working time (for example, short-time working arrangements). 'Flexibility also allows men and women to combine work and care commitments, enhancing in particular the contribution of women to the formal economy and to growth, through paid work outside the home' (European Commission, 2010b: 6).

The Europe 2020 employment targets are further developed in 'An agenda for new skills and jobs' (European Commission, 2010b), with the overall target set of 75 per cent of the population in employment. In 2017, the overall employment rate in the EU reached 72.2 per cent (Eurostat, 2018: 27). In terms of gender, the employment rates are considerably lower for women than men, although the gender employment gap is shrinking (Eurostat, 2018: 27). Overall, for the age group 20 to 64, the gap fell from 17.3 percentage points in 2002 to 11.5 percentage points in 2017 (Eurostat, 2018: 34).

The only stipulated action taken related to gender according to the main document (European Commission, 2010a) is to examine the impact of the employment-relevant non-discrimination directives 2000/78/EC10 and 2000/43/EC (European Commission, 2010b: 16). The directive 2000/78/EC10, called the 'Employment Equality Framework Directive', establishes a general framework for equal treatment in employment and occupation by prohibiting employment discrimination on the grounds of religion or belief, disability, age or sexual orientation. The directive 2000/43/EC, called the racial directive, regulates equal treatment between persons irrespective of racial or ethnic origin. According to EU law, member states are required to align their national legislation with all the requirements of the directives. At the national level, the Treaty provisions and, in particular, the directives must be implemented. This means a transposition of the legal provisions into national law. This is partly done by amending relevant national legislation. According to the European Equality Law Network, all member states have transposed the provisions of the directives in their national legislation, although the directives are not necessarily implemented effectively throughout all member states (Burri and Van Eijken, 2014: 39).

A review of documents related to Europe 2020 and employment shows that gender equality is viewed as an important measure to reach full employment and economic growth. To involve more women in the workforce is a way to increase the overall employment rate in Europe. Only one point in the document includes a reference to gender equality as an important value in itself. Gender equality as an intrinsic value plays a marginal role in the text (European Commission, 2010a: 9). That the strategy of equal treatment is present as the only concrete action stipulated in the document is itself a reflection of the impact of discrimination-related directives. Gender mainstreaming is mentioned, but only in general terms and without detailing how mainstreaming will have an effect on the advancement of women's participation in the workforce.

To make gender equality into an issue related to employment is not a new strategy in the European Union. This had already been seen to be used for example in the Defrenne case. It can, however, be interpreted as an example of political entrepreneurship. To call for work–life-related action in order to increase employment is a way to step outside the limitation set by the provisions in the treaties.

Research and Innovation

The target set for research and innovation is described in detail in the EU flagship initiative 'Innovation Union', which set out to improve framework conditions and access to finance for research and innovation, and by doing so to strengthen the innovation chain and boost levels of investment throughout the Union. Research and development are closely linked to employment, and when gender equality is of concern in the document it is regarding the improvement of working conditions in order to attract women to a research career. Also in the area of research and innovation, the main idea is to use the pool of women to increase the number of researchers.

In Innovation Union, member states are recommended to have strategies to train enough researchers to meet their national R&D targets and to promote attractive employment conditions in public research institutions and '[g]ender and dual career considerations should be fully taken into account in these strategies' (European Commission, 2010e: 12). The Commission stated their intention to support measures to remove obstacles to mobility and cross-border cooperation, and 'ensure through a common approach quality of doctoral training, attractive employment conditions and gender balance in research careers' (European Commission, 2010e: 13). More people need to be engaged in research, and therefore the research career needs to be attractive also to women. The aim for the member states should be that 'frameworks for research careers, including doctoral studies, offer sufficiently attractive conditions to both men and women in comparison to international standards, especially those in the US' (European Commission, 2010e: 36). The interest in increasing the number of women in research is especially focused on the science, technology, engineering and mathematics (STEM) disciplines as the problem of 'too few girls taking science to an advanced level' still exists (European Commission, 2010e: 11).

The overall target for research and innovation sets out to improve the 'conditions for innovation, research and development', in particular with the aim of 'increasing combined public and private investment in R&D to 3 per cent of GDP' by 2020 (Eurostat, 2018: 50). This figure stagnated at around 2.03 per cent and as a result, the target is still far away (Eurostat, 2018: 52). Eurostat statistics show that the numbers of researchers being trained have increased. This is especially the case for STEM disciplines, but large gender gaps still exist. The EU increased its output of tertiary graduates in science and technology (59 per cent between 2003 and 2015), but women still remain underrepresented in these fields of study, as their number was only around half that of male graduates (Eurostat, 2018: 59).

The area of research and innovation is closely linked to employment policy, and in a similar way, gender equality is an instrument for increasing the number of researchers rather than an objective in itself. This impression is strengthened by the fact that the interest of the Commission in R&D is mainly focused on the fields in which research is expected to have an effect of economic growth, that is, the STEM disciplines. As in the rest of the employment area, the strategy of equal treatment is at work, as European Union law also applies in the form of employment-relevant non-discrimination directives. Apart from the anti-discrimination legislation, the main strategies for supporting the member states to increase the number of researchers take place through the use of 'soft' governance tools such as benchmarking, recommendations on best practices and guidelines through the OMC. Focus has been on improving gender-based statistics (for example, the SHE figures) in order to assess the share of women graduating and reaching higher positions as researchers. As the EU does not have any formal right to act in the area of research and development, the inclusion of R&D in the area of employment is a typical example of how the EU expands its powers and can be viewed as an example of political entrepreneurship. To turn the focus of women's underrepresentation in science from a question of justice to a question of recruitment can in a similar way be analysed as an example of political entrepreneurship.

Education

Women and gender equality are not at all in focus in the flagship 'Youth on the move' initiative (European Commission, 2010c), which addresses education; neither gender equality nor women are mentioned in the document, and no targets with a direct connection to gender are set out. However, most of the actions suggested for reaching employment are in fact related to education. In line with this, Europe 2020 does not contain any actions for increasing gender equality per se but does address areas that are expected to improve female participation in the workforce. Women are only mentioned in relation to temporary contracts: their 'higher risk of being hired by temporary contracts' is addressed, and young women are described as 'particularly at risk of falling into this segmentation trap'. The Commission concludes that the use of such contracts should be limited, as it is 'bad for growth, productivity and competitiveness' (European Commission, 2010c: 16).

Despite the lack of explicit references to gender, several of the additional targets set out in the document, particularly the target of strengthening Early Childhood Education (European Commission, 2010c: 9), are highly related to gender. Also the other targets can be analysed from a gender perspective, as performance in education often differs between men and women.

The main targets set out for education are *reducing the school drop-out rate* to less than 10 per cent and increasing the share of the population aged 30–34 that have *completed tertiary education* to at least 40 per cent by 2020 (European Commission, 2010c). On both of these targets, women perform better than men. Reports on the first target, increasing the share of early leavers, indicate a continuous fall from 17.0 per cent in 2002 to 10.6 per cent in 2017. Overall, men leave school earlier than women do, and the rate for women who leave school is already below the headline target, with only 8.9 per cent leaving early in 2017, whereas the rate for men is 12.1 per cent (Eurostat, 2018: 90–91). Also, women have met the target of 40 per cent for *tertiary education* whereas men have not. Between 2002 and 2017, the share of tertiary educated grew from 23.6 per cent to 39.9 per cent. The growth was considerably faster for women, who in 2017 were already clearly above the Europe 2020 target at 44.9 per cent, whereas the number for men was 34.9 per cent (Eurostat, 2018: 96). This indicates a significantly widening gender gap among people with tertiary educational attainment across the EU. Whereas the share of tertiary graduates in 2002 was almost similar for both sexes, the share of female graduates has grown, resulting in a gender gap of 10 percentage points in favour of women in 2017 (Eurostat, 2018: 96).

To support the achievement of the two main objectives, the Commission has set another five benchmarks (Eurostat, 2018: 88): (1) at least 95 per cent of children between the age of 4 and the age at which education becomes compulsory should participate in early childhood education; (2) the rate of underachievement in basic skills for 15-year-olds should be below 15 per cent; (3) the employment rate of recent graduates should be at least 82 per cent; (4) at least 15 per cent of adults should participate in learning; and (5) at least 20 per cent of graduates from higher education and at least 6 per cent of 18–34-year-olds with vocational education should have spent time studying abroad. All of these targets can be discussed from a gender perspective, as they – especially the first target – have important gender implications.

The additional benchmark for *early childhood education* and care states that at least 95 per cent of children between the age of 4 and the age at which primary education becomes compulsory should participate in early childhood education (European Commission, 2011a). This target is closely related to the ambition of increasing the female share of the workforce and enabling more parents, especially mothers, to join the labour market. In Barcelona in 2002, objectives were set to 'remove disincentives to female labour force participation, taking into account the demand for childcare facilities and in line with national patterns of provision, to provide childcare' (European Council, 2002: 2). The participation in early education has been rising more or less continuously in the EU since 2002, reaching 95.5 per cent in 2016 and exceeding the benchmark of 95 per cent (Eurostat, 2018: 94).

The benchmark set to follow up the *reduction of the underachievement in basic skills* stipulates that the share of low-achieving 15-year-olds in reading, mathematics and science should be less than 15 per cent (Eurostat, 2018). The follow-up in 2018 shows that, according to the European Commission's PISA 2015 report, the EU as a whole is seriously lagging behind the 2020 target (Eurostat, 2018: 94).[1] The report indicates a backward trend, with the rate of low achievers increasing. In reading, girls still outperform boys in all EU countries by a large margin. However, compared to previous PISA cycles, this gender gap has shrunk considerably (European Commission, 2016: 12). PISA data show a lack of striking differences in the shares of male and female low achievers in mathematics and science (European Commission, 2016: 12). The result for science is similar: the rate of low achievement in science is slightly higher among boys (20.7 per cent) than it is among girls (20.4 per cent).

The benchmark set for the *employment rate for recent graduates* (20–34-year-olds who have left education and training in the past one to three years and are not in any further education and training) is set as at least 82 per cent. The economic crises hit this group hard; the rate fell from 82.1 per cent in 2008 to 75.4 per cent in 2013. This number slightly increased to 80.2 per cent in 2017. The target is reached by men: 82 per cent of 20–34-year-old men have employment, but the employment rate for women is lower (78.4 per cent) (Eurostat, 2018).

In 2011, the European Council adopted a resolution on a renewed European agenda for *adult participation in learning* (European Council, 2011), including a benchmark that aims to raise the share of adults who participate in learning to at least 15 per cent. Women are more likely to participate in adult learning than men are. In 2017, the share of adult women engaged in learning was 11.8 per cent, compared with 10.0 per cent for men (Eurostat, 2018: 102).

In sum, when the analyses concern education, women mostly perform better than men; when the analyses concern employment, men outperform women. If the underrepresentation of women in employment needs to be addressed primarily by making work possible by adding childcare facilities and reducing discrimination on the labour market, the underrepresentation and underperformance of men in education is likely to be due to different factors. This however is not discussed in the EU 2020 documents.

[1]   Test results were best for reading, with a 19.7 per cent share of low achievers, followed by science with a 20.6 per cent share and mathematics with a 22.2 per cent share. On average, the share of low achievers in reading is 15.9 per cent among girls and 23.5 per cent for boys in the EU. In mathematics, the EU average shows a slightly higher share of low-achieving girls at 23.2 per cent compared to boys at 21.2 per cent. The results for science are slightly higher among boys (20.7 per cent) than they are among girls (20.4 per cent) (Eurostat, 2018).

The Commission views education as an important tool for growth and prosperity in the European Union. One of the important actions for increasing the number of women on the labour market is the spread of early childcare education, which will also empower women, increase their economic independence and thus strengthen gender equality. The objective is not gender equality, but gender equality is the likely result.

None of the targets in the area of education have provisions in the treaty. Education has a weak legal basis in the treaty, as the EU's role is solely to promote cooperation between member states and, when necessary, support and supplement their efforts. The EU can only act through soft tools within the framework of the OMC. The Commission has strategically acted as a political entrepreneur by moving the area of education by creating a link between education policy and employment policy, where education and improvements in terms of gender equality in the sphere were seen as a condition for a competitive EU. This link was central, as it justifies the Union's influence on education as a part of creating jobs, employment and growth.

The Fight Against Poverty

The last flagship initiative discussed in this chapter is the *European Platform against Poverty and Social Exclusion* (European Commission, 2010d). Here, the Europe 2020 target is that 'the number of Europeans living below the national poverty lines should be reduced by 25%, lifting over 20 million people out of poverty' (European Commission, 2010a: 11). Compared to the documents discussed above, the Platform against Poverty and Social Exclusion focuses more on women than on gender equality. Women (together with children, young people, single parents, people with migrant backgrounds, certain ethnic minorities and people with disabilities) are considered parts of the population that are particularly exposed to the risk of poverty (European Commission, 2010d).

As women are at higher risk than men are – primarily due to gender inequalities in the labour market – the Commission emphasizes the gender perspective as a key to understanding poverty. Gender roles, stereotypes and structural inequalities weaken women's opportunities in the labour market and devalue their work. These obstacles mean that women, especially lone mothers, struggle to balance their work and private lives much more than men do. Gender relates to poverty in different ways. The need to care for children prevents many women from working, and traditional views on gender roles affect men's and women's educational choices and future careers. The average employment rate of women is systemically below that of men. Women are nearly four times more likely to work on a part-time basis than men are (32 per cent against 8 per cent), and the inactivity rate of working-age women (20–64 years) is almost twice that of men (30 per cent against 17 per cent). One-fifth of women living in poverty are not active in the labour market due to childcare and domestic responsibilities (European Institute for Gender Equality, 2016: 11). Compared to men, women are hired on temporary contracts more often, and their earnings are often relatively lower, leading to their lower levels of financial independence (European Institute for Gender Equality, 2016).

The Commission highlights two gender-related ways to combat poverty, and both actions and measures are related to employment policy. First, the Commission focuses on anti-discrimination policies as an important way to fight poverty: 'social inclusion policies need to dovetail with effective antidiscrimination policies, as for many groups and individuals the roots of poverty and hardship very often lie in restrictions from opportunities and rights that are available to other groups' (European Commission, 2010d: 9). In line with this, the Commission states that gender equality policies 'are needed to address the gender income gap that is visible in most age groups, and leads to higher rates of poverty in the female population, both in work and out of work' (European Commission, 2010d). Second, poverty will be reduced by raising the number of women who work, thus increasing the economic independence of women. To do this, the Commission will step up efforts to promote the economic independence of women (European Union, 2010d). This was also the first of the five priorities of its strategy for achieving equality between women and men for 2010–15 (European Commission, 2011b:10): 'Poverty and exclusion from the labour market go hand in hand, and this is particularly visible for women and younger people' (European Commission, 2010d: 4), and

> [g]etting a job is the safest route out of poverty for those who can work. This is a difficult message to preach at a time of economic crisis, but as our economies move back to growth our primary focus must be on ensuring sustainable job-intensive growth. Achieving by 2020 the 75% employment rate target for both women and men set for the Union would represent the single biggest contribution to lifting 20 million Europeans out of poverty (European Commission, 2010d: 6).

In Europe 2020, gender equality is put forward as an instrument of combating poverty, mainly by increasing the number of women who work. Similar to the area of employment, the strategies in this area include improving and reviewing the anti-discrimination legislations in the EU, which fall into the category of equal treatment. The other strategy is related to employment policy and involves increasing the number of women who work. Actions here include increasing early childhood education and the number of women in education, which are outside the provisions of the Treaty and fall under the category of soft tools. Signs of political entrepreneurship in this area are less evident.

CONCLUDING REMARKS

Table 9.1 summarises the targets set in Europe 2020 and the extent to which they were completed in 2016.[2] The table shows that the Europe 2020 targets have been reached only in the area of early childhood education. Progress has been made in all other areas, except in reducing poverty: the number of poor people in Europe increased by 0.1 per cent (not shown in the table). Men perform better than women on the overall employment target and on the targets for the employment of the recently graduated. Women perform better than men on the targets of tertiary education, the reduction of the share of early school leavers, underachievement in basic skills and adult participation in learning.

The evaluation of the targets set in Europe 2020 that can be related to gender indicates that many of the targets have not been reached and that important gender differences still exist.

In all areas of Europe 2020, gender equality appears mainly as a tool for change. The instrumentalist perspective on gender is dominant, and gender equality as an intrinsic value is rare. This is however expected, as Europe 2020 is an agenda for growth and a strategy for removing Europe from economic crises. The question that needs to be asked is whether the Commission's instrumentalist view on gender equality will also lead to improved positions for women in Europe and create gender equality also in other ways. In Nordic countries, the increased participation of women in the labour market and improved childcare facilities have had a positive impact on gender equality. For decades, Nordic gender-equality policy has focused on increasing gender equality in working life and has targeted women as a labour force. These focuses in combination with available and affordable childcare have been the main avenues for enabling female labour-market participation (Wikander, 1992). This (instrumental) strategy has put the Nordic countries in the top positions on global indexes of gender equality. In many ways, the European Union is now copying this strategy.

Although gender equality in the EU historically has been characterized by an equal treatment perspective, actions and measures in the Europe

---

[2] Most of the statistics presented in Eurostat (2018) refer to figures of performance measured in 2016. In some cases, the figures have been updated for 2017.

Table 9.1 *Overview of objectives and aims related to gender equality in Europe 2020 and related documents*

AREA	Targets set in Europe 2020	Additional targets set by the Commission	Overall completion in 2016	Men	Women
Employment	Employment rate at 75%		72.2%	76%	63%
Research & innovation	Investment in R&D constituting 3% of the GDP		2.03%	–	–
Education	Share of early leavers under 10%		10.6%	12.1%	8.9%
	Share of people with tertiary education at 40%		39.9%	34.9%	44.9%
		95% of children in early childhood education	95.5%		
		Reduction of underachievement in basic skills to below 15%	Reading 19.7% Maths 22.2% Science 20.6%	23.5% 20.2% 20.7%	15.9% 23.3% 20.4%
		Employment rate of recent graduates at 82%	80.2%	82%	78.4%
		Adult participation in learning at 15%	10.9%	10.0%	11.8%
Poverty	Numbers under the national Poverty line of 96.1 million		118 million	55 million	62 million

Source: European Commission (2016), Eurostat (2018), Eurostat (online data code: sdg_04_50).

2020 strategy tend mostly to rely on soft tools. Very few of the actions that can be related to gender are based on provisions in the treaties. This implies that gender equality in the EU will depend on how well the OMC will work and to what extent it will affect member states' policies. Experiences from other areas, such as education and employment, indicate that the OMC process has had an important impact on policy. In theory, the mainstreaming approach could transform existing structures and institutions. Gender mainstreaming and soft tools are non-binding; this does not mean that no constraints are imposed. Instead, the constraints are cognitive rather than formal, as they are voluntary procedures (Jacquot, 2010). Mainstreaming and the use of soft tools give important cognitive power to the Commission. The work against discrimination and gender inequalities and the focus on gender equality as an element of economic growth and competitiveness – with activities aiming at including the female workforce – can be viewed as examples of the Commission's influence in acting as a political entrepreneur to increase the scope of its mandate.

REFERENCES

Bergmann-Winberg, M. and E. Wihlborg (2011). *Politikens Entreprenörskap – Kreativ Problemlösning och Förändring*. Malmö: Liber.
Burri, S. and Van Eijken, H. (2014). 'Gender Equality Law in 33 European Countries: How are EU rules transposed into national law?' European network of legal experts in the field of gender equality. Brussels: European Commission Directorate-General for Justice Unit.
Calvo, D., Burns, T.R. and Carson, M. (2009). 'Toward a new social order?: Mainstreaming gender equality in EU policymaking'. In M. Carson, T.R. Burns and D. Calvo (eds), *Paradigms in Public Policy: Theory and Practice of Paradigm Shifts in the EU*. Internationaler Verlag der Wissenschaften.
Consolidated version of the Treaty on European Union. OJ C 326, 26.10.2012, pp. 13–390.
Council Directive 75/117/EEC of 10 February 1975 on the approximation of the laws of the Member States relating to the application of the principle of equal pay for men and women.
Council Directive 76/207/EEC of 9 February 1976 on the implementation of the principle of equal treatment for men and women as regards access to employment, vocational training and promotion, and working conditions.
Council Directive 79/7/EEC of 19 December 1978 on the progressive implementation of the principle of equal treatment for men and women in matters of social security.
Council Directive 92/85/EEC of 19 October 1992 on the introduction of measures to encourage improvements in the safety and health at work of pregnant workers and workers who have recently given birth or are breastfeeding (tenth individual Directive within the meaning of Article 16 (1) of Directive 89/391/EEC).

Council Directive 97/81/EC of 15 December 1997 concerning the Framework Agreement on part-time work.

Council Directive 2000/43/EC of 29 June 2000 implementing the principle of equal treatment between persons irrespective of racial or ethnic origin.

Council of Europe (1996). Council Recommendation of 2.12.1996 on the Balanced Participation of Women and Men in the Decision-Making Process (96/694/EC), OJ L 319/10.12.96.

Dahl, Robert, A. (1961). *Who Governs? Democracy and Power in an American City.* New Haven: Yale University.

Defrenne vs Sabena. EJC 8 April 1976. Case 43/75.

Dollar, D. and Gatti, R. (1999). 'Gender inequality, income and growth: are good times good for women?' Mimeograph, Washington, DC: World Bank.

European Commission (2010a). 'EUROPE 2020 – A strategy for smart, sustainable and inclusive growth'. COM(2010) 2020.

European Commission (2010b). 'An agenda for new skills and jobs: A European contribution towards full employment'. Strasbourg, 23.11.2010, COM (2010) 682 final.

European Commission (2010c). 'Youth on the Move – An initiative to unleash the potential of young people to achieve smart, sustainable and inclusive growth in the European Union'. Luxembourg: Publications Office of the European Union.

European Commission (2010d). 'The European platform against poverty and social exclusion: a European framework for social and territorial cohesion'. COM (2010) 758 final, Luxembourg: Publications Office of the European Union.

European Commission (2010e). 'Europe 2020 and the flagship innovation union'. SEC (2010) 1161. Luxembourg: Publications Office of the European Union. Directorate-General for Research and Innovation.

European Commission (2011a). 'Early childhood education and care: providing all our children with the best start for the world of tomorrow'. COM (2011) 66 final.

European Commission (2011b). Gender equality between women and men 2010–2015. Luxembourg: Publications Office of the European Union.

European Commission (2016). 'PISA 2015: EU performance and initial conclusions regarding education policies in Europe'. Luxembourg: Publications Office of the European Union.

European Council (2000). 'European Council Meeting in Lisbon, 23 and 24 March 2000 – Conclusions'.

European Council (2002). 'Presidency Conclusions: Barcelona 15–16 March 2002'. SN 100/1/02 REV 1.

European Council (2011). 'Council Resolution on a renewed European agenda for adult learning' (2011/C 372/01), *Official Journal of the European Union*, 20 December 2011.

European Insititute for Gender Equality (EIGE) (2016). *Promoting Gender Equality in Academia and Research Institutions.* Luxembourg: Publications Office of the European Union.

Eurostat (2018). 'Smarter, greener, more inclusive? Indicators to support the Europe 2020 strategy'. Luxembourg: Publications Office of the European Union.

Hantrais, L. (2008). *Social Policy in the European Union.* Basingstoke: Palgrave Macmillan.

Hix, S. (2005). *The Political System of the European Union.* Basingstoke: Palgrave Macmillan.

Hofmann, Ulrich v. Barmer Ersatzkasse. ECJ 12 July 1984. Case 184/83.
Hoskyns, C. (1996). *Integrating Gender: Women, Law and Politics in the European Union.* London: Verso.
Hyman, R. (2008). 'Britain and the European social model: capitalism against capitalism'. IES Working Paper: WP19. London School of Economics: Institute for Employment Studies.
Jacquot, S. (2010). 'The paradox of gender mainstreaming: unanticipated effects of new modes of governance in the gender equality domain', *West European Politics*, **33**(1), 118–35.
Kabeer, N. and Natali, L. (2013). 'Gender equality and economic growth: is there a win–win?' *IDS Working Papers*, **2013**(417), 1–58.
Klasen, S. (2006). 'Gender and pro-poor growth', in Lukas Menkoff (ed.), *Pro-Poor Growth: Policy and Evidence*, pp. 151–71. Berlin: Duncker and Humblot.
Klasen, S. and Lamanna, F. (2009). 'The impact of gender inequality in education and employment on economic growth: new evidence for a panel of countries'. *Feminist Economics*, **15**(3), 91–132.
Minstrom, M. (2004). *Policy Entrepreneurship and School Choice.* Washington, DC: Georgetown University.
Pollack, M.A. and Hafner-Burton, E. (2000). 'Mainstreaming gender in the European Union'. *Journal of European Public Policy*, **7**(3), 432–56.
Rees, T. (2006). *Mainstreaming Equality in the European Union.* London: Routledge.
Rossilli, M. (ed.) (2000). *Gender Policies in the European Union.* New York: Peter Lang Publishing.
Schneider, M., Teske, P. and Mintrom, M. (1995). *Public Entrepreneurs: Agents for Change in American Government*, Princeton, NJ: Princeton University Press.
Squires, J. (1999). 'Rethinking the boundaries of political representation'. In S. Walby (ed.), *New Agendas for Women* (pp. 169–89). London: Palgrave Macmillan.
Squires, J. (2005). 'Is mainstreaming transformative? Theorizing mainstreaming in the context of diversity and deliberation'. *Social Politics: International Studies in Gender, State & Society*, **12**(3), 366–88.
Verloo, M.M.T. and Lombardo, E. (2007). *Contested Gender Equality and Policy Variety in Europe: Introducing a Critical Frame Analysis Approach.* Budapest: CEU Press.
Walby, S. (1999). 'The European Union and equal opportunities policies'. *European Societies*, **1**(1), 59–80.
Warleigh-Lack, A. and Drachenberg, R. (2011). 'Spillover in a soft policy area? Evidence from the Open Method of Co-ordination in education and training'. *Journal of European Public Policy*, **18**(7), 999–1015.
Wikander, Ulla (1992). 'Delat arbete, delad makt: om kvinnors underordning i och genom arbete. En historisk essä'. In Y. Hirdman and G. Åström (eds), *Kontrakt i Kris: Från Ojämlik till Ojämställd.* Stockholm: Carlssons förlag.
Young, B. (2000). 'Disciplinary neoliberalism in the European Union and gender politics', *New Political Economy*, **5**(1), 77–98.

10. Asylum and migration policies: enabling inclusive growth in the EU?

Anna Parkhouse

The financial crisis in Europe became the catalyst for a new take on finding innovative ways for smart, sustainable and inclusive growth in the light of successfully tackling the crisis. Although inclusive growth, as 'fostering a high employment economy delivering social and territorial cohesion' (EC, 2010: 3) forms the backbone of Europe 2020, there is, however, little reference to the inclusion of migrants. This is surprising seeing as how already in 2005 and in the light of the looming demographic crisis,[1] the European Commission had stressed the need to strengthen the integration of migrants in order to meet labour market needs, contributing to a stronger European economy and to the survival of the welfare state (EC, 2005).

The migration crisis of 2015, in parallel with the increasing demographic crisis, would contribute to strengthen the link between migration and integration. According to Commission action programmes, more effective integration would henceforth also include refugees in so far as the 'full participation and early integration of all third-country nationals, including refugees' (EC, 2016b: 3) is vital in order to ensure both economic growth and social cohesion. The necessity to use the competencies of both migrants and refugees more effectively in order to increase the ratio of active workers versus inactive workers has been brought onto the Commission agenda. However, statistics show that the unemployment rate of migrants is still high and that the over-qualification of migrants doing low skilled work remains a barrier towards more effective integration (EC, 2011: 3). This has led some to argue that what many have termed the 'refugee crisis' in fact is more of a migration governance crisis or a 'crisis of Europe and its institutions rather than one of European migra-

---

[1] The demographic crisis refers to an ageing population, longer life expectancies and a declining working age population (EC, 2011: 2).

tion' (Parkhouse and Strömblad, 2018; Zimmermann, 2017: 88). This perspective is based on two arguments: on the one hand the demographic crisis means that Europe is lacking in labour force and increased labour mobility; on the other hand, neither national nor European institutions seem to have the capacity to integrate migrants and refugees into the respective Member State societies (Zimmermann, 2017: 88).

Although the linkage between migration flows and the policies to handle them is arguably evident (Lulle and King, 2016: 22), research focusing on the role of migration policies linked to more effective integration has been negligible. This is surprising seeing as how institutional factors seem to be partly responsible 'for their weak performance in the labour market' (Zimmermann, 2017: 96). Institutions can broadly be defined as a 'set of rules and practices that guide the interactions of actors in a given structural context' (March and Olsen, 1998: 948; Trauner and Ripoll Servent, 2016: 1419). Against the backdrop of Europe 2020, this chapter will explore the role of asylum and labour migration policies and whether they are enabling to respond in a flexible way to the priorities and needs of EU Member States' labour markets. Another aim is to explore what potential roles political entrepreneurs have in policy-making and policy development, creating more effective and innovative paths to labour market integration and inclusive growth in Europe. Adhering to the definition used in the book, a political entrepreneur is someone who

> operates beyond traditional and routinized procedures and is innovative and creative in using formal and informal institutions and networks to improve the public sector's activities towards entrepreneurs and entrepreneurship by developing and promoting new norms that have not been embedded in traditional day-to-day public activities (see Chapter 1 in this volume).

By migration, we mean movements of people across state borders. These movements can take place in both directions, that is, they can deal with both emigration and immigration. In this chapter, we are only concerned with EU asylum and labour immigration policies. After an overview of the policy areas, the chapter moves on to analyse asylum and migration policies and the potential role of political entrepreneurs in creating more effective and innovative paths to labour market integration and inclusive growth in the EU.

THE EU ASYLUM AND MIGRATION POLICY CONTEXT

History and Development of the Policy Area

Within the framework of Justice and Home Affairs, asylum and migration policy became a new policy area in the Treaty of Maastricht in 1993 (Ucarer, 2013). The establishment of the policy area should be seen as a *spillover* from the completion of the single market and therefore as a logical consequence of the passport-free union (Nugent, 2010). Subsequently, a strengthened Schengen cooperation was also integrated into the EU institutional framework. However, the effectiveness of border protection was hampered by the fact that membership in Schengen is neither complete nor restricted to the EU Member States.[2] These shortcomings were legally reinforced by the Treaty of Nice (2003), which extended the principle of flexible integration to apply also to the area of asylum and migration policy. This meant that Ireland and the United Kingdom were given judicial rights to stand outside the cooperation, in so-called 'opt-out clauses' (Nugent, 2010). The five-year Tampere programme (2000–2005) was to be the first of a number of strategic action programmes in the launching of the policy area. In parallel with increasing the rights and the free movement of those legally staying in the EU, the fight against illegal immigration was strengthened. The Tampere programme was also the starting point for the Common European Asylum System (CEAS), designed to harmonise national asylum systems. Minimum levels of legislation combined with poor compliance with the regulations resulted in the Tampere Programme's goals also becoming priority objectives in the subsequent policy programmes in the Hague (2005–10) and in Stockholm (2010–14) (Collett, 2014). In 2009, the CEAS was institutionalised in the Treaty of Lisbon (Art. 78 [1] TFEU, Lisbon). At the same time, the solidarity clause and the principle of fair division of responsibility between Member States were institutionalised (Art. 222, TFEU, Lisbon). The right to asylum is based

---

[2]   The Schengen cooperation is composed of 22 EU Member States and 4 countries not having EU membership. Apart from Ireland and the United Kingdom, having opt-out clauses, Bulgaria, Croatia, Cyprus and Romania are not yet part of the cooperation. When in compliance with the membership criteria, they are obliged to become members. Non-EU member states, such as Iceland, Lichtenstein, Norway and Switzerland are associate members of the Schengen cooperation. Although not *de jure* members of Schengen, Monaco, San Marino and the Holy See are de facto members, keeping their borders to neighbouring states open (Ucarer, 2013).

on the Geneva Convention[3] and is governed by the EU Charter of Human Rights (Article 18 of the EU Charter).

In 2015, and in order to strengthen more effective migration management, the Commission took a more holistic approach by proposing the European Agenda on Migration.[4] The objective of the third pillar is the development of a more robust CEAS. The fourth pillar focuses on developing the policy for legal migration, thus strengthening the economic and social integration for the purposes of addressing labour market needs as well as social cohesion (EC, 2015a). The considerably large migratory influx, which played out on European soil during the autumn of 2015, made it evident that the commitments of both the CEAS and the solidarity clause were not upheld. The political turmoil that followed, subsequently leading some EU Member States to reintroduce national territorial border controls and more restrictive migration policies, also contributed to further embed the policy area in the larger EU foreign policy and developmental nexus. With the aim of responding to the crisis, the Commission roadmap of 2017 was an effort to build a collective engagement on a comprehensive deal on migration. The roadmap is based on key action areas, such as tackling the structural causes of migration, reinforcing external border management and the strengthening of the work on readmission and relocation. The strategy of strengthening relations with international actors and neighbouring countries has therefore become key after the EU–Turkey Statement of March 2016, which led to the drastic decrease[5] of migrants going from Turkey to Greece (EC, 2018; Zimmermann, 2017: 97). In the European Council meeting in June 2018, the lack of a collective engagement from the EU Member States continues to be hampering any comprehensive deal on migration.

Conceptualisation of Migrants and Refugees

The asylum and migration policy area is based on a paradox in so far that in order to guarantee the free movement of people within the EU, this requires more rigorous control and regulation of those who are outside,

---

[3]   The Geneva Convention of 1951 and its 1967 Protocol are the international legal documents regulating the rights of displaced people and the obligations of the sovereign states having signed and ratified the documents (Zimmermann, 2016: 3).

[4]   The Agenda consist of four pillars. The aim of the first pillar is to reduce the incentives for illegal migration. Linked to this, the aim of the second pillar is to strengthen the border management by creating smart borders, necessitating the better use of IT systems, such as the Schengen Information Systems (SIS) (EC, 2015a).

[5]   The EU–Turkey Statement has meant a drastic reduction in the number of migrants going from Turkey to Greece, from an average of 10 000 to circa 80 on a daily basis (EC, 2018).

who in EU terminology are called third-country nationals or migrants, referring to 'persons born in a country outside the EU and persons born in the EU but not holding the citizenship of a Member State' (EC, 2011: 3).[6] Whereas a migrant normally is a person who is leaving his country of his own free will, seeking a better life abroad and usually for economic reasons, commonly referred to as a labour migrant, refugees and asylum-seekers are forced to emigrate in order to seek protection from another 'sovereign country abroad' (Constant and Zimmermann, 2016: 3). The difference between a refugee and an asylum-seeker is that a refugee, upon arrival in the host country, already has a pre-approved protective status, either from the new host country or from a humanitarian organisation. Asylum-seekers, on the other hand, are unprotected and usually arrive in the host country as illegal immigrants or as displaced persons who seek asylum upon entry to the host country. Upon approval of the application, the status of the asylum-seeker changes into that of a refugee (Constant and Zimmermann, 2016: 3). Whereas asylum-seekers, refugees and labour migrants historically have been categorised separately, the increasing and more complex migratory movements are arguably making the distinction between the categories[7] more fluid, paving the way for the term 'mixed migration' (Lulle and King, 2016: 23). This also has a bearing on the temporal dimension since the distinction between temporary and permanent is becoming less relevant as refugees tend to stay and many of them acquire citizenship in the host country (Lulle and King, 2016). This means that the policy area is politically sensitive to the extent that it is strongly associated with issues of national sovereignty and questions about citizenship and asylum, that is, who is entitled to live, work and use the State's welfare system, issues which traditionally belong to the state's responsibilities. Consequently, the policy area is closely tied to other policy areas, such as integration, foreign, security and development policy.

EU Competences

Having been established as a strict intergovernmental cooperation in the Treaty of Maastricht (1993), the policy area initially developed very quickly. In the Treaty of Amsterdam (1999), and largely due to the impending Eastern enlargement, asylum, border controls, visa and migration

---

[6] In EU parlance, the definition of a migrant also sometimes includes second and third generation migrants, legally residing in EU territory (EC, 2011: 3).

[7] In EU parlance, categories such as asylum migration, labour migration, family migration and irregular migration are used. Other categorisations in use are: international/national migration; forced/voluntary migration; temporary/permanent migration; legal/illegal migration and low-skilled/high-skilled migration (Lulle and King, 2016).

issues were transferred to the first supranational pillar (Nugent, 2010). Up until the ratification of the Treaty of Lisbon (2009), the division of competences in the policy area remained according to the pillar structure introduced by the Treaty of Maastricht. Even though the whole policy area was 'communitarised' in the Treaty of Amsterdam, unanimity in the Council of Ministers was guaranteed over a transitional period of five years (Ucarer, 2013). Subsequently, this meant that the legislative powers of the European Parliament were still severely limited.[8] This changed in 2004 when the legislative powers of the European Parliament were equated with those of the Council of Ministers. The European Court of Justice would also receive a mandate to interpret and judge in litigation. However, although a considerable part of the decision-making was transferred to the supranational level, the rules and regulations of the Treaty of Amsterdam were an example of complex 'legal engineering'[9] (Ucarer, 2013: 285), for the purpose of political ends. The Treaty of Lisbon also involved significant reforms in this policy area and in decision-making. With the disappearance of the pillar structure, shared authority was introduced as a legislative principle (Art. 4 TFEU Lisbon). This means that the competence is divided between the EU and its Member States and that the EU can legislate and adopt binding acts in significant parts of the policy area (Art. 4 TFEU Lisbon). The complexity of the multi-level governance in terms of coordination and consistency, however, became evident in the migration crisis of 2015. In the following, we investigate asylum and migration policies and the role of political entrepreneurs in creating more effective and innovative paths to labour market integration and inclusive growth in the EU.

EU 2020: ASYLUM AND MIGRATION POLICIES, LABOUR MARKET INTEGRATION AND INCLUSIVE GROWTH IN THE EU

Integration is a contested concept and encompasses a broad range of policies and issue areas, such as for instance the labour market, education, culture and citizenship rights (Zimmermann, 2017: 103–104). Broadly defined, integration refers to 'the process of becoming an accepted part of society' (Penninx and Garcés-Mascarenas, 2015). The Commission

---

[8] By using the consultation procedure, in which the European Parliament only has an advisory role, in parallel to using the unanimity principle in decision-making in the Council of Ministers, the legislative powers of the European Parliament were limited (Ucarer, 2013).

[9] The maze of the rules and regulations in the area created a system that was difficult to comprehend even for legal experts (Ucarer, 2013).

refs to the integration process as a dynamic two-way process between the immigrants and the EU citizens (EC, 2005; 2016b). In the EU Member States, a variety of models of integration exist, spanning from the pure assimilationist, based on the complete incorporation of the migrant into the host society, to the very multiculturalist, based on the celebration of cultural differences.[10]

Migration policies have been on the EU agenda for more than two decades. In the EU 2020 Strategy and in the aftermath of the most serious recession in the history of the European cooperation, inclusive growth and social and territorial cohesion were emphasised as indispensable in the recovery towards a sustainable and smart economy. Even though the inclusion of migrants is only briefly addressed in the Strategy on Europe 2020, the need for a comprehensive labour migration policy which would 'respond in a flexible way to the priorities and needs of the labour markets' (EC, 2010: 17) is emphasised. In particular, five areas of concern are emphasised, of which the low unemployment rate of migrants, and particularly that of migrant women, is foremost. Another prioritised area is the problem of over-qualified migrants doing low-skilled work (EC, 2011: 3).[11] With the increasing demographic crisis in parallel with the migration crisis, the link between migration and labour market integration has been further intensified. In the light of labour and skills shortages due to the shrinking and ageing population in Europe,[12] the Commission has emphasised that the EU needs to become more competitive in attracting highly skilled competence with a view to meeting EU labour market needs (EC, 2016a). Skills, defined as 'what a person knows, understands and can do' (EC, 2016a: 2) are at the very heart of competitiveness, innovation and the creation of future jobs and growth. With increasing migration, the need to integrate migrants and refugees more effectively into the labour markets of host societies is therefore emphasised (EC, 2016a; 2016b). In the literature on political entrepreneurship, crises are seen as

---

[10] Whereas France, the Netherlands and the UK have been countries of extensive immigration, the majority of countries in Eastern Europe have little experience of immigration (Lulle and King, 2016: 52). The traditionally assimilationist policy of France was severely questioned after the Parisian riots of 2005. The multiculturalist policy, which became predominant in Sweden at the beginning of the 1970s has been resistant to the criticism which has become more systematic after the increasing migratory influx in recent years (Borevi, 2010).

[11] Other areas highlighted were higher risks of social exclusion among migrants; gaps in educational achievement; and last, the problem of public attitudes on the lack of integration of migrants (EC, 2011: 3).

[12] According to the 2015 Aging Report, although the population is forecasted to increase in the EU between 2013 and 2060 (from 507 million to 523 million), in parallel, there will be a decrease in the working population (from 211 million to 202 million) (EC, 2015b: 1.2).

potential opportunities where political entrepreneurs, by way of innovative measures, can promote formal and informal institutions in order to respond to new societal challenges. However, since the decision-making power, as set out in the Lisbon Treaty (Art. 79 (4) TFEU), within the realm of integration lies primarily at Member State level, how likely is it that innovative measures are promoted and implemented effectively? In the following, we investigate asylum and migration policies and the role of potential political entrepreneurs in creating more effective and innovative paths to labour market integration in the EU. Labour market integration is investigated in relation to the right to work, the right to be self-employed and the right to study.

Migration Policies

When it comes to formulating a sustainable strategy for developing common policies for labour immigration and more effective integration in the EU, progress has been rather slow. It was only in the Stockholm programme (2010–14), with the aim of making the EU more competitive, that an action programme for a more demand-driven labour immigration, which would also include more effective integration policy measures, was formulated (Collett, 2014). Linked to the necessity of ensuring sustainability of both welfare systems and economic growth in EU Member States, the fourth pillar of the European Agenda on Migration is centred on strengthening effective policies for legal immigration, specifically focusing on the necessity to attract both students and 'other talented and highly-skilled persons' (EC, 2015a; Lulle and King, 2016: 22). Since the skills shortage, especially pertinent in sectors like ICT, health and engineering (EC, 2016d), has the potential to limit growth, productivity and innovation, the focus on how to use migrants' skills in a more efficient and sustainable way has become key (EC, 2016a).

Back in 2009 and in view of facilitating highly skilled third country nationals to migrate to the EU, the Commission launched the *Blue Card directive*.[13] Apart from the higher education requirement, three years of working experience is required to qualify to become a Blue Card holder (2009/50/EC). By combining the residence and work permit, the *Single permit directive* was adopted as a complement to facilitate the administrative procedures and to further strengthen possibilities to be a Blue Card holder (2011/98/EU). The *Intra-corporate transfer directive*

---

[13]   The Blue Card directive was adopted in May 2009 and pertains to all Member States except Denmark, Ireland and the United Kingdom, Member States that have opt-out clauses and that therefore are not bound by the directive (2009/50/EC).

is centred on facilitating multinational companies to relocate their staff temporarily for a maximum period of three years (2014/66/EU). Another directive to strengthen legal migration is the recast *Students and researchers EU directive* whose aim it is to make it easier for third-country nationals to study, do research and train or volunteer in the EU (2016/801/EU). Other directives aimed at facilitating third-country nationals to migrate to the EU are the *Family reunification directive*, regulating admission and residence of family members of third-country nationals (2003/86/EC) and the *Long-term residents recast directive*. The objective of the latter directive is to make it easier for those third-country nationals having legally resided in an EU Member State for at least five consecutive years, to obtain an 'EU long-term resident status' (2011/51/EU) and associated rights. Another directive, more short-term, is the *Seasonal workers directive* whose aim is to simplify entry and residence in more low-skilled professions, especially in sectors of services, care, industry and agriculture. The directive, which was adopted in February 2014, regulates both housing and working conditions for the seasonal worker who may legally stay in a Member State between five and nine months (2014/36/EU).[14]

Taking into consideration that by 2025 nearly half of the jobs on the EU labour market will require highly skilled competencies (EC, 2016a), in parallel to the labour shortages, the inefficiency of the Blue Card directive has been particularly problematic. In 2016, and in order to strengthen the competitiveness of the EU, the Commission proposed the revision of the Blue Card directive (EC, 2016e). By focusing on introducing more flexible rules and procedures and by proposing to extend the scope of future Blue Card holders to two new categories, the Commission seems intent not only on increasing possibilities of attracting highly skilled third-country nationals, but at the same time on facilitating highly skilled intra-EU mobility. Indeed, and clearly in view of addressing the large influx of asylum-seekers and refugees in 2015 and to strengthen their right to work, the scope of future Blue Card holders is proposed to be extended to include 'beneficiaries of international protection and non-EU family members of EU citizens' (EC, 2016e). Admittance of the last category is, however, conditional upon having the right to work according to EU asylum rules and the qualification recast directive (2011/95/EU). To pave the way for more effective integration of refugees is understandable, seeing that in 2014, 22 per cent of the refugees of working age[15] in the EU had at least tertiary

---

[14]   The time limit is Member State competence (2014/36/EU).
[15]   Working age according to Eurostat indicators is in the range of 15–64 years (EC 2015b).

education (Tanay and Peschner, 2017: 4).[16] When it comes to introducing the category of EU citizens in a reformed Blue Card, this is arguably an attempt by the Commission to take action against the problematically low levels of intra-EU mobility. Another innovative measure proposed by the Commission, and in line with supporting entrepreneurship 'as a vital channel to foster third-country nationals' contribution to economy and society as a whole' (EC, 2016c), is to enable future Blue Card holders to have the right to be self-employed in parallel with having highly skilled employment. Last, by way of preventing fragmentation of the system, the reformed Blue Card would replace any national schemes running in parallel (EC, 2016e).

In view of more effectively meeting the priorities of an EU labour market in need of increased highly skilled labour, there is also a need to make the European higher education landscape more competitive in order to both attract but also retain foreign students. Investing in the human capital that students and researchers form for 'ensuring smart, sustainable and inclusive growth' (2016/801/EU), thereby contributing to achieving the goals of Europe 2020, is emphasised by the Commission (EC, 2010). By taking a more holistic approach to the attraction and retention of third-country students and researchers, it is clear that the perspective of the recast directive is to link measures to promote educational programmes more closely to labour market programmes and career possibilities. By increasing employment opportunities for students during their study period as well as facilitating access to the labour market for graduates, the directive would strengthen the competitiveness of the European higher education landscape at the same time as meeting the priorities of the EU labour markets. At the same time, it is clear that access to the labour market is conditional upon the level of unemployment rates of the Member State, thus Member State competence (2016/801/EU). The recast directive is also introducing faster application procedures, from a maximum of 90 days to 60 days and, in line with the reformed Blue Card, is integrating the category of EU citizens in order to increase intra-EU mobility rights (2016/801/EU).

It is certain that a reformed Blue Card directive contains important and innovative changes in view of strengthening the legal rights of migrants, but also of refugees, to take up highly skilled employment and to be self-employed in the EU. Whether these changes will make an impact in terms of meeting the priorities of the EU labour market more effectively, and to strengthen inclusive growth, is however less certain. Indeed, even though a reformed directive would provide Blue Card holders with the

---

[16] This figure is to be compared with 30 per cent within the group of non-EU born and 29 per cent of native born having at least tertiary education (Tanay and Peschner, 2017: 4).

same rights as a Member State national in terms of 'working conditions, education, recognition of qualifications, social security' (2009/50/EC), there are intrinsic shortcomings. They are intrinsic in so far as there is not one integrated labour market in the EU but 28 different national systems with widely differing practices on, for instance, the recognition of qualifications from outside of the EU (Parkhouse and Strömblad, 2018). In this context, even though the reforming of the European Qualifications Framework would mean a more comparable and consistent system for the recognition of qualifications, the impact of this Commission proposal is highly uncertain. It is uncertain in the sense that the in-built conservatism of national educational institutions, as shown by the failure of implementing the Bologna process within the higher education institutions, is sure to hamper the development of a more efficient common European system for the recognition of qualifications and skills that would have an impact in the 28 Member States, but also as a supplier of competencies and skills that the labour markets need. Indeed, according to a survey from 2011, 'over two thirds of students and recent graduates perceive a mismatch between the supply of graduates and the knowledge and skills the economy needs' (EC, 2016a: 16). This picture was also confirmed by approximately 50 per cent of the higher education providers (EC, 2016a). The mismatch, and the misuse, of competencies and skills of third-country nationals are equally challenging. Indeed, even though 25 per cent of third-country nationals are highly skilled, as many as 75 per cent of this group are 'inactive, unemployed or overqualified for their jobs' (EC, 2016a: 10). It is therefore positive that the tackling of future skills mismatches forms one of the four key goals in the renewed Agenda for higher education, adopted by the Commission in May 2017 (EC, 2017b).[17] It is clear that the role of higher education institutions, as arenas of knowledge production and dissemination, are central building blocks of innovation systems in ensuring smart and sustainable growth. Since inclusive growth forms the backbone of Europe 2020, specifically translated into the three flagships of 'Innovation Union', the 'Agenda for new skills and jobs' and also the 'European platform against poverty' (EC, 2010: 3–4), the fact that the refugees in the recast directive for more competitive higher education institutions in the EU are not specifically included is surprising, viewed that this category is the most vulnerable in terms of labour market integration (Zimmermann, 2017: 93).

---

[17] The renewed EU Agenda for higher education identifies four key goals for a strengthened cooperation in higher education. Apart from the tackling of skills mismatches and the promotion of excellence in the development of skills, the other key goals are: the building of inclusive and connected higher education systems; the focus on higher education institutions as contributors to innovation; and last, the support of more effective higher education systems (EC, 2017b).

Although it is certain that the Commission has taken its traditionally entrepreneurial role a long way to strengthen the legal rights of highly skilled migrants and refugees to have access to highly skilled employment, self-employment and higher education, it is less clear whether these innovative reforms will actually lead to more effective labour market integration and inclusive growth. Indeed, due to the fact that much of the decision-making power is Member State competence, as institutionalised by the Treaty of Lisbon (Art. 4 TFEU, Lisbon), the leeway of the Commission is undercut and limited to promoting and supporting Member States in the area of integration (EC, 2016c). This furthermore means that even though the EU can legislate and adopt binding legal acts in significant parts of the policy area, decisions regulating 'who enters, on what basis, for how long and in what number' (Geddes, 2015: 78), are still essentially Member State competence. In this context, it is important to remember that even though the demographic and the migration crisis are European phenomena, the differences in national interests and varying economic, judicial and political prerequisites are preventing a common European solution. Indeed, ever since the Eastern enlargement in 2004, the EU-15 have attracted workers particularly from the Central and Eastern European Member States. This has created large discrepancies and a fragmentation of labour markets, creating an unbalanced labour mobility intra-EU, paradoxically contributing to intra-EU competition and a brain-drain *problematique* (EC, 2016a).

This fragmentation, fuelled also by the migration crisis and the considerable differences in Member States' willingness to receive asylum-seekers in 2015, is clearly hampering the efforts of the Commission to strengthen both coordination and coherence of the policy areas. Consequently, this is also leading to enhanced flexibility where many Member States have national schemes running in parallel[18] to the Blue Card and which, in many cases, have proven more successful (EC, 2017a). This has created a situation where Member State governments as well as regional and local actors are pressurised into finding innovative ways for more effective labour market integration, such as promoting and implementing their own national schemes to attract 'highly skilled workers as part of the global competition for talent' (EC, 2018: 11). With an increasing number of asylum-seekers seeking refuge in the EU Member States, it has become important to integrate this category in labour market programmes as well, with the aim of offering them both possibilities of employment but also of further education. In the following, we investigate asylum policies and

---

[18]   For instance, Austria, Germany and the Netherlands had national schemes to attract highly skilled third-country nationals (EC, 2017a; EC, 2018).

the role of political entrepreneurs in creating innovative paths to labour market integration.

Asylum Policies

From its inception, the asylum policy area has been based on the protection pillar, as provided by the Geneva Convention and the EU Charter of Human Rights (Art. 18, EU Charter). With increased asylum immigration,[19] in parallel with the mismanagement of the migratory influx, this has led to the securitisation of the policy area.[20] This development is potentially a threat to the protection pillar since it is restricting to the right to seek asylum, a fundamental principle of international law and EU law.[21] At the same time, where the protection of the receiving Member States tends to move from a temporary to a permanent commitment, the early inclusion of asylum-seekers and refugees in labour market integration programmes has become necessary (EC, 2016b: 3). This would however require that the policies regulating the legal rights of asylum-seekers facilitate access to both employment and further education.

Since legislation had initially provided only minimum levels of protection, they were to be revised with a view to strengthening the Common European Asylum System (CEAS). The *qualification directive*, which was first adopted in 2004 and revised in 2011 (2011/95/EU), establishes rules for what is considered to be the basis for international protection. Also, the directive sets out rules and regulations as to rights to housing, access to employment and education as well as to healthcare and welfare. In 2005, the EU adopted the *asylum procedures directive*, setting out rules for a fair and efficient asylum process. The *reception conditions directive,* adopted in 2003, sets out minimum criteria for living conditions, ensuring rights to food, housing, employment and to healthcare upon arrival in the host country. Both directives were amended in 2013 (2013/32/EU; 2013/33/EU). The *Dublin Convention* of 1997 and its recasts, the *Dublin II Regulation* of 2003 and the *Dublin III Regulation* of 2013, form

---

[19]   Asylum immigration to the EU has increased considerably over the last decade. In 2008, the number of first-time asylum-seekers was 153 000. In 2015, this number had increased to 1.3 million (Tanay and Peschner, 2017: 2).

[20]   With increasing asylum immigration, the policy area is becoming closely tied to policies to combat irregular immigration. In the European Agenda on Migration, the Commission has proposed more effective efforts to counter irregular immigration, for example by combating the trafficking in human beings within the framework of the Common Security and Defence Policy (EC, 2015a).

[21]   The principle of non-refoulement guarantees asylum-seekers the right not to be sent back to a country where their lives would be threatened (Art. 33, Geneva Convention; Zimmermann, 2017: 95).

the basis of the CEAS, focusing on determining a responsible Dublin State to test asylum applications. The *Eurodac Regulation* was adopted in 2000 as a fingerprint database for a more efficient application of the Dublin Convention (Constant and Zimmermann, 2016: 4–5). In 2011, the European Asylum Support Office (EASO) was set up with the aim of enhancing the cooperation between Member States. The migration crisis in 2015 would lead the Commission to propose the reforming of the legislative acts, of which a strengthened *Qualification regulation* and an amended *Eurodac regulation* are in the process of being negotiated by the European Parliament and the Council of Ministers (EC, 2018: 6). If amended, the proposal for a new qualification regulation would provide for easier access to employment (Art. 30) as well as facilitated procedures for the recognition of qualifications and validation of skills (Art. 32) (EC, 2016f). In a reformed *Reception conditions directive*, incentives for asylum-seekers to have easier access to the labour market, such as 'to let asylees[22] work within six months after their application at the latest' (Constant and Zimmermann, 2016: 6) are proposed by the Commission. In addition, it is emphasised that access to the labour market should be in full compliance with the standards of the labour market (EC, 2016f).

However, just as in labour immigration policy, the failure of the Commission to be able to enforce any supranational power also in the domain of asylum policy is hampering any effective impact. Subsequently, even though the Commission is promoting innovative measures in the domain of early inclusion of asylum-seekers in the labour markets, the policies and rules regulating their rights to take up employment during the application procedure are Member State competence. Therefore, there is great variation, both in terms of flexibility in the policies as well as how entrepreneurial the policy-makers are. Indeed, whereas asylum-seekers have the legal right to start working from day one in Latvia and Sweden, the waiting time is longer in Germany (3 months) and even longer in Estonia and the United Kingdom (12 months) (Constant and Zimmermann, 2016: 13). However, whether the differences in these regulations have any tangible impact on more effective labour market integration is difficult to ascertain since domestic factors, such as unemployment rates of the host country, as well as the level of education and level of host language skills of the asylum-seekers are important preconditions for labour market integration (Lulle and King, 2016; Parkhouse and Strömblad, 2018). Even though Germany and Sweden are

[22] Asylee is the term used for an asylum-seeker having lodged an application which is under consideration (Zimmermann, 2016: 13).

comparable in terms of reception of asylum-seekers in 2015, proportional to their population sizes,[23] there is a large discrepancy with regard to labour market integration outcomes. Indeed, whereas the unemployment rate of non-EU born in 2017 amounted to 15.4 per cent in Sweden (to be compared with 4.5 per cent of native born), that figure was only 6.4 per cent in Germany (compared with 3.3 per cent of native born) (OECD, 2018).

Indeed, even though Swedish regulations give asylum-seekers the legal right to take up employment from day one, 'high labour market entry thresholds, spatial segregation, and bottlenecks in migrant settlement' (OECD, 2017: 2) are barriers to more effective labour market integration. In Germany, in contrast, a more flexible system has been introduced of customised integration paths with more effective ways for labour market integration for asylum-seekers with good prospects to remain (Grote, 2018).[24]

The early inclusion of asylum-seekers and refugees in Member States' labour markets is challenging seeing that it takes them up to 20 years to reach a similar employment rate to the native born of the host country (OECD, 2016; Tanay and Peschner, 2017). Even though 22 per cent of this category in 2014 had tertiary education, 'the return on higher education in terms of better employment prospects is lower for refugees than for the rest of the population' (Tanay and Peschner, 2017: 1). Seeing as there are labour shortages in an increasing number of highly skilled sectors, the more effective inclusion of highly skilled asylum-seekers and refugees in EU labour markets in view of more inclusive growth is necessary. In this respect, there is a need to remove a certain number of obstacles, such as the discrimination of these categories in the labour markets, which would necessitate a change of mindset, both on the individual level as well as on the organisational level (EC, 2016a). It is equally important to reform the national institutions for the more effective recognition of qualifications and skills, as emphasised in the reformed Qualification regulation (Art. 32). At the same time, asylum-seekers and refugees, as compared to other non-EU born migrants, are overrepresented in the category of those having the lowest level of education,[25] which would put pressure on comprehensive training and integration support (Tanay and

---

[23]   In 2015, Germany received 476 510 asylum-seekers and Sweden received 162 450 (EC, 2018: 25).

[24]   The system of customised integration paths meant the categorisation of asylum-seekers into those with a good prospect of staying and vice versa those with little or no prospect of staying (Grote, 2018: 5).

[25]   A high level of education refers to people having at least tertiary education. A medium level of education refers to those having finished upper secondary and post-secondary non-

Peschner, 2017: 4). Thus, it is certain that the more effective integration of asylum-seekers and other non-EU migrants would require the reforming of national educational institutions, particularly in terms of more effective validation of qualifications and skills. It would also require more effective language learning since command of the host language is key, not only to more effective labour market integration, but also to social cohesion.

CONCLUDING REMARKS

In the EU 2020, inclusive growth was not specifically equated with the inclusion of migrants in EU labour markets. This would however change with the migration crisis since the large influx of asylum-seekers would lead to urgency regarding the early inclusion of both migrants and refugees in the EU labour market. Even though the Commission, as the supranational political entrepreneur *par excellence*, has been promoting a forward-looking policy agenda, with initiatives that strengthen the legal rights of both migrants and refugees to have access particularly to highly skilled employment, self-employment and the right to study, there are intrinsic shortcomings. Indeed, owing to the fact that the policies regulating labour market integration are Member State competence, the political leverage of the Commission is heavily weakened on behalf of the Member States.

Thus, the focus of the Commission to strengthen both the attraction and the retention of highly skilled competencies to the EU is understandable and indeed indispensable in view of meeting the needs and priorities of the EU labour markets. By increasing the support to attract foreign students and researchers, the EU and its Member States could gain access to international competencies and that way be able to compensate for the skills shortages intra-EU, especially pertinent in certain sectors such as ICT, health and engineering. Indeed, to use the influx of new competencies from migrants and asylum-seekers more systematically, would arguably be of valuable support in the development of innovative systems, new technologies and future sustainable and inclusive growth, in parallel with alleviating the effects of an ageing population. This would compensate for the inability of higher education institutions to supply EU Member States' labour markets with the skills needed for innovation, productivity and growth. Also, the mismatch and the misuse of competencies is a clear

---

tertiary education. A low level of education pertains to those who have completed up to lower secondary school level (Tanay and Peschner, 2017: 4).

indication of the need to modernise the European landscape of higher education institutions.

The better matching of competencies puts pressure on the national institutions in need of reform and a change of mindset, with more effective, that is, labour market oriented, validation of qualifications and skills. Furthermore, even though the Commission's focus has been on facilitating integration of highly skilled migrants and asylum-seekers, the large majority of the latter group belong to the category having a low level of education. To integrate this category in the labour markets more effectively, there is a need for policy makers at Member State level to devise policies and systems, facilitating access also to low skilled employment. In Germany, for instance, political entrepreneurs were quick to adjust their earlier systems to a more flexible system based on customised integration paths, that way facilitating asylum-seekers with good prospects of staying to integrate more rapidly. In Sweden, in contrast, the high thresholds have been criticized as hampering easier access to the labour market.

Indeed, since labour market integration is Member State competence and because there are wide variations as to both national interests and preconditions, the fragmentation of the 28 national labour markets, including the persisting brain-drain *problematique*, is certain to continue to prevent any serious sustainable development for inclusive growth at EU level. Therefore, even though the entrepreneurial role of the Commission did strengthen with the migration crisis, paradoxically, the response of the Member States has rather been the strengthening of fragmentation, as evidenced not only by the failure to reach a collective engagement for the management of migration but also by the upcoming Brexit.

REFERENCES

Borevi, K. (2010). 'Dimensions of citizenship: European integration policies from a Scandinavian perspective', in B. Bengtsson, P. Strömblad and A.H. Bay (eds), *Diversity, Inclusion and Citizenship in Scandinavia*. Newcastle upon Tyne: Cambridge Scholars Publishing.

Charter of Fundamental Rights of the European Union (2000/C 364/01), 18 December 2000.

Collett, E. (2014). 'Future policy development on immigration and asylum: Understanding the Challenge'. Migration Policy Institute Europe, Policy Brief Series, No. 4.

Constant, A.F. and K.F. Zimmermann (2016). 'Towards a new European refugee policy that works'. *CESifo DICE Report*, 4/2016.

Council directive 2013/32/EU, *Asylum procedures recast directive*, 26 June 2013.

Council directive 2009/50/EC, *Blue Card directive*, 25 May 2009.

Council directive 2003/86/EC, *Family reunification directive*, 22 September 2003.

Council directive 2014/66/EU, *Intra-corporate transferees directive*, 15 May 2014.
Council directive 2011/51/EU, *Long-term residents recast directive*, 11 May 2011.
Council directive 2011/95/EU, *Qualification recast directive*, 13 December 2011.
Council directive 2016/801/EU, *Recast students and researchers directive*, 11 May 2016.
Council directive 2013/33/EU, *Reception conditions recast directive*, 26 June 2013.
Council directive 2014/36/EU, *Seasonal workers directive*, 26 February 2014.
Council directive 2011/98/EU, *Single permit directive*, 13 December 2011.
Council regulation (EC) 343/2003, *Dublin Convention*, 18 February 2003.
Council regulation (EC) 2725/2000, *Eurodac regulation*, 11 December 2000.
European Commission (2005). *A Common Agenda for Integration Framework for the Integration of Third-Country Nationals in the European Union*. Brussels: COM(2005) 389 final.
European Commission (2010). *Europe 2020. A strategy for smart, sustainable and inclusive growth*. Brussels: COM(2010) 2020.
European Commission (2011). *European Agenda for the Integration of Third-Country Nationals*. Brussels: COM(2011) 455 final.
European Commission (2015a). *A European Agenda on Migration*. Brussels: COM(2015) 240 final.
European Commission (2015b). *The 2015 Ageing Report. Economic and budgetary projections for the 28 EU Member States (2013–2060), in European Economy 3/2015*. Luxembourg: Publications Office of the European Union, 2015.
European Commission (2016a). *A New Skills Agenda for Europe. Working together to strengthen human capital, employability and competitiveness*. Brussels: COM(2016) 381 final.
European Commission (2016b). *Action Plan on the integration of third country nationals*. Brussels: COM(2016) 377 final.
European Commission (2016c). *Evaluation and Analysis of Good Practices in Promoting and Supporting Migrant Entrepreneurship*. Guide Book. Brussels, 15 September 2016.
European Commission (2016d). *Press release on reforming the Blue Card directive*.
European Commission (2016e). *Commission proposal on reforming the Blue Card directive*. Brussels: COM [2016] 378.
European Commission (2016f). *Commission proposal on a new qualification regulation*. Brussels: COM [2016] 466.
European Commission (2017a). 'Annual Report on Migration and Asylum'. *European Migration Network*. Brussels, 25 April 2017.
European Commission (2017b). *Commission communication on a renewed agenda for higher education*. Brussels: COM [2017] 247 final.
European Commission (2018). 'Annual Report on Migration and Asylum 2017'. *European Migration Network*. Brussels, 15 May 2018.
Geddes, A. (2015). 'Migration: Differential institutionalization and its effects', in F. Trauner and A. Ripoll Servent (eds), *Policy Change in the Area of Freedom, Security and Justice: How EU Institutions Matter*. London: Routledge.
Geneva Convention on the Status of Refugees, 28 July 1951.
Grote, J. (2018). 'The changing influx of asylum seekers in 2014–2016: Responses from Germany'. *Focused Study by the German National Contact Point for the European Migration Network* (EMN). Working Paper 79.
Lisbon Treaty (2009). Accessed 14 September 2018 at https://eur-lex.europa.eu/eli/treaty/lis/sign.

Lulle, A. and R. King (2016). *Research On Migration: Facing Realities and Maximising Opportunities: A Policy Review.* Luxembourg: Publications Office of the European Union.

March, J.G. and J.P. Olsen (1998). 'The institutional dynamics of international political orders'. *International Organization,* **52** (4), 943–69.

Nugent, N. (2010). *The Government and Politics of the European Union.* Basingstoke: Palgrave Macmillan.

OECD (2016). 'How are refugees faring on the labour market in Europe?' *Working Paper, 1/2016.* Paris: OECD Publishing.

OECD (2017). *OECD Economic Surveys: Sweden 2017.* Paris: OECD Publishing.

OECD (2018). *International Migration Outlook.* Paris: OECD Publishing.

Parkhouse, A. and P. Strömblad (2018). 'Exploring preconditions for political entrepreneurship and integration in European societies', in C. Karlsson, C. Silander and D. Silander (eds), *Governance and Political Entrepreneurship in Europe. Promoting Growth and Welfare in Times of Crisis.* Cheltenham, UK and Northampton, MA, USA: Edward Elgar Publishing.

Penninx, R. and B. Garcés-Mascarenas (eds) (2015). 'The concept of integration: towards an analytical and policy framework', in R. Penninx and B. Garcés-Mascarenas (eds), *Integration of Migrants into What? Integration Processes and Policies in Europe.* Cham: Springer.

Tanay, F. and J. Peschner (2017). 'Labour market integration of refugees in the EU'. *LFS workshop,* Copenhagen, 4–5 April.

Trauner, F. and A. Ripoll Servent (2016). 'The communitarization of the area of freedom, security and justice: why institutional change does not translate into policy change'. *Journal of Common Market Studies,* **54** (6).

Ucarer, E.M. (2013). 'The area of freedom, security and justice', in M. Cini and N. Pérez-Solórzano Borragán (eds), *European Union Politics.* Oxford: Oxford University Press.

Zimmermann, K.F. (2016). 'Refugee and migrant labour market integration: Europe in need of a new policy agenda'. Paper to be presented at the EUI Conference on the Integration of Migrants and Refugees, 29–30 September.

Zimmermann, K.F. (2017). 'Refugee and migrant labour market integration: Europe in need of a new policy agenda', in R. Bauböck and M. Tripkovic (eds), *The Integration of Migrants and Refugees. An EUI Forum on Migration, Citizenship and Demography.* Robert Schuman Centre for Advanced Studies.

11. Climate and environmental politics: resource efficient

Martin Nilsson

Since the economic crisis began in 2008–09 across Europe, the EU has tried to determine how best to cope with the crisis in many ways. One overall strategy has been Europe 2020, which includes all sorts of actions to develop Europe into a modern economy, including emphasis on sustainable development. During this period, the EU has also implemented various climate change and environmental policies (that is, related to mitigation, adaptation and capacity building) in order to reduce the future risk of climate change as well as to promote entrepreneurship and thereby smart, sustainable and inclusive growth across Europe. Although there have been some criticisms of the EU's climate policy, the EU has also been recognised as being at the forefront of international efforts toward a new and more comprehensive global climate agreement, such as the most recent Paris Agreement (see Schreurs and Tiberghien, 2007; Delbeke and Vis, 2015; Strielkowski et al., 2016).

In 2010, the EU launched its Europe 2020 initiative to promote sustainable growth. Europe 2020 could be understood as a European socio-economic model with strong emphasis on climate change policies, and it incorporated several already-existing climate change targets and objectives. In particular, one flagship of the Europe 2020, 'Resource efficient Europe', has a strong focus on climate change issues and sustainable development (European Commission, 2010). However, though the entire process of Europe 2020 can mostly be seen as a process initiated from above, with the European Commission as the key actor as a political entrepreneur, it also involves other important actors, such as member states in the Council, the European Parliament, the industrial sector, and also the member states' ability to implement policies taken by the EU.

Therefore, the aim of this chapter is to explore reforms by the EU as a political entrepreneur in the field of climate change, to produce sustainable growth, and to analyse challenges to achieve these goals in Europe 2020. The first two sections elaborate both on the background of the EU's climate policy and its relation to Europe 2020, and continue with the EU's contemporary climate change policies and its relation to Europe 2020. In the next section, the chapter discusses the idea of political entrepreneurship and the entrepreneurs behind these policies in promoting economic growth through environmental and climate policies. Finally, the chapter also discusses constraining factors in accomplishing the policy outcomes of Europe 2020, and some final remarks.

BACKGROUND: ENVIRONMENT, CLIMATE CHANGE AND EUROPE 2020

While most traditional Western European states' history of establishing environmental policies dates back to the mid-20th century, nowadays, the European Union has undoubtedly taken the leading role in Europe at a supranational level to tackle environmental and climate change issues (Pavese and Torney, 2012; Jordan et al., 2012; Downie, 2013; Babonneau et al., 2014). In the Lisbon Treaty (2007, in force 2009), environmental and climate change policies were introduced as a shared competence area, which means that on one hand, each member state could still set its own environmental laws, but on the other hand, the EU also makes laws and regulations at a supranational level, which all member states have to follow and implement according to the acquis communautaire. Within the EU's different competence policy areas, the EU also has to embed a certain degree of environmental aspects to reduce environmental damage (Wysokinska, 2016). Still, while the member states have to implement all the binding EU requirements, each member state is still allowed to establish even more demanding national environmental laws, at least as long as they do not clearly violate the EU's common market rules (Benson and Jordan, 2016).

In recent years, the EU's environmental policies have been embedded into the broader idea on how to combat climate change. As in the case of environmental laws, each member state also has its own parallel national strategies on how to deal with climate change issues. The EU's climate change agenda includes a system of 'multilevel reinforcement' or Europeanisation, by which the EU's laws and directives affect national legislation and have also become 'an organising focus for virtually all of its policies' (Jordan et al., 2010: 58), including 'varieties of market-based policy' (see Meckling and Jenner, 2016: 853; Jordan et al., 2012; Böhringer et al., 2016). As far back as 1996, the guiding principle of reducing the rise of global temperatures to a maximum of 2°C was spread among EU countries (Delbeke and Vis, 2015). In 2000, the EU established its first European Climate Change Programme (ECCP) and became the vehicle to achieve the objectives set in the Kyoto Protocol (European Commission, 2018d). During the 2000s, the EU worked on various policies related to mitigation, adaptation and capacity building in order to reduce the future risk of climate change.

When the most recent treaty, the Treaty of Lisbon (2007), was negotiated during the mid-2000s, it became clear at an early stage that environmental issues were about to get an upgraded role in the forthcoming treaty, and later became a so-called shared competence area between the EU and the member states. This means that the EU at a supranational level can set a certain standard on most important environmental issues, while member states still can take a harder stance so long as they avoid contradicting the fundamental values of the EU's common market principle. Consequently, and together with the EU's somewhat new role in signing international treaties, the EU has, in accordance with its international obligations, talked with one voice on the international scene on climate change issues, and also implemented several mitigation and adaptation policies and measures at the EU level.

In addition, long before the Europe 2020 strategy was established, the EU adopted a clear vision of how to develop a sustainable future economy. By 2007, in accordance with the Lisbon agenda and later in Europe 2020, the European Commission established a much more comprehensive approach to climate change, which still is accurate and aims to integrate clean energy, transportation, production and consumption, natural resources, public health, social cohesion, and other socioeconomic sustainability challenges into its climate change policies (Wysokinska, 2016). In the '2007 EU climate and energy package', it was also decided, by 2010, to reduce greenhouse gas emissions and energy consumption by 20 per cent, and to increase the share of renewable energy by 20 per cent in the near future (year 2010, from 1990) (European Commission, 2018c; Skjærseth, 2016). The long-term objective was to be 100 per cent carbon free, and as a step toward this goal, greenhouse gas emissions must be reduced by 80 per cent by 2050. Besides these goals, it also stipulated a transition toward a smart and greener economy.

Despite the fact that a lot of criticism has been raised against the EU's climate change policies, the EU is no doubt internationally recognised as a frontrunner in the global work to combat climate change, and the EU was one of the key actors behind the most recent Paris Treaty (Bäckstrand and Elgström, 2013; Downie, 2013; Babonneau et al., 2014). During 2016, the EU also established its new comprehensive global strategy, the Global Strategy, in which internal and external EU security is supposed to be even more intertwined, and where climate change is also seen as one of many security threats (European Commission, 2018a).

However, parallel to this development of the EU's environmental and climate change policies in the 2000s, in 2010 the EU also launched the broader Europe 2020 for sustainable growth, where global climate issues are important to achieve overall objectives for smart, sustainable and inclusive growth. The second target, as the Commission stresses, relates to sustainable growth and to 'promoting a more resource efficient, greener and more competitive economy' (European Commission, 2010: 3). In reality, it means that the EU aims to construct a green and competitive economy on the world market based on resource efficiency, and smart and green technology.

CLIMATE CHANGE POLICIES AS A PART OF EUROPE 2020

During the past two decades, the EU has been seen as one of the frontrunners around the world to tackle the global climate change threat as well as the establishment of global climate agreements, such as the 2015 Paris Agreement. The EU has also decided to act as one actor representing all the member states on the global scene, which means that the member states have at least partially given up this individual authority (Pavese and Torney, 2012; Damro et al., 2008).

However, despite the fact that the EU is acting with one voice, today the EU's climate change policies are a somewhat complex issue in many aspects. One aspect is that not all EU laws or other measurements are directly or significantly connected to climate change issues as an objectives part of the climate agenda. For example, the EU has many specific directives and regulations on issues related to water protection, air quality and noise, waste, chemicals, genetically modified organisms and biodiversity, which all seem to be important environmental issues, though they are not an explicit part of the EU's climate change policies or Europe 2020 (Langlet and Mahmoudi, 2016). A second issue is that climate change policies are a part of other broader EU policy agendas, such as Europe 2020 (2010) and, since 2016, also a part of the EU's official foreign and security policy strategy (Meckling and Jenner, 2016: 853; European Commission, 2018b). A third issue is that only about 50 per cent of the EU's own supranational legislation controls the output in terms of greenhouse gas emissions, which means that about 50 per cent depends on the EU's ability to co-work with its member states, mainly through mainstreaming climate change policies into other policy areas. Consequently, this means that the output also depends on how much the member states are willing to commit to combat global climate change issues (Delbeke and Klaassen, 2015: 79).

In recent years, the EU has undertaken measures to uphold its climate policies that are regulatory (for example, CO2 emissions from cars), market-based (for example, upper and lower limits for national fuel taxes), informational (for example, ecolabels), and voluntary (for example, the previous existing voluntary system for emission from cars) (see Jordan et al., 2012; Skjærseth, 2016). Furthermore, the EU's climate change policies have also become a natural part of the EU's Europe 2020. One of the top priorities in Europe 2020 states: 'The "20/20/20" climate/energy targets should be met (including an increase to 30% of emissions reduction if the conditions are right' (European Commission, 2010: 3).

This objective is particularly connected to one of the seven EU flagship initiatives, named 'Resource efficient Europe'. This flagship deals with issues related to sustainable growth through climate and energy policies: the EU's climate change policies are the major part of this achievement, where the European Commission stresses the importance of: '"Resource efficient Europe" to help decouple economic growth from the use of resources, support the shift towards a low carbon economy, increase the use of renewable energy sources, modernise our transport sector and promote energy efficiency' (European Commission, 2010: 4).

In Europe 2020, when the Commission is referring to the prospect of smart, sustainable and inclusive growth, one of three top priorities is connected to the EU's climate change policies, where the EU stresses that sustainable growth means 'promoting a more resource efficient, greener and more competitive economy' (European Commission, 2010: 8). One of the EU's overall 2020 targets has also the same kind of ambition that the EU has had in the past decades in its climate change policy: 'Reduce greenhouse gas emissions by at least 20% compared to 1990 levels or by 30%, if the conditions are right; increase the share of renewable energy sources in our final energy consumption to 20%; and a 20% increase in energy efficiency' (European Commission, 2010: 8).

The EU's climate policies, both as a part of Europe 2020 and in their own right, can be structured around distinct supranational policies to mitigate climate change as well as mainstreaming adaptation measurements, in which for the latter it is harder to know whether or not they are achievable.

Mitigation, Energy and the Emissions Trading System (ETS)

With the Lisbon Treaty, the EU also decided to incorporate energy policy as a policy area. Therefore in Article 194, it is stated that the EU, in solidarity, should ensure the functioning of the energy market, promote energy efficiency and saving and develop new forms of energy. In February

2015, the Commission outlined an energy strategy around five dimensions regarding an Energy Union. In the 'resilient Energy Union with a forward looking climate policy' the Commission argued that a strategy has to be built around five dimensions (European Commission, 2015a; 2015b, see also European Commission, 2018a; 2018b):

1. Energy security, solidarity and trust: the European Commission has the ambition to prevent shortages of gas supply from abroad in times of crisis, such as during the Ukraine crisis. This will be accomplished through several actions that will coordinate gas supply between member states and with external countries. It also includes an approach to improve energy efficiency and the use of renewable energy, that is, developing sustainable heating and cooling systems.
2. A fully integrated European energy market: includes actions such as developing a future electricity market in which people are empowered and have the right to choose between different sustainable options.
3. Energy efficiency: includes the idea of reducing the reliance on external suppliers, which will contribute to moderation of demand and also help the environment, including various actions to boost energy efficiency in old and new buildings, co-generation of heat and power, establishing an EU energy efficiency measure for products that will save money and energy, mobilising private financing for investments, and developing heating and cooling systems.
4. Decarbonising the economy: includes the EU's overall ambition to enable the European economy to transition in a new, more climate-friendly, low-carbon direction, in which the most important action is the flagship EU Emissions Trading System (ETS), which is supposed to tackle climate change to achieve the overall objective of reducing emissions by 40 per cent by the year 2030.
5. Research, innovation and competitiveness: the EU has invested public money in research and innovations in low-carbon technology through different programmes and action plans, such as the European Strategic Energy Technology Plan and Horizon 2020. In addition, the EU also encourages private investors to contribute to clean technology and renewable energy sources.

Consequently, over a couple of years the EU has made several resolutions to increase the use of renewable energy and to improve energy efficacy, such as combining heat and power installations, energy efficiency in buildings (private and public) and reducing CO_2 emissions in new cars and from landfills (European Commission, 2018b). Three of these warrant more attention.

The first and perhaps most well-known, and the cornerstone of the EU's climate actions, is the ETS, which has been running since 2005 and now covers 31 countries and includes about 45 per cent of all emissions within its covered sectors (European Commission, 2018f). Most of the sectors engaged are related to carbon dioxide and sectors that can be 'measured, reported and verified' with high accuracy, including power and heat generation in industry sectors such as oil refineries, steel works and production of iron, aluminium, metals, cement, lime, glass, ceramics, pulp, paper, cardboard, acids and bulk organic chemicals, and commercial aviation. The entire system works on the principle of 'cap and trade', which means that companies within the cap receive and can buy emissions allowances on the market, and if a company does not surrender enough allowances every year, they must pay a huge fine. Between 2013 and 2020, the ETS is developing its third phase aiming to include even more sectors and more types of gases beyond carbon dioxide.

The second resolution is 'The Renewable Energy Sources Directive' (European Commission, 2009), which requires 10 per cent of all energy in the transport system to come from renewable sources by 2020, including biomass fuels (ethanol, biodiesel) and the use of electricity for transport in trains and other vehicles. The directive also aims to develop renewable energy sectors such as wind, solar, hydropower, wave power and biomass energy, including energy generated through heat pumps and renewable electricity in the transportation system. As with many of its other aims, the goal is to increase the share of renewable energy by 20 per cent.

The third is the new 'Energy Efficiency Directive' (European Commission, 2018g), which replaced most of the previous directives on energy efficiency. This new directive aims to increase energy efficiency for the renovation of residential, commercial and public buildings. It includes all sorts of policies for the member states to only buy products and services with high-energy efficiency whenever possible. It also includes obligations for enterprises to undergo energy audits on a regular basis, 'insofar as this is consistent with cost-effectiveness, economic feasibility, wider sustainability, technical suitability, as well as sufficient competition' (Delbeke and Vis, 2015: 79).

According to Delbeke et al. (2015), the EU has been quite successful in its mission to increase the share of renewables, increasing it to 15 per cent in 2015, and is about to reach the 20 per cent target by 2020. While the EU seems to be on the right track towards improving energy efficiency, it seems to be harder to reach the overall climate targets of Europe 2020. Besides having made several resolutions to mitigate climate change, the EU has also adopted mainstreaming efforts.

Mainstreaming, Adaptation and Capacity Building: the Effort Sharing Decision for the non-ETS Sectors

The sectors outside the ETS constitute around half of the EU's greenhouse gas emissions, and include emissions from smaller industrial installations, services, transport, agriculture, waste and households. Reductions for these non-ETS sectors are made legally binding by the Effort Sharing Decision.

To cope with these sectors and tackle climate change, the EU has also adopted several mainstreaming adaptations and capacity-building actions (see Skjærseth, 2016). This process has been parallel to the development of the EU's mitigation policies, and began when the European Commission's 'White Paper' report was released, 'Adapting to Climate Change: Towards a European Framework for Action' (Commission of the European Communities, 2007; 2009). This report contains all possible actions one could imagine in terms of necessary support to share knowledge and information between the member states. By 2020, the EU has foreseen the costs of adaptation measurement as 100 billion euros, but it will save lives. In 'The EU Strategy on Adaptation to Climate Change' (European Commission, 2013b), the EU shows how one could integrate adaptation into all sorts of EU policies, but also promote how member states could proactively adopt adaptation measurement to tackle climate change.

However, compared to mitigation policies, it's harder to deal with adaptation measurement, and to further complicate the issue, in 2016 the European Commission also launched its new broader foreign and security policy strategy, 'Shared Vision, Common Actions: A Stronger Europe' (European Commission, 2016), of which climate change is a natural part. Besides having more regular foreign and security policy objectives, it also has the ambition to establish a much clearer linkage between internal and external security, as well as the goal to seek energy and environmental resilience for the EU. In the strategy, the EU also confirms that 'The EU will lead by example by implementing its commitments on sustainable development and climate change' (European Commission, 2016: 40).

The EU has framed its mainstreaming adaptation policies around three dimensions (European Commission, 2013b; Skjærseth, 2016). The first is how the EU can integrate climate change issues into their own laws and policies through the European Regional Development Fund, the Cohesion Fund, and into policy areas such as the Common Agricultural Policy (CAP), the fisheries policy and the action plan for a maritime strategy, and to policy areas that are closely connected to issues such as water resources, carbon sequestrations, flood protection, soil erosion mitigation, and to weather-related disaster risks due to climate change.

The second dimension is the EU's ability to promote member states acting independently on climate change, including national strategies to support the capacity to deal with these issues. As late as 2015, only 20 out of 28 member states had developed such plans (European Commission, 2013a; 2013b; 2015a: 14). Finally, besides the adaptation of EU policies and promoting member states to act through national plans, the EU has also established its programme for research and innovation, Horizon 2020. Horizon 2020 is a cross-cutting issue for climate change, and aims to strengthen the member states' resilience to climate change, including several core actions (European Commission, 2013a; 2013b).

As one consequence of the EU's strategies on mitigation, adaptation and capacity building, it is clear that the EU understands global climate change both as a policy area itself and as an integrated part of the entire agenda, including aspects such as economic growth, innovation and sustainable development.

POLITICAL ENTREPRENEURSHIP: ACTORS BEHIND CLIMATE CHANGE POLICY

Within the EU system, the Directorate-General for Climate Action has taken the leading role to combat challenges presented by climate change, which is also a huge part of Europe 2020. During the last decade, the European Commission has taken several actions within its broader missions, such as formulating and implementing policies, leading international negotiations on climate change issues, implementing the EU's ETS, and monitoring them at the national level, as well as generally stimulating and promoting low-carbon adaptation measures.

During this process, the European Commission has been a very important political entrepreneur, particularly the Commissionaires for both the Environment and the Energy Directorates working together to promote all the climate change ideas (Boasson and Wettestad, 2017: 51; Christianson and Wettestad, 2003). In addition, the Head of the Commission at that time, President Barroso, did not become devoted to climate change issues until the late 2000s, which means that in the early days in the 2000s, all the ideas about climate change as a broader and overall agenda came mainly from the Directorates of Environment and Energy. In general, when it came to all important decisions, the Commission's influence on the agenda and the drafts between different readings with the Council and the European Parliament was significantly high. However, the European Parliament has been an important and reliable ally to the Commission in their ambition to initiate, develop and shape the EU's climate change policy at a supranational level (Burns and Carter, 2011; Oberthur and Dupont, 2011; European Parliament, 2001; 2006).

However, within this broader conclusion, there are some slight differences among the important directives, such as the ETS, Renewable Energy and Energy Efficiency, which are all related to the objectives of Europe 2020. The first important directive is the ETS, which, according to Boasson and Wettestad (2017: 51; see also EURELECTRIC, 2007; Gullberg, 2008) was not initiated by the industry; rather, it was driven by the Commission, whose entrepreneurial skills were crucial in getting it on the agenda. However, once it was on the EU policy agenda, the industry itself became more eager to play an important role in shaping a more concrete outcome. Still, the more high-intensive energy industry was against the idea and tried to obstruct much of the development during the first years, but did not get any support from the member states. Meanwhile, the European Parliament was in favour of the directive; most of the member states were also in favour, and did not support the parts of industry that tried to stop the establishment of regulations in the ETS system (European Parliament, 2008a; 2008b; Gullberg, 2008). Therefore, the Commission managed to initiate the ETS as a policy entrepreneur, and stayed in control of the ideas that finally led to the 2009 ETS directive.

A second important directive is the renewable energy directive, which as in the case of ETS was not initiated by the industry itself, but by the Commission as early as the 1980s. At the time, it became a discussion when barely any clean energy industry existed, but when it became larger, it also became devoted to stimulate its own energy sector: renewable energy. However, as a contrast to the ETS, the renewable energy sector did not want to have the market-oriented system that the Commission favoured, and garnered support from several member states and the European Parliament (see Boasson and Wettestad, 2017; Oberthur and Dupont, 2011; European Parliament, 2008b). Thus the Commission was the key actor to initiate the issue, and the renewable industrial actors shaped it.

Finally, a good example of a somewhat unsuccessful political entrepreneurship is the energy policies for buildings (see Boasson and Wettestad, 2017). As in the other cases, the Commission was behind it, and a more symbolic policy had already been made in the 1990s. However, since most of this building construction sector was driven by national interest in each country, the member states were not eager to support a centralisation of this issue at the EU level. The somewhat vague Directive (2012) is a consequence of this antipathy. Therefore, though the Commission put a lot of emphasis on this issue in the 1990s and early 2000s, nowadays it comes up mostly in official policy documents related to climate change, but with no real commitment.

To summarise, the EU as an organisation can be seen as a frontrunner in the global community to combat global climate change, and since most components of these policies are also a part of the EU's Europe 2020 to establish and develop a more sustainable development and create economic growth, the EU may also be seen as a key actor in this aspect. The European Commission, as the government of the EU system, is the most important political entrepreneur, but the European Parliament and some of the member states (the Nordic countries, Germany and the Netherlands) also belong to this category. The industrial complex seems more to be re-active when it needs to play along with contemporary trends in the climate change agenda, while some member states, such as the Visegrad countries, are more reluctant on most climate change policies, including those who are a part of the EU's Europe 2020.

MISSION COMPLETED OR FURTHER CHALLENGES?

The question then is how far the European Union has come in its mission to reach the 20/20/20 climate objectives according to Europe 2020. In this case, it also means how well the European Commission has succeeded as the most important political entrepreneur to promote climate change in order to create innovations, jobs and economic growth. So far, since the objectives have not yet been achieved, the issue is also what kind of remaining challenges the EU has to overcome to be able to reach all the central objectives, and whether they have stimulated innovation and economic growth. When it comes to an evaluation of how well the objectives have been met, one could conclude that the EU might achieve all three climate objectives by 20/20/20 according to Europe 2020. However, the EU might fall short in some aspects.

First, when it comes to the issue of reducing greenhouse gas emissions by 20 per cent compared to 1990, the EU will most likely achieve this objective. Back in 2014, the EU had already reduced their emissions below their goal of 20 per cent reduction, also in a context with economic growth. The European Commission's own 2017 report concludes: 'The EU continues to successfully decouple its economic growth from its emissions . . . From 1990 to 2016, the EU's GDP grew by 53%, while total emissions fell by 23%' (European Commission, 2017: 4).

According to the Climate Action Network – the major NGO coalition on climate issues – based on the EU's gradual improvement over time, this objective will most likely be achieved by 2020 (CAN, 2018). Still, the Climate Action Network (2018) has raised some concerns and concludes that 'No single EU country is performing sufficiently in both ambition and progress in reducing carbon emissions. Countries can and must to do more to achieve the goals of the Paris Agreement' (CAN, 2018: 4).

Regarding the second objective, to increase the share of renewable energy sources to 20 per cent by 2020, the EU seems to have some problems. In the most recent follow-up 2017 report, the European Commission states that, by 2014, about 16 per cent of total energy consumption came from renewable energy sources (European Commission, 2017). The estimation for 2016 was that the share would be 17 per cent. In the 2017 report, the European Commission presented key conclusions such as:

> In its final energy consumption, the EU as a whole achieved a 16% share of renewable energy in 2014 and an estimated 16.4% share in 2015. . . . The vast majority of EU countries are well on track to reach their 2020 binding targets for renewable energy, but all countries will have to continue their efforts to meet these targets. . . . The transport sector achieved a 6% share of renewable energy in 2015, so some EU countries will have to intensify their efforts to reach the 10% binding target for transport by 2020. (European Commission, 2018e)

In the 2018 report, Eurostat (2018) confirmed that the EU reached a level of 17 per cent renewable energy, which means that the EU might have problems reaching the 20 per cent target by 2020. However, the European Commission seems to be aware of the fact that the EU might not achieve this renewable energy objective.

The third part of the EU's climate change objectives in Europe 2020 is to increase energy efficiency by 20 per cent between 1990 and 2020. This objective is the one that the European Commission believes is the hardest one to really achieve, mainly because economic growth seems to lead to higher demand for energy use, and also because weather conditions with cold winters are somewhat crucial for energy savings. The achievement went well up until 2014, but recent years show some worrying signs. As the European Commission (2017: 2) concludes:

> If the declining trend observed since 2005 continues in the coming years, the EU should still be on track to achieve the 2020 target [. . .] for both primary and final energy consumption. However, if the increases observed in recent years reverse the trend, achieving the 2020 targets will require additional efforts.

In the 2018 report, Eurostat confirms this scenario:

> To meet its target, the EU must reduce primary energy production by an additional 3.9% over the four years from 2016 to 2020. Even though the 2020 target for final energy consumption was reached temporarily in 2015, a subsequent

rise in consumption in 2016 means an additional 2.0% fall is required by 2020. (Eurostat, 2018: 80)

As indicated by the European Union's own reports and predictions, and other independent sources, there seem to be some remaining challenges for the European Commission as a political entrepreneur in favour of climate actions to reach the objectives of Europe 2020. Furthermore, the European Environmental Agency (EEA, 2017) also came to the same kind of conclusion in their progressive report, 'Trends and Projections in Europe 2017 – Tracking Progress towards Europe's Climate and Energy Targets'. In 2015, it was estimated that there was a minor decline in greenhouse gas emissions; still, the overall conclusion of the EEA's report is that the EU might reach its 2020 targets. In the Eurostat assessment of 2017 and 2018, it noted a minor increase of emissions over the last few years, but an overall significant decrease over time, leaving the EU with a great chance to meet the Europe 2020 target by 2020. Eurostat explained such EU progress in terms of reduction of gas emissions in all sectors except fuel combustion in transport and aviation as follows: 'The share of renewable energy in gross final energy production, the Europe 2020 strategy's second climate change and energy target, increased from 16.7% in 2015 to 17.0% in 2016. Therefore, the EU remains 3.0 percentage points below the Europe 2020 renewable energy target of 20 per cent' (Eurostat, 2018: 10).

At the same time, whether or not the objectives are achieved, both the European Union's supranational policy actions and the member states' own initiatives have been successful in creating new technology and innovations to reduce emissions in most sectors, such as renewable energy (European Commission, 2018c). In addition, these actions have also stimulated economic growth, which on the other hand seems to present its own challenge, since economic growth demands more electricity consumption and thereby decreases the possibility of reducing the overall level of energy consumption. There are still some remaining challenges for the EU to fully achieve the 20/20/20 objectives.

One challenge is that most of the policy areas in the EU budget at the supranational level, such as agriculture, fisheries, and structural and regional funds, normally have more negative than positive effects on the environment. In addition, these policy areas' share of the EU budget is not much related to contemporary climate change actions. For example, by 2015, it was estimated that only about 20 per cent of the EU's budget, one way or another, was linked to climate actions (European Commission, 2015a: 16). Most climate actions in these policy areas are therefore handled through the adaptation mainstreaming EU approach, in which the agricultural sector is particularly crucial for both the climate change and sustainability aspects of Europe 2020. Agriculture is very much connected to the greenhouse gas effect, and very much dependent on clean natural resources of soil, air and water, and on weather conditions. As a consequence, the EU understands it as a twin challenge to both produce environmentally sustainable food and to try to reduce the emission of greenhouse gases.

A second challenge is that many important policy areas for global climate change seem to fall between the EU system and respective national legislation in its 28 member states. This means that when the EU is about to use mainstreaming policies in shared competence areas such as the common market, agriculture, fisheries, transportation, environment, research and innovation, it only affects EU decisions. Meanwhile, at the national level, it is still up to the member states to take their own path and decisions related to combat climate change, which means that there is variation among the member states and respective governments to be more or less proactive about climate change. In addition, most greenhouse emissions are in the sectors of energy production or transportation, which are a long way from reaching their objectives of having 10 per cent coming from renewable energy (Böhringer et al., 2016; Strambo et al., 2015; European Commission, 2015a). Therefore, despite the EU's various climate actions and adaptions measures, important sectors that are connected to either energy or greenhouse emissions, such as transportation, agriculture, housing and waste, are mostly dealt with at the national level. It means that these are partly out of the EU's wider control, and EU strategies cannot really reach the objectives while it is up to the member states to deal with these issues in concrete terms (see the Treaty of Lisbon, 2007; Fellman et al., 2017).

Third, while the EU has clear objectives and a strategy for adaptation to climate change that seem to be headed in the right direction, some member states have still failed to adopt national agendas on climate change. So far, by 2018, most member states, but not all 28, have implemented their national agendas, but there is also variation in their objectives (European Commission, 2018c; 2018e; 2018f). Therefore, one problem is that the entire system is constructed around the principle of differentiated burden sharing, by which some, that is, richer Western European member states, have to accomplish the climate change and Europe 2020 objectives better than others (Jordan et al., 2012). In reality, these richer states have to be much more ambitious than the others, both in the EU system and their respective national agendas. Some member states still do not have a national climate change agenda, or a more ambitious agenda. In addition, almost half of the member states do not have a specific budget with which to implement their national agendas, which is an indication of whether or not they would prefer to prioritise climate change. This disparity within the EU system, in fact, is the same as on the question of migration, meaning that in particular, some of the Visegrad countries (Hungary, Slovakia, and Poland), the Baltic States, Romania and Bulgaria are not hesitating to increase the EU's efforts to combat climate change or reach the 2020 Agenda, and these countries are in favour of more burden-sharing among the member states (Bocquillon and Maltby, 2017; Braun, 2014; Wysokinska, 2016; Marcinkiewicz and Tosun, 2015). In the long run, relatively speaking, it means that the Nordic countries, Germany and the Netherlands, among others, have to accomplish more than other countries. However, it also means that the Visegrad countries, among other member states less friendly on climate change actions, could slow down the entire EU climate change process, and consequently the EU's climate change actions in Europe 2020.

In addition, there are major challenges in implementing Europe 2020, including global climate change, which is also the case in most other EU policy areas (see Antimiani et al., 2016). The EU's entire Europe 2020 Agenda, and the parts that include climate change actions, has very ambitious targets and many different actions, but the main problem is that a lot of these are dependent on conditions beyond the EU systems' magnitude. The EU has a relatively weak capacity to implement or to manage everything initiated in documents such as Europe 2020 and regarding most climate actions (Jordan et al., 2012).

Finally, and perhaps most importantly, it is hard to really understand, in concrete terms, to what extent the achievement of the 20/20/20 climate objectives, as in Europe 2020, will lead to solid economic growth, particularly in relation to actions other than climate change. However, since most of the actions are related to new innovations, it will definitely stimulate new ideas and innovations in various sectors, no matter whether the objectives themselves are fully achieved or not.

CONCLUDING REMARKS

On the global scene, the EU has been a frontrunner for some time regarding climate change policies. In particular, the European Commission has been seen as the key actor as a political entrepreneur when it comes to promoting climate change actions.

Since the economic crisis in 2008–09, most of the EU's previous climate change policies were also embedded into Europe 2020, to promote smart, inclusive and sustainable growth across Europe. As such, the EU seems to be on a path to more or less achieve its ambitious 20/20/20 climate and energy targets for 2020 and 2030, but whether they also will stimulate economic and sustainable growth in the long run is still an open question. Several challenges remain for the EU to be able to mainstream and adopt all policies based on the principle of sustainability, and several member states also need to do more to follow this route. For example, the EU's budget is connected to policy areas in which greenhouse emissions are very high, such as the agricultural sector, but it is still very much up to the member states to follow the EU approach of adaptation mainstreaming policies at the national level. It is up to each member state to implement various measures for climate actions, which is a major challenge, because the ambition among the member states differs from the Nordic countries to the Visegrad countries. To all these challenges, one could also add a more controversial challenge, which is that the entire EU system is based on the free market principle, with free movement of goods, which in a way stimulates the highly energy demanding transport sector by moving goods between the member states within the internal market. Aside from all these challenges, the EU's 2020 strategy is still more than less based on the principle of sustainability compared to the time before Europe 2020 was established.

REFERENCES

Antimiani, A., V. Costantini, O. Kuik and E. Paglialunga (2016), 'Mitigation of adverse effects on competitiveness and leakage of unilateral EU climate policy: An assessment of policy instruments', *Ecological Economics*, **128**, 246–59.
Babonneau, F., A. Hauri and M. Vielle (2014), 'Assessment of balanced burden-sharing in the 2050 EU climate/energy roadmap: a metamodeling approach', *Climatic Change*, **134** (4), 505–19.
Bäckstrand, K. and O. Elgström (2013), 'The EU's role in climate change negotiations: from leader to "leadiator"', *Journal of European Public Policy*, **20** (10), 1369–86.
Benson, D. and A. Jordan (2016), 'Environmental policy', in M. Cini and N. Pérez-Solórzano Borragán (eds), *European Union Politics* (5th edn), Oxford: Oxford University Press.
Boasson, E.L. and J. Wettestad (2017), *EU Climate Policy Industry, Policy Interaction and External Environment*, Abingdon: Routledge.
Bocquillon, P. and T. Maltby (2017), 'The more the merrier? Assessing the impact of enlargement on EU performance in energy and climate change policies', *East European Politics*, **33** (1), 88–105.
Böhringer, C., A. Keller, M. Bortolamedi and A.R. Seyffarth (2016), 'Good things do not always come in threes: on the excess cost of overlapping regulation in EU climate policy', *Energy Policy*, **94**, 502–508.
Braun, M. (2014), 'EU climate norms in East-Central Europe', *Journal of Common Market Studies*, **52** (3), 445–60.

Burns, C. and N. Carter (2011), 'The European Parliament and climate change: from symbolism to heroism and back again', in R.K.W. Wurzel and J. Connely (eds), *The European Union as a Leader in International Climate Change Policies*, Abingdon: Routledge, pp. 58–74.

CAN (Climate Action Network) (2018), *European NGO coalition on climate and energy 2018. Off target Ranking of EU countries' ambition and progress in fighting climate change*, June 2018, Brussels, accessed 10 September 2018 at http://www.caneurope.org/publications/press-releases/1619-eu-countries-off-target-in-fighting-climate-change.

Christianson, A.C. and J. Wettestad (2003), 'The EU as a frontrunner on greenhouse gas emission trading: how did it happen and will the EU succeed?', *Climate Policy*, **3** (1), 3–18.

Commission of the European Communities (2007), *Green Paper. Adapting to climate change in Europe – options for EU action*, Brussels, 29 June (2007), COM (2007) 354 final.

Commission of the European Communities (2009), *White Paper. Adapting to climate change: Towards a European framework for action. Brussels*, 4 April (2009), COM (2009) 147 final.

Damro, C., I. Hardie and D. MacKenzie (2008), 'The EU and climate change policy: law, politics and prominence at different levels', *Journal of Contemporary European Research*, **4** (3), 179–92.

Delbeke, J. and G. Klaassen (2015), 'Framing member states' policies', in J. Delbeke and P. Vis (eds), *EU Climate Policy Explained*, London, UK and New York, USA: Routledge, pp. 79–93.

Delbeke, J. and P. Vis (2015), 'EU's climate leadership in a rapidly changing world', in J. Delbeke and P. Vis (eds), *EU Climate Policy Explained*, London, UK and New York, USA: Routledge, pp. 4–24.

Delbeke, J., G. Klaassen and S. Vergote (2015), 'Climate-related energy policies', in J. Delbeke and P. Vis (eds), *EU Climate Policy Explained*, London, UK and New York, USA: Routledge, pp. 61–91.

Downie, C. (2013), 'Shaping international negotiations from within the EU: substate actors and climate change', *Journal of European Integration*, **35** (6), 705–21.

EEA (European Environmental Agency) (2017), *Trends and projections in Europe 2017 – Tracking progress towards Europe's climate and energy*. Copenhagen: EEA.

EURELECTRIC (2007), 'Position paper – review of the EU Emissions Trading Directive (2003/87/EC) and the Linking Directive (2004/101/EC)'. July, Brussels: EURELECTRIC.

European Commission (2009), *Directive 2009/28/EC of the European Parliament and of the Council of 23 April 2009 on the promotion of the use of energy from renewable sources and amending and subsequently repealing Directives 2001/77/EC and 2003/30/EC*, accessed 10 August 2018 at http://eur-lex.europa.eu/legal content/EN/TXT/PDF/?uri=CELEX:32009L0028&from=en.

European Commission (2010), 'EUROPE 2020 – A strategy for smart, sustainable and inclusive growth', Brussels, 3.3.2010, COM (2010) 2020.

European Commission (2013a), *An EU Strategy on adaptation to climate change*, Brussels, 16 April, 2013, COM (2013) 216 final.

European Commission (2013b), *The EU Strategy on adaptation to climate change. Climate Action*, accessed 10 November 2016 at https://ec.europa.eu/clima/publi cations/docs/eu_strategy_en.pdf.

European Commission (2015a), *Climate Actions Progress report 2015*, Climate Action. Publications Office, November 2015, accessed 10 November 2016 at https://ec.europa.eu/clima/sites/clima/files/strategies/progress/docs/progress_report_2015_en.pdf.

European Commission (2015b), *A Framework Strategy for a Resilient Energy Union with a Forward-Looking Climate Change Policy*, Brussels, COM (2015) 80 final, 25/02/2015.

European Commission (2016), *Shared Vision, Common Action: A Stronger Europe. A Global Strategy for the European Union's Foreign and Security Policy*, June, 2016, European Union Global Strategy.

European Commission (2017), *2017 Assessment of the progress made by Member States towards the national energy efficiency targets for 2020 and towards the implementation of the Energy Efficiency Directive as required by Article 24(3) of the Energy Efficiency Directive 2012/27/EU*, Report from the Commission to the European Parliament and the Council. Brussels, 23.11.2017, COM (2017) 687 final.

European Commission (2018a), *Climate Action. Causes of Climate change*, accessed 10 August 2018 at http://ec.europa.eu/clima/change/causes_en.

European Commission (2018b), *Climate Action. What we do*, accessed 10 August 2018 at https://ec.europa.eu/clima/about-us/mission/index_en.htm.

European Commission (2018c), *Climate Action. 2020 climate & energy package*, accessed 10 August 2018 at http://ec.europa.eu/clima/policies/strategies/2020_en.

European Commission (2018d), *First European Climate Change Programme*, accessed 10 August 2018 at https://ec.europa.eu/clima/policies/eccp/index_en.htm.

European Commission (2018e), *Progress Report*, accessed 10 August 2018 at https://ec.europa.eu/energy/en/topics/renewable-energy/progress-reports.

European Commission (2018f), *Climate Action: EU Emissions Trading System (EU ETS)*, accessed 10 August 2018 at https://ec.europa.eu/clima/policies/ets_en.

European Commission (2018g), *Climate Action: 2020 climate & energy package*, accessed 10 August 2018 at https://ec.europa.eu/clima/policies/ets_enhttps://ec.europa.eu/clima/policies/strategies/2020_en.

European Parliament (2001), *II Recommendation for Second Reading on the Proposal for a European Parliament and Council Directive on the Promotion of Electricity from Renewable Energy Sources in the Internal Electricity Market*, Brussels, COM 2000, 79, 22 June, final A5-0227/2201.

European Parliament (2006), *Reports with Recommendations to the Commission on Heating and Cooling from Renewable Sources of Energy*, Brussels, 2005/2122, 1 February 2006. Final A6-0020/2006.

European Parliament (2008a), *Compromise Amendments 1-25 on the Proposal for a Directive of the European Parliament and Council Amending Directive 2003/87/EC*, Draft Report, Brussels, 2008/0013 (COD), 5 October.

European Parliament (2008b), *Draft Report on the Proposal for a Directive of the European Parliament and of the Council on the Promotion of the Use of Energy from Renewables Sources*, COM 2008: 0019, 2008/0016, Committee on Industry, Research and Energy, 2006/0016 (COD), 13 May.

Eurostat (2018), *Smarter, greener, more inclusive? Indicators to support the Europe 2020 strategy*, Luxembourg: Publications Office of the European Union.

Fellmann, T., P. Witzke, F, Weiss, B. Van Doorslaer, D. Drabik, I. Huck, G. Salputra et al. (2017), 'Major challenges of integrating agriculture into climate change mitigation policy frameworks', *Mitigation and Adaptation Strategies for Global Change*, **22** (124), 451–68.

Gullberg, A.T. (2008), 'Lobbying friends and foes in climate policy: the case of business and environmental interest groups in the European Union', *Energy Policy*, **36** (8), 2964–72.

Jordan, A., H. van Asselt, F. Berkhout and D. Huitema (2012), 'Understanding the paradoxes of multilevel governing: climate change policy in the European Union', *Global Environmental Politics*, **12** (2), 43–66.

Jordan, A., D. Huitema, H. van Asselt, T. Rayner and F. Berkhout (2010), *Climate Change Policy in the European Union: Confronting the Dilemmas of Mitigation and Adaptation?*, Cambridge: Cambridge University Press.

Langlet, D. and S. Mahmoudi (2016), *EU Environmental Law and Policy*, Oxford: Oxford University Press.

Marcinkiewicz, K. and J. Tosun (2015), 'Contesting climate change: mapping the political debate in Poland', *East European Politics*, **31** (2), 187–207.

Meckling, J. and S. Jenner (2016), 'Varieties of market-based policy: instrument choice in climate policy', *Environmental Politics*, **25** (5), 853–74.

Oberthur, S. and C. Dupont (2011), 'The Council, the European Council and international climate policy', in S. Oberthur and T. Gehring (eds), *The European Union as a Leader in International Climate Change Policies*, Abingdon: Routledge, pp. 74–91.

Pavese, C.B. and D. Torney (2012), 'The contribution of the European Union to global climate change governance: explaining the conditions for EU actorness', *Revista Brasileira de Política Internacional*, **55**.

Schreurs, M.A. and Y. Tiberghien (2007), 'Multi-level reinforcement: explaining European Union leadership in climate change mitigation', *Global Environmental Politics*, **7** (4), 19–46.

Skjærseth, J.B. (2016), 'Linking EU climate and energy policies: policy-making, implementation and reform', *International Environment Agreements*, **16** (4), 509–23.

Strambo, C., M. Nilsson and A. Månsson (2015), 'Coherent or inconsistent? Assessing energy security and climate policy interaction within the European Union', *Energy Research & Social Science*, **8**, 1–12.

Strielkowski, W., E. Lisin and I. Gryshova (2016), 'Climate policy of the European Union: what to expect from the Paris Agreement?', *Romanian Journal of European Affairs*, **16** (4), 68–77.

Treaty of Lisbon (2007), *Treaty on European Union, 2007. Part of the Treaty of Lisbon amending the Treaty on European Union and the Treaty establishing the European Community*, signed at Lisbon, 13 December 2007 (2007/C 306/01). Lisbon, 17 December.

Wysokinska, Z. (2016), 'The "new" environmental policy of the European Union: a path to development of a circular economy and mitigation of the negative effects of climate change', *Comparative Economic Research*, **19** (2), 57–73.

PART IV

Concluding remarks

12. European political entrepreneurship: Europe 2020 to an end

Daniel Silander

On 12 September 2018, Jean-Claude Juncker, the President of the European Commission, presented the State of the Union 2018 address to the European Parliament. He asked, 'What is the State of the Union today in 2018?' and followed up by stressing the following:

> Ten years after Lehman Brothers, Europe has largely turned the page on an economic and financial crisis which came from outside but which cut deep at home. Europe's economy has now grown for 21 consecutive quarters. Jobs have returned with almost 12 million new jobs created since 2014. 12 million – that is more jobs than there are people in Belgium. Never have so many men and women – 239 million people – been in work in Europe. (Juncker, 2018: 4)

Juncker further declared his enthusiasm for the economic progress in the EU within the context of the preceding global and European crisis. He stressed the vitality of the EU as an economic actor and argued that the EU is a global trade power:

> The European Union now has trade agreements with 70 countries around the world, covering 40% of the world's GDP. These agreements – so often contested but so unjustly – help us export Europe's high standards for food safety, workers' rights, the environment and consumer rights far beyond our borders. (Juncker, 2018: 4)

Jean-Claude Juncker's 2018 State of the Union address also re-emphasised the importance of a unified Europe, both in dealing with internal growth and promoting social cohesion within the Single European Market (SEM), as well as in relation to growing global competition. As one European market, one political voice and one integrated European community, Europe can continue to provide for its own prosperity, wealth, freedom and cohesion:

> Only a strong and united Europe can protect our citizens against threats internal and external – from terrorism to climate change.

Only a strong and united Europe can protect jobs in an open, interconnected world.
Only a strong and united Europe can master the challenges of global digitisation. It is because of our single market – the largest in the world – that we can set standards for big data, artificial intelligence and automation. And that we are able to uphold Europeans' values, rights and identities in doing so. But we can only do so if we stand united.
A strong and united Europe is what allows its Member States to reach for the stars. (Juncker, 2018: 5)

The President of the Commission explicitly stated the importance of shared sovereignty in Europe. United European states, he argued, stand taller and are more powerful when dealing with contemporary changes and challenges than individual member states.

In 2010, the Commission called for united European governance to address the European economic crisis in the European Commission Communication, 'Europe 2020 – A strategy for smart, sustainable and inclusive growth'. Through European governance and political entrepreneurship at all levels of authority among European institutions, member states, EU agencies, regional and local authorities and the private sector, Europe could seek new paths in the 21st century (see Silander, 2018; European Commission, 2010: 4; see also Eurostat, 2018). The Commission addressed the economic crisis not only as a major challenge to European wealth and prosperity, but also as an opportunity for integration (see Silander, 2018; Karlsson et al., 2016).

Mai'a K. Davis Cross, in *The Politics of Crisis in Europe* (2017), addressed how historical and contemporary European crises from the 1950s to the early 2000s have been debated, perceived and addressed in European politics. Crisis, defined as an unusual event that poses serious and unexpected threats to founding structures, norms and values and places stress on a system to act under time pressure and uncertain circumstances, has at times been a force for change (see Cross, 2017: 23; Ikenberry, 2008; see also Rosenthal et al., 1989). The author argues that European integration has developed based on both real and/or perceived crisis. Over the decades, European crises have often referred to key member states' reluctance to maintain membership; the dismantling of deepened integration in the European economy; or halted integration in core policy areas such as the Euro, the Common Foreign and Security policy, enlargement, the SEM, Schengen or asylum and migration. Despite these 'crises', the European project has continued to develop over the decades, using contemporary crises to transform Europe into a peace-prone region, the largest trading bloc in the world, an outspoken green power on environmental issues and the largest contributor of humanitarian assistance. Internally, the European project has not only survived real and perceived crises, but has deepened in more policy areas while expanding geographically with a growing number of member states. As Cross states,

> [d]espite this dark cloud hanging over Europe's image, the region is today arguably stronger, wealthier, and more integrated than ever. It has the largest economy in the world and is the United States' biggest trading partner and investor. Its member states continue to sign new treaties, solidifying new levels of integration in a wide spectrum of policy areas, from foreign policy to finance and internal security. The membership of the EU continues to grow with countries to the east . . . formally seeking to become candidates or members. (Cross, 2017: 2)

Shared European challenges and crises have resulted in common debates, negotiations, policies and laws providing for European integration. These challenges and crises have not always been easy to address, taking into account European nation-states' diverse histories, cultures and political legacies, but the contemporary EU is a major symbol of European unity amidst diversity. This is not to say that a European crisis cannot result in distrust, disengagement and finally disintegration. There have been and will be serious structural and systematic hindrances in politics and economics, but European integration trends over the last 75 years suggest that Europe's development has embedded political entrepreneurship by treating crises as opportunities. European leaders, both now and in a post-World War II and post-Cold War context, have continued not only to survive European crises, but to view them as opportunities for change (see Cross, 2017: 4). Europe faces serious challenges and potential crises in internal political debates over right-wing populism, illiberalism, asylum and migration policies, Russia and weakened transatlantic ties, among other issues. As European history has shown, the EU and its member states must address such challenges and potential crises to prevail as one community and continue European integration.

This book has dealt with the Commission Communication Europe 2020, which was a direct result of the global economic crisis that began in 2007. The authors' aim has been to explore the role of European political entrepreneurship in debating, shaping and implementing the Europe 2020 strategy within the EU. The focus has been on European political entrepreneurship and how Europe 2020 has been debated, decided on and implemented from a European governance perspective, including EU institutions, member states, EU agencies and regional and local authorities. As stated elsewhere in this book, Europe 2020 was a Commission initiative to deal with the crisis by promoting smart, sustainable and socially inclusive growth. The political entrepreneurship within the Commission was intended to become a driving force for political entrepreneurship on all levels within European governance. As it has done in the past, the Commission addressed the economic crisis of 2007–08 not only as an existential threat to European wealth and health, but also as an opportunity to promote necessary changes to build a prosperous Europe in the 21st century.

The first part of the book, 'Europe 2020 and framework of study', introduced the reader to the context and content of Europe 2020 and the overall aim of this book. Chapter 1, 'The European Commission and Europe 2020: smart, sustainable and inclusive growth', by Daniel Silander, introduced the Commission Communication Europe 2020 to the reader and explained the meaning of smart, sustainable and social inclusive growth. It also addressed how European political entrepreneurship on the part of the Commission, as the driving engine for EU interests and objectives, was linked to expected and necessary political entrepreneurship within other EU institutions, member states, agencies and regional and local authorities. The Commission called for bold and innovative European leadership to halt the ongoing economic crisis and help Europe become economically and socially great again. The focus on potential and existing European political entrepreneurship aiming for growth and employment in Europe was introduced to the reader. Political entrepreneurship, in this case, refers to new, innovative activities beyond day-to-day practices that challenge and change traditional institutions in favour of smart, sustainable and socially inclusive growth.

Chapter 2, 'EU, Europe 2020 and a social market economy', also written by Daniel Silander, explored the founding norms and values of European integration and the historical and political roots of the Commission Communication on smart, sustainable and socially inclusive growth. Overall, the chapter explored the meaning of the European social market economy model and the historical, political and entrepreneurial visions behind such a model. This project, which has promoted a unique form of political entrepreneurship, has resulted in a more international Europe that advocates for liberal order, state collaboration, common institutions, democratic governance and a social market economy. Silander further argued in this chapter that the economic recession of 2007–08 challenged years of European progress and destabilised economic and social structures between and within EU member states. The Commission called for unified European actions based on a legacy of common norms and values to promote Europe's social market economy for the 21st century. It required member states to focus on relevant issues, such as unemployment, social exclusion, poverty and limited education. The EU's strong roots in the spirit of democracy, freedom and solidarity through common institutions were a foundation on which to build the world's most competitive, dynamic and knowledge-driven economy while promoting internal economic and social cohesion. A social market economy provided for human-centred economic growth. The EU Commission strives to continue to promote a unique European model in which democracy, peace and socioeconomic growth are essential elements. The social aspects of European growth have become more explicit, with growing interests in European collaboration on social policy issues and the top-down push for social integration among member states. The EU is a political and democratic community with a single European market, but progress must still be made to become a solid social economic model.

Part II: 'Core Actors on Europe 2020' included four chapters dealing with core European actors' debates and decisions to implement reforms to achieve smart, sustainable and socially inclusive growth. Chapter 3, 'Policy-making in the European Council and the Council of the EU on Europe 2020: the presidency effect', authored by Brigitte Pircher, addresses how the 2007 economic crisis resulted in the Commission's developing five target policy areas linked to flagship initiatives to promote smart, sustainable and social inclusive growth in Europe. In her study, Pircher explored whether intergovernmental institutions have functioned as political entrepreneurs and, if so, how. She also examined individual member states' stands on Europe 2020. Pircher argues that political entrepreneurship was explicitly present in the actions taken by Herman van Rompuy, elected president of the European Council in 2009, and Commissioner president José Manuel Barroso. Together, they initiated the development of Europe 2020 and became driving engines behind Europe 2020 despite major differences among member states in employment, social inclusion, agriculture and education. The presidency in the Council of the EU challenged previous day-to-day activities and institutional structures through innovative approaches.

Chapter 4, 'The European Parliament and the Europe 2020 strategy: an arena for public debate or political entrepreneurship?', by Mats Öhlén, addressed another core actor within the EU in the European Parliament. The European Parliament is the only directly elected EU institution and is therefore an important institution to bring legitimacy to Europe 2020 and the EU ambition to promote smart, sustainable and social inclusive growth in all EU member states. This chapter addressed the European Parliament's plenary debates, resolutions and reports on Europe 2020 to identify possible political entrepreneurship in the ideas and attempts to influence the content and the implementation of Europe 2020. The author focused on two plenary debates in the European Parliament: in

February 2010, when the European Council presented the first draft of Europe 2020, and in October 2015, on the mid-term review of the strategy. The author focuses on ideas presented by political groups, conflicting interests among political groups and founding ideological arguments in contrast to technical aspects of Europe 2020. The author also examined whether there are signs of political entrepreneurship among individual politicians, party groups and the Parliament itself. Mats Öhlén identifies a Left–Right and EU-integration conflict in the European Parliament, but also notes concerns over the Greek crisis and the overall relation between the European Parliament and the European Council. Öhlén highlighted how the European Parliament has found itself somewhat neglected in its involvement in Europe 2020, with only minor impact on strategy due to its limited formal authority. However, the author identified elements of political entrepreneurship both on an individual level, among members of the European Parliament, and an institutional level, through the actions taken by the Parliament.

Chapter 5, 'Local and regional involvement in Europe 2020: a success story?', authored by Brigitte Pircher, addressed the importance of local and regional authorities to Europe 2020 from a multilevel governance perspective. Pircher addressed how, in the late 1980s, the EU initiated partnerships tied to regional policies on funding and how the Europe 2020 embedded such an approach by engaging national, local and regional authorities to ensure the realisation of the strategy. The partnership included actions and programmes to be used to reach national targets in the specific policy area. This chapter focused on potential political entrepreneurship on a local and regional level within member states and their impact on the implementation of Europe 2020. Pircher argued that such an approach is a forgotten dimension to explore, as the focus of most analysis of Europe 2020 has been on the Commission and member states. This chapter therefore asked the following questions: what characterises the governance architecture of the Europe 2020 strategy, and to what extent are local and regional authorities involved in the implementation of the strategy? The chapter also explored whether their involvement will have an impact in policy outcome and if there has been room for political entrepreneurship. Pircher argued that Europe 2020 can only be successful if addressed and implemented on all levels, including local and regional ones. It is further argued that local and regional engagement has varied considerably between member states and that high engagement has led to improved results on a national level. EU member states, with a tradition of local and regional self-government, have engaged local and regional actions to implement Europe 2020. In addition, local and regional engagement is important for member state performances on employment, research and development and waste management. It is on the local and regional level that room for political entrepreneurship is obvious.

Chapter 6, 'Europe 2020, EU agencies and political entrepreneurship', developed by Helena Ekelund, focused on Europe 2020 and the role of three EU agencies: the European Centre for the Development of Vocational Training (Cedefop), the European Foundation for the Improvement of Living and Working Conditions (Eurofound) and the European Agency for Health and Safety at Work (EU-OSHA). The author also asked the following research question: To what extent are the activities and initiatives the agencies engage in with regard to Europe 2020 expressions of political entrepreneurship? Ekelund argued that none of the agencies have the authority to formulate policy officially, but may influence policymakers both before decisions are made and during the implementation phase. It is argued in the chapter that all three agencies have acted entrepreneurially when addressing Europe 2020 through their expertise and networks. Europe 2020 called upon all actors within the system of European governance to participate in the initiative. It was also important to make use of social dialogue with all social partners. Cedefop, Eurofound and EU-OSHA are agencies with a tripartite governance structure, including member state authorities, employers' organisations and employees' organisations, resulting in close ties to social partners. These agencies play a vital strategic role by acting as political entrepreneurs to promote collaboration between individual member states, stakeholders and themselves. In particular, the author highlighted how the agencies have developed a wide range of methods for gathering and analysing data in their specific areas based on their expertise and ability to make use of such expertise to favour entrepreneurship in Europe. The expertise embedded in the agencies is also utilised through existing networks in which research findings are informed by and through new technology.

Part III: 'Policies on smart, sustainable and inclusive growth', focused on important policy areas for European growth by addressing Europe 2020 in essential policy areas, such as industrial policy, research and innovation, gender equality, asylum and migration and environmental and climate policies. Chapter 7, 'Policy evaluation in competitiveness: towards more results-oriented industrial policies', co-authored by Charlie Karlsson and Sam Tavassoli, focused on industrial policies and the growing concerns within the EU regarding how to develop a competitive industrial policy in a globalised order of emerging economies and a new geography of growth, production and trade. It is also argued that Europe is facing challenges in the new geography of innovation with the diffusion of information technologies and larger investments in science and technology in developing countries. Additionally, the chapter explored how climate change puts pressure on European governments and EU institutions to develop a new 'green' economy in a context of the recent economic recession. In Europe 2020, the EU has highlighted the importance of transforming European industrial policies into smart, sustainable and inclusive growth by increasing competitiveness, among other things. Research on industrial policy, has, however, disagreed on what role and design such a policy may have for economic growth in developed and developing economies. This chapter identified hindrances to policy evaluations in general and industrial policies in particular with reference to the Europe 2020 strategy and set out the role of policy monitoring and evaluation in an industrial policy life cycle model to improve policymakers' and researchers' understanding of existing challenges to design result-oriented assessments. The results presented in the chapter take the form of policy advice to EU institutions and member states on how the presented model would improve the industrial policy processes and make these policies more results-oriented, improve evaluations and increase policy learning.

Chapter 8, 'Research and innovation', developed by Anne Haglund-Morrissey, explored the role of the European Commission and its Directorate-General for Research and Innovation in advocating for Europe 2020. It is stated that the European Commission has been active in promoting research and innovation since the global and European crisis of 2008. Research and innovation have been stressed as important tools not only to recover European economies, but also to promote a future competitive European economy based on smart, sustainable and inclusive growth. The Commission has stated that research and innovation are essential and strategically important to develop new products, processes and services to boost the European economy. This chapter addressed the Commission's efforts to reach Europe 2020 objectives using innovative initiatives focusing on new investments, member state research and innovation systems and increased funding for EU programmes. The Commission has also promoted actions and monitoring instruments to help individual member states improve both the level and the quality of investments and to facilitate the exchange of best practices between member states based on the Open Method of Coordination. Overall, the Commission and the Directorate-General for Research and Innovation have played a key role by outlining, developing and implementing policies, but the Commission is dependent on the willingness and capacities of member states in the research and innovation area. Due to the shared competence, Europe 2020 on research and innovation is dependent on individual member states' public and private sector investments.

Chapter 9, 'Gender equality policy', written by Charlotte Silander, analysed Europe 2020 from a gender perspective by exploring the gender strategies embedded in the strategy and related documents. The author addressed previous research on EU and gender equality that, on the one hand, pointed to developments in gender equality as an important part of social cohesion and inclusion within the EU, but, on the other hand, primarily focused on women's employability and through neo-liberal capitalist strategies. Risks of this approach include weakened social protections for women in the name of a market-oriented economy. Overall, therefore, the chapter examined whether gender equality is viewed as an objective in itself in Europe or as a tool for encouraging economic growth. Such focus included a discussion on how Europe 2020 and related documents provided by the EU define gender equality, what strategies are defined to promote gender equality, what impact such strategies have had on EU member states, and political entrepreneurial tools used within the EU to advocate for improved gender equality throughout Europe. The author provided a historical discussion not only on the idea of equal treatment within the EU and the lack of gender equality, but also on how the previous treaties and articles have gradually addressed salaries, social benefits, equal opportunities, pension rights, discrimination, and health and safety for pregnant and breastfeeding women. The author argued that the Commission and the Council of Ministers have played an important role through the use of soft power and the open method of coordination on gender equality and related social issues. It is also, however, argued that Europe 2020 primarily addresses gender equality in terms of its role as a tool for economic growth and welfare. Europe 2020 mainly focuses on women's participation in the workforce and how it is crucial for a dynamic economy to make full use of all societal groups, including women. Europe 2020, it is argued, concerns itself with why and how women must be employable for the EU to meet its economic growth objectives.

Chapter 10, 'Asylum and migration policies: enabling inclusive growth in the EU?', developed by Anna Parkhouse, highlighted how the European Commission stressed the importance of dealing with demographic changes and challenges in Europe by improving the possibilities of integrating migrants into the labour market, promoting a more prosperous European social and economic development. The author explored asylum and migration policies based on Europe 2020 and the role of political entrepreneurship in providing better and more innovative paths to labour market integration and social inclusion in the EU. The aim of the study was to analyse the role of asylum and labour migration policies and determine whether these policies meet the needs of EU member states' labour markets. The author also set out to study how political entrepreneurs influence and shape the policy-making process to improve labour market integration and inclusive social growth. This chapter identified the Commission's role

as a political entrepreneur in initiating reforms to improve the legal rights
of migrants and refugees to access skilled employment, self-employment
and education. The author, however, identified remaining challenges in
EU member states' domestic labour markets due to national competence
in this policy area. Overall, although the Commission acted to increase the
ratio of active workers to inactive workers, data shows that unemployment among migrants continues to be high and that qualified migrants
pursue low-skilled labour, leaving EU member states with dual challenges
of social exclusion of newcomers and a consistent demographic pressure
for labour force mobility.

Chapter 11, 'Climate and environmental politics: resource efficient',
authored by Martin Nilsson, explored potential political entrepreneurial
reforms to promote sustainable growth in Europe within the context of climate change. The analysis focused on changes and challenges within Europe
to meet the objectives set out in Europe 2020. Nilsson argued that the main
actors behind climate and environmental politics framed by Europe 2020
have been the Commission and the European Parliament, although the
Council of Ministers, individual member states and the industrial sector
have played important roles in implementing Europe 2020. The Commission
in particular has acted as political entrepreneur both on a European and
global level. Together, these actors have acted as political entrepreneurs
to achieve identified objectives by focusing on mitigation, adaptation and
capacity building. The Europe 2020 flagship 'Resource efficient Europe'
has specifically addressed climate change and sustainable growth. Martin
Nilsson stressed that the EU is close to meeting the 20/20/20 climate and
energy objectives through climate and environmental actions. However, the
EU must still overcome obstacles concerning financial challenges, political
reluctance from some member states to implement necessary climate change
actions and the transport sector's high energy demands related to the free
movement of goods throughout the single European market.

Part IV: 'Concluding remarks' contains this final Chapter 12, 'European
political entrepreneurship: Europe 2020 to an end', written by Daniel
Silander. It has highlighted the main objectives of the book and the
different contributions to the discussion and analysis of Europe 2020
by focusing on European political entrepreneurship from a multi-level
governance perspective.

Europe 2020 is soon ending. In September 2015, the 2030 Agenda was
adopted at the United Nations Sustainable Development Summit. The
EU was a driving force behind the agenda titled *Transforming our world:
the 2030 agenda for sustainable development* (United Nations, 2015). The
agenda consisted of 17 sustainable development goals and 169 related
targets. In November 2016, the EU Commission published the commu-

nication *Next steps for a sustainable European future: European action for sustainability* (European Commission, 2016), setting out a strategy to meet the targets set out in the 2030 Agenda. The communication stressed two paths: first, to integrate sustainable development goals with Commission priorities and, second, to identify and develop Europe's long-term goals. The 10 European Commission priorities symbolised decades of European efforts towards a democratic, social market integration in which smart, sustainable and socially inclusive growth are essential. It is for the future to tell whether Europe and the EU will develop to promote a sustainable European future. Whatever the method, however, it will most certainly require political entrepreneurship in a multi-level governance structure.

REFERENCES

Cross, M.K.D. (2017). *The Politics of Crisis in Europe*. Cambridge: Cambridge University Press.

European Commission (2010). *Communication from the Commission: Europe 2020: A Strategy for Smart, Sustainable and Inclusive Growth*. Brussels, 3.3.2010. Brussels: European Commission.

European Commission (2016). *Next Steps for a Sustainable European Future: European Action for Sustainability*. Accessed 12 October 2018 at https:// ec.europa.eu/europeaid/commission-communication-next-steps-sustainable-european-future_en.

Eurostat (2018). *Smarter, Greener, More Inclusive? – Indicators to Support the Europe 2020 Strategy*. Luxembourg: Publications Office of the European Union.

Ikenberry, J. (2008). 'Explaining crisis and change in transatlantic relations: an introduction'. In J. Anderson, J. Ikenberry and T. Risse (eds), *The End of the West? Crisis and Change in the Atlantic Order*. Ithaca, NY, USA and London, UK: Cornell University Press.

Juncker, J.C. (2018). *State of the Union 2018 – The Hour of European Sovereignty*. Accessed 13 October 2018 at https://ec.europa.eu/commission/news/state-union-2018-hour-european-sovereignty-2018-sep-12_en.

Karlsson, C., C. Silander and D. Silander (eds) (2016). *Political Entrepreneurship: Regional Growth and Entrepreneurial Diversity in Sweden*. Cheltenham, UK and Northampton, MA, USA: Edward Elgar Publishing.

Rosenthal, U., M.T. Charles and P. 't Hart (1989). *Coping with Crises: The Management of Disasters, Riots, and Terrorism*. Springfield: Charles C. Thomas.

Silander, D. (2018). 'European governance and political entrepreneurship in times of economic crisis'. In C. Karlsson, C. Silander and D. Silander (eds), *Governance and Political Entrepreneurship in Europe: Promoting Growth and Welfare in Times of Crisis*. Cheltenham, UK and Northampton, MA, USA: Edward Elgar Publishing.

United Nations (2015). *Transforming our World: the 2030 Agenda for Sustainable Development*. Accessed 12 October 2018 at https://sustainabledevelopment. un.org/post2015/transformingourworld.

Index